Hugh Mackay is a social researcher and bestselling author. *Australia Reimagined* is his nineteenth book. His research career has spanned six decades, including 25 years as research director of *The Mackay Report*, publishing quarterly reports on all aspects of Australian life. Among many other appointments, he has been deputy chair of the Australia Council for the Arts, chairman of trustees of Sydney Grammar School and the inaugural chair of the ACT government's Community Inclusion Board, and is currently a patron of the Asylum Seekers Centre. He is a Fellow of the Australian Psychological Society and has been awarded honorary doctorates by five Australian universities. In 2015, he was appointed an Officer of the Order of Australia. He lives in Canberra.

www.hughmackay.net.au

Other books by Hugh Mackay

AUSTRALIA REIMAGINED

Towards a more compassionate, less anxious society

HUGH MACKAY

MACMILLAN
Pan Macmillan Australia

First published 2018 in Macmillan by Pan Macmillan Australia Pty Ltd
1 Market Street, Sydney, New South Wales, Australia, 2000

A catalogue record for this
book is available from the
National Library of Australia

Typeset in 12.5/16.5 pt Bembo by Midland Typesetters, Australia
Printed by McPherson's Printing Group

The author and the publisher have made every effort to contact copyright holders
for material used in this book. Any person or organisation that may have been
overlooked should contact the publisher.

The paper in this book is FSC® certified.
FSC® promotes environmentally responsible,
socially beneficial and economically viable
management of the world's forests.

It is so much easier to venture far – not just in distance but also in terms of your willingness to experiment, take risks, and reach out to the other – when you know that you're still tethered to a place called home, and to a real community.

Thomas L. Friedman, *Thank You for Being Late*

Preserving social cohesion is our biggest challenge.

Michael Kyrios, Past President, Australian Psychological Society

Gross national product counts air pollution, and cigarette advertising, and ambulances to clear our highways of carnage. It counts special locks for our doors and the jails for the people who break them . . . Yet the gross national product does not allow for the health of our children, the quality of their education, or the joy of their play; it does not include the beauty of our poetry or the strength of our marriages, the intelligence of our public debate or the integrity of public officials. It measures neither our wisdom nor our learning, neither our compassion nor our devotion to our country. It measures everything, in short, except that which makes life worthwhile.

Robert F. Kennedy, Remarks at the University of Kansas, 18 March 1968

To Sheila

Contents

INTRODUCTION

Compassion changes everything

Sometimes, when I talk to people about 'the state of the nation', they wonder if I'm some kind of prophet of doom. Nothing could be further from my intent. I love Australia and am full of optimism about its future, especially as the rising generation of young Australians – more nimble, adaptable and open-minded than the rest of us – gradually take over. But if, as I suspect, we are in more trouble than many of us realise, the best starting point for course correction is to acknowledge where we are now, and how we got here.

As a social scientist, I'm inviting you on a journey into the heart of the nation, to take a look at what's really going on beneath the surface noise. I'm also encouraging you to consider the possibility that the clearest signs of the health of a society are to be found in the life of its local neighbourhoods and communities. And I'm urging all of us to bring more compassion to our discourse – both public and private – about the kind of society we want to become.

The book examines our troubling epidemic of anxiety and its causes; the damage done to our social fabric by attacks on our cultural diversity; the hazards we face if we surrender too much control to emerging information technology; and the ways our social cohesion is threatened by the onrush of social change and the widening fault lines of social and economic inequality. The underlying theme is that we are suffering from a deficit of compassion.

After 26 years of continuous economic growth, income inequality is increasing, national and household debt are at unsustainable levels, we are quibbling about the entitlements of welfare recipients (particularly those for whom we can't find work), we are asking students to bear an ever-greater proportion of the cost of their tertiary education, and we have been shutting young first-home buyers out of the housing market. How did that all happen?

At a time when there are 65 million refugees and displaced persons in the world, how did a society like ours, with a history of commitment to the 'fair go' and the 'second chance', become so heartless in our treatment of asylum seekers? How did we manage to degrade our public schools to the point where overall education standards are in decline? How come we haven't made more progress towards genuine gender equality?

Part of the answer is that we, like many Western societies, are in the midst of a period of such rampant individualism and material-ism that we have become more self-absorbed, more competitive and more socially fragmented. As a result, we no longer engage with such issues as we once did.

But these trends are not irreversible. Our capacity for hard thinking, tempered by compassion – the powerful combination former NSW premier Nick Greiner described as 'tough minds, tender hearts' – is what has always prevented us from descending into chaos, and it can keep on preventing us.

In writing this book, I have been inspired by the many com-munities and individuals who are showing us how to become a more generous, more compassionate, more cohesive and more harmonious society. Their example reminds us that the state of the nation actually starts in our own street.

PART I

THE WAY WE ARE

1

We need more courage than luck

If you do not change direction, you may end up where you are heading.

Lao Tzu

Do you ever find yourself pondering questions like these:

Will my job be replaced by a robot?

Will cash disappear?

Will terrorism threaten our way of life?

Is religion really on the way out?

Why has politics become so annoying?

Will climate change decimate the human population?

Will artificial intelligence take over?

Are gender distinctions becoming irrelevant?

Which are the real 'rogue states'?

Will I be able to understand what my grandchildren are talking about?

Perhaps you find yourself trying *not* to ponder such questions. We humans have an inbuilt tendency towards inertia – leaving things as they are; staying put; keeping on doing what we've always done. Habits, rituals, repetitive practices . . . our attachment to the familiar can be a source of comfort, but sometimes familiarity can send us the wrong signal, reassuring us that everything can go on as it is even when *other* signals are telling us the very opposite. This is one of those times: the quote from Lao Tzu at the top of the chapter precisely captures the dilemma we are now facing.

Two seminal facts about Australia, taken together, suggest we are in urgent need of some course correction. Fact number one: thanks to our rate of relationship breakdown, our shrinking households, our busy lives, our increasing income inequality and our ever-increasing reliance on information technology, we are a more fragmented society than we have ever been. Fact number two: we are in the grip of an epidemic of anxiety. Two million of us suffer an anxiety disorder in any one year, and the closely related epidemics of depression and obesity swell that number even more.

Those two facts are so closely connected we should think of them as two sides of the same coin. Heads, we're more fragmented; tails, we're more anxious. Much more needs to be said about the stories that lie behind these twin facts and about the societal context in which they exist, but it doesn't take much imagination to see the link: because we are herd animals by nature, we become anxious when we are cut off from the herd and our anxiety, in turn, induces the kind of self-absorption that further inhibits social interaction. It's a vicious circle.

There is no cause for despair (yet), but there is certainly a reason to reflect on ways we might live differently – as individuals, as neighbours and as citizens – if we are to cope with life in a world that looks a bit like a spinning kaleidoscope whose patterns keep changing too quickly for us to read them. The challenge of coping with change is magnified when personal relationships are more transient, fragile and increasingly mediated through technology. It's harder to deal with upheavals in our personal or working life if we're not supported by a caring and compassionate family, or a stable network of friends, neighbours or colleagues. It's harder to stay calm about the future if we don't have someone we can share our concerns with, or if we're living with an empathy deficit.

Social cohesion, grounded in compassion and mutual respect, is the key to true greatness for any society. By contrast, social fragmentation – exacerbated by rampant individualism and competitive materialism – inevitably damages the social fabric and diminishes our capacity for greatness.

That potent blend of materialism and individualism tends to undermine social cohesion by overemphasising competition for personal 'success', and by encouraging the pursuit of the kind of happiness that can only exist in a bubble of narcissism. And here's a darker twist: a culture of excessive individualism is like a hothouse for psychopaths. In *Taming Toxic People*, David Gillespie quotes international research showing that psychopaths thrive in individualistic societies (such as ours has become), where people tend to place their own interests ahead of the community's and to be always asking: 'What's in it for me?' In more cooperative, communitarian cultures (such as we once were, and could become again) psychopaths are less likely to be tolerated and their influence more contained.

It would be a tragedy for Australia if we failed to grasp the importance of social cohesion not only to our mental and emotional health as individuals, but also to the health of our society. Michael Kyrios, executive dean of the College of Education, Psychology and Social Work at Flinders University and a former president of the Australian Psychological Society, put it to me unequivocally: 'Preserving social cohesion is our biggest challenge.' In the US, a similar warning was issued by Professor Julianne Holt-Lunstad, speaking at the 125th Annual Convention of the American Psychological Association in August 2017: 'Social isolation could be a greater threat to public health than obesity.'

In countries like Australia, we are at more risk of antisocial behaviour from people who are socially isolated and mentally ill than we are from ideologically based acts of terrorism. Melbourne's 2017 Bourke Street Mall and Flinders Street car attacks on pedestrians, and the earlier Hoddle Street and Port Arthur massacres, are extreme examples of that. Even in the case of Sydney's 2016 Lindt Café siege, psychologist Steve Biddulph has argued strongly that the gunman responsible was far from being a terrorist, only using ISIS as a cover story in an attempt to bolster his self-importance in the context of a socially incoherent life.

Fortunately, there are signs that we might be rising to the challenge described by Professor Kyrios. When enough of us feel bewildered by the accelerating rate of social, cultural, economic and technological change; when we feel deeply troubled and, in some cases, angry about the increasingly divided state of the nation, with income inequality now a serious issue for us; when we lose faith in our institutions, and despair at the parlous state of federal politics; when there seems no clear sense of where all this is taking us . . . this might be the moment when we find the courage to tackle issues from which we have been insulated by our own complacency.

Disruption can bring out the best in us

Try this out for an idea. Think of someone you know (it might even be you) who has had to face a big personal trauma – a life-threatening illness, say, or an extended period of depression, or a retrenchment followed by unemployment, or the repossession of their home, or the acrimonious breakdown of an intimate relationship. People who go through such turbulent episodes will often tell you that while this was happening to them, they felt they could barely cope. Everything seemed to have been turned on its head; the world seemed to be against them; their prospects looked bleak; they might even have felt as if they were finished and that life was hardly worth living.

After such experiences, not surprisingly, some people fall apart and never quite recover. But others look back on the trauma and say, almost in a spirit of disbelief, that it was the making of them. In retrospect, they see it as having been a time of such disruption that they were forced to rethink their priorities, their values, and the very purpose of their life. They had to decide what really mattered to them. And then they felt as if they had been handed a blank slate on which they could write a new story.

Many people who have survived and even prospered after a trauma like that have concluded that there had to be a period of brokenness before they could rebuild their lives. In retrospect, the breaking-down seemed *essential* to the outcome. That idea of redemption through destruction and renewal is central to Christianity's resurrection metaphor, and occurs in many other religious and pagan traditions, often inspired by the seasonal cycles in nature.

Analogies can be too glib, especially analogies between traumatic changes in an individual's life and upheavals in a society. Yet the British philosopher A.C. Grayling argues in *The Age of Genius* that Europe's seventeenth-century Enlightenment was a direct consequence of the disruptions, dislocations and displacements caused by the Thirty Years War. Closer to home, many older Australians believe that the Great Depression, for all its horrors, taught their parents' generation the value of prudence, thrift and loyalty. And we are regularly made aware of the positive social effects of natural disasters like floods and bushfires that first traumatise and then unite communities, generally bringing out the best in people.

Whether or not you think the analogy works, there's a growing body of opinion among social, economic and political analysts and commentators that 'something's gotta give'; that a serious break with the past is needed if we are to face the future with the kind of mindset that will equip us for dealing with its challenges.

The UK has had to think big in the wake of its surprise Brexit vote and the subsequent general election that turned conventional wisdom on its head; many US citizens are still questioning the integrity of a system that brought them President Trump; the French surprised themselves by electing a president who represents neither of the political parties that have dominated French politics for 50 years and by then going on to grant Macron's brand-new party unassailable power in the National Assembly.

Perhaps we, too, will need to do something bold to repair the damage to our social fabric and to prepare ourselves to face the threats to our way of life already appearing on the horizon.

Strange as it may seem, upheavals, disruptions, ambiguities and uncertainties are good for us. We don't welcome those things, of course: no one hopes for a retrenchment, a life-threatening illness or a failed relationship – for ourselves, or for our loved ones. No one chooses to live with uncertainty. Yet it is the unexpected events that crash into our lives that keep us alert, alive and open to fresh possibilities. Learning to live with insecurity is one of the primary challenges of being human: after all, we cling to existence itself by the merest thread, and unexpected twists and turns are the stuff of life. We are defined not by how we cope with the familiar and the comfortable but by our reaction to the unusual, the disruptive, the surprising. How we respond in the face of a challenge tells us far more about who we really are than all our rhetoric about attitudes, values or aspirations. Nothing clarifies our priorities like a crisis, and nothing keeps the brain active like an encounter with the unexpected.

Neuroscience confirms this. From the very beginning of our lives, according to Mark Johnson, co-director of the Centre for Brain and Cognitive Development at Birkbeck, University of London, postnatal brain development is a dynamic, plastic process in which a child actively seeks out novel information to stimulate the brain. And it's not just babies: we now know that brain plasticity can be maintained well into old age and that unpredictability is the key. We don't have to want change, let alone welcome it, to know that we must adapt to it. The rate of change is not going to slow down; on the contrary, every prediction tells us we are heading for such profound disruptions to the ecology, the economy and the culture that we can't easily imagine what the future will be like even twenty or thirty years hence. And we are not the hapless victims of changes thrust upon us: in fact, many of the disruptions are of our own making – such as those caused by our excessive consumption of natural resources, our excessive mobility generating excessive carbon emissions (especially air travel, where we dump our emissions straight into the stratosphere), our excessive demand for choice, our excessive accumulation of *stuff* we probably don't need and possibly can't afford, our excessive reliance on digital technology, and even our excessive assertions of independence that fly in the face of our nature as social beings who need each other.

Do we need a shock to the system?

Many Australians are angry, or simply in despair, about the state of politics, or their fading prospect of home ownership, or the widening chasm between wealth and poverty, or the swiftly changing job market that threatens to disadvantage so many of us. Many are fearful of the looming threat not only to jobs but to our way of life, from the rapid development of artificial intelligence, robotics, and ever more sophisticated information and communication technology. Many of us have lost our faith in the institutions – federal parliament, the big banks and 'big business' more generally, the church, the mass media, the trade unions – that were once regarded as positive symbols and instruments of our way of life. There's a widespread mood of disillusionment and disenchantment.

In this kind of mood, we are often tempted to take refuge in small-scale, self-centred concerns; to focus on things we feel we can control, when so much else seems beyond our control. We might try to distract ourselves via the trivialities and banalities of everyday life, such as the Quest for the Perfect Latte. In fact, you could think of this reaction as QPL syndrome, typified by that particular quest but also manifested in any of our pleasantly distracting quests for perfection: the interminable search for the perfect taps to set off the bathroom renovation; prolonged tinkering with the plans for a new barbecue setting complete with outdoor sink; a radical new hairstyle, a tattoo, or perhaps a bit of cosmetic surgery to lift the spirits along with the face; or even a relentless quest for the perfect school for our offspring. QPL syndrome is a form of Utopia complex. In a more serious vein, we might devote ourselves to Pilates, yoga or mindfulness training, perhaps in pursuit of greater physical fitness or a more 'spiritual' frame of mind that will calm our anxieties and provide welcome distraction from life's uncertainties and frustrations.

None of this is to be mocked or discouraged. All these are perfectly natural, healthy and rational strategies for dealing with the disquieting sense that all is not as it should be. But their relentlessly inward focus may contribute to a sense of disengagement that blinds us to some larger realities and allows us to forget that, as citizens, we bear some responsibility for the direction our society is taking.

When you listen to the surface noise, you can get the impression that things are going pretty well – apart from the obligatory grizzles about politics. The state of disengagement is a state of insulation; a kind of cocooning. So if we *can* find the perfect latte, get the outdoor sink installed in the barbecue area *and* find a terrific yoga teacher, it's easy to imagine things are going pretty well. Fifty years ago, it was that kind of cruising, coasting, narrow-focused acquiescence that led one of our most famous iconoclasts, Donald Horne, to make the scathing assessment that we were merely a 'lucky country', getting ahead more by good luck than good management; a lucky accident on a national scale.

Horne was particularly critical of Australia's political and business leaders at the time. Today, the tendency towards luck-dependency is even more widespread, partly reflected in our world-leading per capita gambling losses. We have become more generally complacent, more generally inclined to cling to the 'she'll be right' attitude, more likely to think of 'lucky' as a compliment, because we manage to keep the big questions off our personal agenda, most of the time.

Many of us don't like or support Australia's treatment of asylum seekers, for example, but very few of us kick up a fuss about it, either because we manage not to think about it too much or prefer not to imagine what it must be like to *be* an asylum seeker – especially one languishing in an offshore detention centre, or waiting in limbo to see if a temporary protection visa could ever become permanent.

We don't really know what to make of the alleged threat of international terrorism, so we accept that 'border protection' is a really big issue, and thank goodness someone has it under control. We're a very pro-immigration society – how could we be otherwise, given our history? – but we still tend to fall for simplistic slogans that conflate immigration with our refugee program and imply (absurdly, falsely) that we are at risk of opening our gates to an entire orchard of bad apples.

All the sweet talk about the mining boom – until it ended – and then about our record run of economic growth has lulled us into thinking that everything must be okay if we're doing so well.

It can be tempting to equate prosperity with virtue. Even if we ourselves, as individuals, can't actually feel the buoyancy of increased prosperity in our own little balloon, especially if we're on the receiving end of flatter wage growth or prolonged underemployment, we still feel entitled to share in this vaunted prosperity. For the past twenty years, a popular solution to that disjunction between national and personal prosperity has been to use our credit cards to live *as if* we're wealthier than we are, so we can feel like participants in the boom times. That's a strategy bound to end in tears when house values fall or interest rates go up, or both, or when an episode of unemployment hits us.

An alarming disconnect

It's as if there are two narratives running in tandem here, though they are actually contradictory. One says everything is fine, the borders are safe, the economy is strong, I should just get on with my more-or-less lovely life. The other says there are big questions about what's happening to Australian society. There are grounds for deep disquiet about our failure to prepare for everything from climate change or the next wave of the IT revolution to the impact of an ageing population and the approaching tsunami of demand for aged care; mental health is a growing issue and that can't be a good sign; the allegedly strong economy appears to be having the effect of increasing inequality; women are still far from equal to men in our boardrooms, our parliaments and our workforce generally; our public school system is in dire straits; the Royal Commission into Institutional Responses to Child Sexual Abuse seems to be the tip of a really big, really jagged iceberg. No surprise, then, that a 2015 OmniPoll survey about quality of life in Australia reported that only 16 percent of Australians thought life was getting better, 35 percent thought it was staying about the same and 49 percent thought it was getting worse.

Richard Eckersley, Australia's internationally respected social analyst, explored that idea of contradictory narratives in 2014 when he alerted us to some research data so significant, I regard it as a clanging alarm bell. According to Eckersley, while most Australians will say they are satisfied with their personal life, pessimists outnumber optimists when it comes to assessing Australia's overall 'quality of life', taking into account social, economic and environmental trends. How disconnected from the nation's social and economic destiny we must be if we can judge that our individual futures are rosy while *Australia's* is not – and how disconnected from our biological destiny as social beings who need each other!

This points to one of the great hazards of a more fragmented society; a sign of just how far off course our rampant individualism has blown us. It suggests that many of us have lost sight of our true nature as people who *belong* to this society. We are, each of us, organically linked to the whole; its problems are our problems; the pain of any is the pain of all. We cannot remain aloof from it unless we have found a way of hiding in a cocoon of self-absorbed individualism. Indeed, if we choose to remain aloof, in what sense can we call ourselves Australians?

Our remarkably sustained period of economic growth may well have contributed to the current mood of disengagement and self-absorption – a mood I described in *Advance Australia . . . Where?* (2007) as our Dreamy Period. Eminent political scientist Ross Garnaut calls it the Great Australian Complacency. The *Sydney Morning Herald*'s political and international editor Peter Hartcher, writing in mid 2017, noted that 'the more we have enjoyed the fruits of economic reform, the more reluctant we've become to accept any further economic reform'. He quoted former Treasury secretary Ken Henry: 'We had drifted into a state of complacency in the years before the GFC [global financial crisis of 2007-8]. Remarkably, the GFC didn't shock us out of it.'

This dangerous complacency is often associated with a kind of blind optimism that, at its most crass, comes out as 'she'll be right', as though good luck will save us, yet again. The distinguished Australian science writer Julian Cribb, reflecting on the many existential threats now facing us, warns that 'it is the blind optimists, rather than the realistic pessimists, who imperil our future', since they are the ones closing their ears to the bad news about the state of the planet. The same might be said of the futility of blind optimism in the face of other disturbing trends, such as our growing inequality of income.

When it comes to our ecological, social, cultural and economic future, misplaced optimism is as dangerous as blind faith. What is needed is the courage to face the way things are, and the wisdom and imagination – informed by the best available evidence – to work out how to make things better.

Given our paradoxical blend of dissatisfaction and complacency, it might require even more serious instability, perhaps amounting to chaos, to convince us to look for more imaginative solutions to the problems that beset us and make us the troubled nation we are.

We saw plenty of political chaos in 2017, but perhaps not enough to convince us that there must be a better way of governing ourselves than the present system of adversarial party-based parliaments, sloganistic elections and career politicians. As long as MPs are seen to represent their party rather than their electorate, and to settle into politics for the long haul, the 'political class' inevitably becomes ever more detached from the society it is meant to serve, a process not helped by unseemly behaviour in the parliament that might amuse the players themselves and their devoted cheersquads, but either bores or repels the rest of us.

Perhaps we'll need even more extended bushfire seasons and more extreme weather events to convince us that drastic measures are required to repair some of the long-term planetary damage caused by the grim, destructive history of carbon-based energy production. Whatever you may think are the causes of global warming, it's clear the planet won't let us go on living, working, travelling and squandering resources the way we have been.

Perhaps we'll have to see educational standards fall even further before we realise that our present school-funding arrangements are ill-conceived, our priorities are wrong, and that it's possible to do it all differently.

Perhaps banks and other business corporations, churches, trade unions and other institutions will have to experience even more of the opprobrium now engulfing them before they start to act differently or face the prospect of new types of institution eroding their power or even supplanting them – as the internet's assault on traditional mass media has already demonstrated.

Perhaps it will require some serious 'breaking down', analogous to a crisis or trauma in the life of an individual, before we are convinced of the need to reset our priorities and rethink our values. Peter Hartcher certainly thinks so; he concluded his 2017 analysis of the effects of our long period of economic growth by wondering: 'If success has bred this complacency, does Australia need a crisis to jolt it back to reality?'

Yet even without one specific crisis – ecological, economic, political or military – the looming challenges to our current way of life will require some seriously imaginative and creative rethinking, restructuring and rebuilding. Dealing with all this will need more courage than luck.

Looming discontinuities

The changes now on their way are not like those that so destabilised us through the 1980s and 90s when we were starting to adapt to the implications of the women's movement, the embryonic IT revolution, the restructure of our economy, the sense of ourselves as a truly, unambiguously, multicultural society and as part of an increasingly globalised world, both economically and culturally. That was challenging enough – radical in its way – but compared to what lies ahead, it was relatively easy to absorb because the world still looked like a familiar place.

The world is rapidly becoming a less familiar place. UK filmmaker Terence Davies, director of *Quiet Passion* (the story of US poet Emily Dickinson), told Australian film reviewer Julian Wood at *FilmInk*: 'Oh, I can't do anything contemporary simply because I can't understand the world now. I can't use any of the technology – none of it. It is almost a denial of modern life. And to be truthful I am a little afraid of it.'

Davies is not alone in feeling a little afraid of the modern world. Tectonic shifts in our way of life will occur in response to growing concern about the ailing health of the planet itself, with prolonged drought and ever-higher temperatures apparently an inevitable feature of our near future. A new round of geopolitical upheavals and realignments has revived the threat of nuclear war. Our growing reliance on super-sophisticated artificial intelligence will make our present modes of living and working seem unimaginably clunky, inefficient, reckless and perhaps even downright stupid, yet perhaps rather more recognisably human than what lies ahead.

In some ways, these early years of the current century are reminiscent of the early years of the twentieth century, when the revolutionary technologies unleashed in the late-nineteenth century were transforming Western societies domestically, industrially, economically and militarily. In 'Economic possibilities for our grandchildren', an essay written in 1928, the economist John Maynard Keynes identified such innovations as 'electricity, petrol, steel, rubber, cotton, the chemical industries, automatic machinery and the methods of mass production' not only as transformative, but also as signposts to even greater technological revolutions to come. He might well have added powered flight to his list, but he was certainly right about the revolutions to come.

In our fast-approaching future, it won't just be a matter of driverless electric or hydrogen-powered vehicles that relieve us of the responsibility for controlling the speed and direction of today's dangerous cars with their poisonous emissions; our computers and other appliances, including our personal robots, will talk to us and expect answers. Perhaps more significantly, they will talk to each other as well. A device will be there to make conversation with us when we're lonely, or to play the music we feel like hearing, or to read us a bedtime story when no one else is around to do it for us – and all that activity will be recorded and transmitted to a central data store and from there, to where? A new academic discipline is already exploring the ethics of our relationships with robots: a 'be kind to robots' campaign is bound to be in our future. In the not-too-distant future, implanted chips might well facilitate the transfer of thought, rendering mobile phones irrelevant for the communication of some types of messages.

Crypto-currencies like Bitcoin may well revolutionise the world of financial transactions, making many current banking and legal services superfluous, and replacing the need for trust in the system with the almost incorruptible and ineradicable 'blockchains' that transparently record and archive every single transaction.

It's already the case that our smartphones can know more than our GP or medical specialist about our state of health and wellbeing – including our mental health. Writing in *The Atlantic*, David Dobbs describes research undertaken by Thomas Insel, the former director of the US National Institute of Mental Health and now president of a new biotech company called Mindstrong, that has led Insel to believe a smartphone can become a diagnostic instrument capable of detecting a deteriorating state of mind and triggering an appropriate treatment response. We need to remember, of course, that anything our smartphones can tell us about ourselves, they can also tell those mysterious, unidentified others to whom our phones and other devices are constantly sending data about us.

In the future, medical technology will not just prolong life, but will give many of us the option of choosing how long we would like to live, and may alleviate pain altogether. Surgery will increasingly be handled by robots under human supervision (initially, at least), and artificial intelligence will supersede the human variety in areas as diverse as accounting, stockbroking, bricklaying, warfare . . . most of whatever you can imagine will become possible.

On top of all that, there's the prospect of artificial intelligence making the great leap to what psychologists would call artificial *general* intelligence – the point where machines will have acquired the ability to 'think' beyond the boundaries of whatever particular tasks they were designed to perform and will appear to possess what we call 'consciousness'. When that moment arrives, they will be able to modify their own programs and create new machines to do ever more sophisticated tasks, far beyond the capacity of the human mind and in ways that may force us to rethink the whole idea of consciousness. As long ago as 1960, anticipating the day when this would happen, US philosopher of science Michael Scriven concluded a paper called 'The compleat robot: A prolegomena to androidology' by posing the question: 'Could an artifact be a person? It seems to me the answer is now clear . . . A robot might do many of the things we have discussed in this paper and not qualify. It could not do them all and be denied the accolade. We who must die salute him.' Scriven's point was not only that when machines reached this stage they would be smarter than humans, but also that, unlike us, they would *not* die.

Now that day has drawn so much closer, some of the smartest minds in the field of artificial intelligence – people like Bill Gates,

Stephen Hawking and Elon Musk – have grown uneasy. As Rachel Botsman reports in *Who Can You Trust?*, far from saluting the new machines, innovators and thought-leaders like those three are actually fearful of the future the machines point to: Hawking has told the BBC that 'the development of full artificial intelligence could spell the end of the human race' – partly because of the possibility of the world's arsenals coming under the control of AI. This is not what we normally mean when we anticipate 'the end of civilisation as we know it', nor how we typically imagine the demise of the human species. We're more likely to think of an ecological disaster, or a human-initiated nuclear war, rather than being dispensed with by our own inventions.

In the case of warfare, the present trend will no doubt continue: a move away from the full-on engagement of armies on defined battlefields towards a blend of terrorist attacks on civilians, and targeted assassinations and bombings via long-range missiles and drones (and other as-yet-unimagined weaponry), controlled by people seated at computer consoles half a world away. Whatever you might think about the idea of a 'morality of war', that morality – just like the morality of our relationships with AI – will be scrambling to keep up with the technology. Dare we hope that, in such a world, conventional armed forces will primarily be deployed for peacekeeping and the dispensing of humanitarian aid, including the building and repair of infrastructure?

On the economic front, there's already serious talk about the possible death of neoliberalism, with its uncritical worship of free markets and its determinedly wasteful consumerist culture – described by former Australian prime minister Paul Keating as having reached a dead end. Perhaps the threat to neoliberalism is part of an even greater upheaval. Perhaps, after 200 years or more, we are actually within sight of the demise of modernity itself, with its emphasis on materialism and individualism, and what Australian theologian Scott Cowdell identifies as its three key features: the desire for closure, for certainty and for control. (May I urge you to stop worshipping that deeply flawed and increasingly irrelevant trinity? This is, after all, the age of discontinuity: closure, certainty and control are in shorter supply than ever.)

Modernity's offspring, postmodernism, has only compounded the problems created for society by the culture of individualism. The worship of postmodernism's twin deities – subjectivity and relativity – has encouraged the idea that everyone's opinion is as valid as everyone else's and, in the process, has eroded the authority of experts: trawl the internet, or even the shelves of your local library, and you can find theories about everything from climate change to diet and health proposed by amateurs, and you're bound to come across a rebuttal to any expert opinion you don't happen to like. All this has led, logically, to the point where 'fake news' and 'real news' are conflated; where any message encountered on the internet, no matter how inane or unreliable, is likely to be taken seriously by *someone*, simply because it's there, it exists, it has the status of being 'a message'.

'Do your own thing' and 'everything's relative' may be simplistic misreadings of postmodernism, but when they became enshrined in contemporary folk wisdom, they took us to the outer limits of individualism. In the process, thanks to those same propositions, social cohesion came to seem less important. When 'it's all about me', and when 'what I think' is just as important as what anyone else thinks, the communitarian spirit is inevitably diminished if not crushed.

In *Fantasyland: How America Went Haywire*, Kurt Andersen argues it was the information explosion that carried the notion of relativity to its present point of cultural dominance. The situation he describes is more extreme than in Australia, but it sounds like a warning of where we, too, are heading: 'Today, each of us is freer than ever to custom-make reality, to believe whatever and pretend to be whoever we wish. Which makes all the lines between *actual* and *fictional* blur and disappear more easily. Truth in general becomes flexible, personal, subjective.'

The good news is that this period in our cultural and economic evolution can't last forever, simply because it represents such a contradiction of our essential human nature as cooperative, interdependent, social beings.

Our present levels of anxiety and discontent – and even our self-protective disengagement – could therefore be read as signs of the discomfort we feel when we live in ways that depart so radically from our true nature. In many contexts, and in many countries, people have become fond of saying: *We are better than this.* That claim rings true; our anxieties and insecurities may well be harbingers of yet another radical culture shift as we seek pathways towards our 'better selves'.

The unique intersection of ecological, biological and economic imperatives may finally be bringing us to the point where we will be forced to abandon the pursuit of certainty and control; where we will see through the twin vanities of individualism and consumerism; where we will begin to understand that not all opinions are equal and that some suitably credentialled people actually know more about their field of expertise than the rest of us do; where we will begin to embrace a more communitarian, cooperative ethos. It might not be a choice; our survival as a species might depend on it.

A reflection

On everyone's desire to be taken seriously

Why did so many Americans vote for Donald Trump to be their president? Why did so many Brits vote to leave the European Union? Why do young men from relatively prosperous Western societies like Australia go off to Syria or Iraq to join ISIS and fight in a war that seems to have nothing to do with them? Why do so many rural and regional Australians vote for Pauline Hanson's One Nation and other splinter parties? Why do so many people keep working beyond the point where they need the money?

A single thread runs through the answers to all those questions, and it relates to one of the most basic drivers of human behaviour: the desire in all of us – young and old – to be taken seriously; to be acknowledged, accepted, respected, appreciated, noticed, heard.

That desire explains why we are so grateful to people who will listen to us when we have something to say; why belonging to a stable friendship circle is so important to us; why eye contact matters so much.

It explains why we're more likely to buy from a salesperson who invites us to talk about ourselves and our needs rather than one who only wants to describe the features of the product. It explains why people will sometimes go on working, long after their use-by date, because their workplace (including colleagues and perhaps clients or customers) satisfies their desire to be taken seriously in a way that nowhere else does.

And it explains why Donald Trump is president of the USA. As a man steeped in marketing lore, Trump instinctively knew he had to talk to his audience about *them*, not about himself or even much about policies. Carl Jung explained Adolf Hitler's appeal to Germany in the 1930s thus: 'He is the loudspeaker that magnifies the inaudible whispers of the German soul until they can be heard in the German's unconscious ear.' Trump could be said to have performed the same role for the American soul. But the soul of which American? US academic and author Joan Williams believes Trump's decisive appeal was to the long-neglected white working class.

In a 2016 article for the *Harvard Business Review*, partly based on insights gleaned from her own family background, Williams argued that members of the white working class had been feeling so alienated, overlooked and marginalised for so long, they were waiting for someone who would acknowledge their frustration, appear to hear their concerns and speak for them. In other words, someone who would appear to take them seriously after years of feeling they had not been taken seriously enough, or at all.

Williams observed that, from the beginning of the presidential election campaign, Trump was bridging the class culture gap in a way that Hillary Clinton was not. Indeed, Clinton stood for the very class from which this huge bloc of voters felt so alienated. In the words of Williams, she epitomised 'the dorky arrogance and smugness of the professional elite . . . Worse, her mere presence rubs it in that *even women* from her class can treat working-class men with disrespect.' Once this bloc of working-class voters had decided Trump was their man, Clinton's derogatory remarks about him sounded, by association, as if she were being condescending and dismissive towards *them* – an impression strongly reinforced by her reference to certain Trump supporters as 'deplorables'.

Drawing on the example of her own father, Williams describes the importance of 'dignity' to a working-class person, and the suspicion felt towards liberals, hipsters and the college-educated professional class: 'Trump promises a world free of political correctness and a return to an earlier era, when men were men and women knew their place. It's comfort food for high-school educated guys who . . . feel like losers – or did until they met Trump.' And it was not only the men: white women without a college degree also voted for Trump over Clinton by 62 to 34 percent.

Well beyond the white working class, Trump's pitch that he was listening, that he understood people's pain, resentment and sense of alienation, packed a powerful emotional punch. By positioning himself as a Washington outsider who would 'drain the swamp', Trump connected with all those who felt remote from the political process and from the politicians who were supposed to represent them – even including those voters (especially women) who felt uneasy about aspects of his personal behaviour. His policy proposals, his simplistic attitude to international relations and trade, his promise to build the infamous wall along the Mexican border . . . all seemed irrelevant beside the one central and irresistible proposition: *I am taking you seriously. I am on your side. We are in this together.*

And Brexit? Same idea. The Leave campaign was based on the proposition that the UK had been so dominated by the rules and regulations imposed on it by the European parliament, and so culturally distorted by the free flow of immigrants from Europe, that many Britons felt they were no longer being taken seriously. Added to that was the sense – felt most keenly in the disadvantaged north of England – that the British government was 'out of touch' (shorthand for 'not taking us seriously; not hearing our voice'). And so, if the government was in favour of staying, they would vote to leave.

Separatist movements ranging from the Kurds to the Catalans – and even to the secessionists of Western Australia – spring from the same source: the frustration of their desire to have their voices heard as distinctive, authentic voices.

In Australia, analysis by the Grattan Institute's John Daley has demonstrated that there is noticeably more political discontent in regional and rural areas than in metropolitan areas. Daley acknowledges that this is hardly new, and is partly the result of slower economic growth in the regions than in the cities (as Judith Brett showed in her 2011 Quarterly Essay *Fair Share*). The resultant decline in rural populations has meant that regional towns often grow 'only by draining population from their hinterland'. Yet, Daley says, it is not obvious why these long-term economic trends should translate into different politics at this particular moment in our socioeconomic and political evolution. He suggests that the rise of minor parties, not only in the regions, is a reflection of falling trust in governments and politicians, rising insecurity fuelled by sluggish economic growth, and a reaction to constant discussion of terrorism. (Incidentally, the rise is spectacular: in the 2016 election, about 35 percent of primary votes for the Senate were cast in favour of minor parties, up from 15 percent in 2010.)

That sense of economic uncertainty is more palpable in the regions than in the major cities, and the Queensland support for Pauline Hanson in the 2016 Senate election reflected that; Daley has calculated that she won less than 4 percent of the vote in the six electorates within twelve kilometres of the Brisbane GPO, and more than 10 percent of the vote in eight of the nine electorates located more than 100 kilometres from Brisbane.

The strong support for the new splinter parties in the regions is not only driven by economics; there's a strong emotional driver as well. Splinter parties have provided a welcome vehicle for the expression of frustration, sometimes amounting to rage, among people outside the major cities who have felt for a very long time that they are not being taken seriously enough – not only by politicians, but by the rest of the country. The closure of rail lines, the withdrawal of educational, medical and administrative services from rural areas, and the flight of young people from regions to cities for higher education and jobs all create an impression that regional populations are mere 'country cousins' who don't warrant as much attention as people in the big cities.

When the desire to be taken seriously is frustrated, patterns of behaviour – including voting behaviour – tend to change, and the so-called splinter parties have opened up a new pathway for that to happen. As Daley wisely says: 'In a democracy, if governments lose the trust of the electorate, then electorates will ultimately rebuild governments' – as, indeed, they have done in France.

The case of young people who leave a stable Western society to travel to the Middle East to train and fight with ISIS is more complex and difficult to explain than the behaviour of voters in an election. But the same underlying factor is almost certainly at work.

Try to imagine that you are a young Muslim man, born in Australia to parents who were migrants – perhaps refugees – from a Middle Eastern country. You're living in the western suburbs of Sydney. You might not have a strong Muslim faith and you might not feel strongly attached to the congregation at the local mosque. You might not have an extended family in Australia. You might be having trouble getting work, and you might have the uneasy sense that your job applications fail because of your Middle Eastern appearance, or even your religion, though no potential employer would dare admit that.

You're conscious of the many statements of Australian politicians that seem designed to conflate the terms 'Muslim' and 'extremist' as part of a general attempt to maintain fear of terrorism in the community, and you've been told that NSW Police has a dedicated Middle Eastern crime taskforce, so you're not surprised when police seem to automatically adopt an attitude of suspicion towards you. You've heard abuse muttered at you on trains and buses, or shouted at you in the street. You've seen Muslim women being mocked or insulted for their way of dressing. You reach the conclusion that you are considered an outsider in this society. Worse, although you were born here, you are not really welcome. Some of your abusers have made that explicit.

Now imagine how you might react to messages delivered either online or in person that suggest there is another community in which you would not only be welcome, but fully embraced as 'one of us'. You would have a clear sense of purpose in your life; a vision; a mission. Best of all, you'd be with people who want you to be with them; who will take you very seriously indeed.

Imagine all that and then ask yourself: in that young man's shoes, would you be tempted?

2

The epidemic that affects us all

Existence floats in an ambience of Love which anxiety pollutes:
Not in an ambience of anxiety which Love clarifies.

Meredith Ryan, 'The Theory of Equanimity'

Fourteen years after he wrote it, Meredith Ryan's beautiful sentiment reads more like an expression of hope than reality. Although we can think of anxiety as an intensely private affliction, when two million Australians are affected each year, the issue is clearly societal as well as personal. And, since this is not a uniquely Australian problem, we have to conclude that something about the nature of life in a 21st-century Western society has caused the incidence of anxiety to reach epidemic proportions. Even if we ourselves are not personally struggling with anxiety, someone in our family, friendship circle or workplace probably is and, in any case, an epidemic of this size affects all of us; the character of our entire society is bound to be influenced by the sheer numbers of people in our midst who are dealing with mental health issues – anxiety chief among them.

The nature of our anxieties might change, and the epidemic might be new, but anxiety itself is hardly a recent phenomenon. We humans have always been an anxious bunch, and why not? Life is mysterious, unpredictable and fragile. Though we crave control and certainty, doubt is the very air we breathe; uncertainty and ambiguity are everywhere. Everything seems transient – even our most intimate relationships offer no guarantee of stability, let alone permanence. Accidents happen, apparently randomly. We fall ill through no fault of our own. Bad guys threaten us with violence. And the most serious questions we ever ask – *Why are we here? What does it all mean? What happens when we die?* – are unanswerable, so we must either shelve them or make up answers that satisfy us.

Although existential angst is an ever-present background rumble to human existence, we are quite adept at smothering its low growl with the noise of other, closer-to-home worries: *Did I turn the stove off? Have I locked the car? Will my daughter pass her exam? What if I lose my job? Will I ever be able to afford a house?*

You could argue, of course, that given the threats to human civilisation posed by the rapid rate of global warming and its potentially catastrophic consequences, high anxiety is a perfectly appropriate response, especially if we can't work out what we, as individuals, can do about it, and there seems to be a disquieting lack of urgency in our leaders' responses. But even without the gradual dawning of that reality on our imagination, the modern world has had plenty of lesser ways of fuelling our anxieties until they reach, as they now have, epidemic proportions.

Brief bursts of anxiety before sitting an exam or delivering a speech or a performance of some other kind can help sharpen us with a bit of perfectly appropriate nervousness. But prolonged anxiety is never good for us. So-called generalised anxiety disorder involves a more or less permanent sense of gnawing uneasiness, sometimes triggered by particular situations but sometimes a persistent state.

Some of us are inclined to confuse the effects of our own anxiety with the effects of the thing we're worrying about. 'Sick with worry' is a good description of the problem. Fear of the effect of wind turbines is one contemporary example of that: if you allow yourself to become sufficiently anxious about living near a wind farm, your anxiety can itself produce symptoms of illness that you can easily blame on the wind farm rather than your anxiety.

One of our favourite ways of dealing with our anxieties, insecurities and uncertainties is to find something that will distract us. Two of our most popular distractions are consumerism and nostalgia.

Consumerism

In modern capitalist societies, consumerism offers the most popular distraction from deeper questions, via the quick-fix benefits of retail therapy and the sophisticated pandering of the marketing industry to the interminable yearnings of our material aspirations: *When we get the new kitchen . . . The next iPhone will be even more awesome than this one . . . There's nothing like a new car to lift your spirits – almost as good as a new romance . . . If only I had a Prada bag for spring . . .* (For some unknown reason, I have started receiving a stream of emails from an online retailer telling me I need a new handbag for spring. I confess the thought had not previously crossed my mind.)

Unfortunately, the blandishments of materialism sow their own seeds of disappointment; the lessons of history tell us that the acquisition of more stuff never creates a deep or enduring sense of satisfaction, and while compulsive spending can be as enjoyable as any other addiction, it contributes nothing to the sense of our life's meaning. Yet many people in societies like ours seem trapped on that merry-go-round: forever borrowing so we can spend even more; forever wondering if the *next* thing we buy will be the one that finally sweeps us across the threshold of the consumer's nirvana into a state of blissful satiation where we finally have everything we want.

As long ago as 1957, US theologian Reinhold Niebuhr was describing 'our gadget-filled paradise suspended in a hell of international insecurity'. Back then, our gadgets were far less sophisticated than they are now, and perhaps the 'hell of international insecurity' is driven by fewer immediate fears now than it was then, when the world seemed on the very brink of nuclear war, but that still serves as a pretty good description of modern madness.

We all know that life's deepest satisfactions never come from gazing lovingly at 'gadgets', whether we own them or merely covet them, but the dirty little secret at the heart of consumerism is that while it promises satisfaction, and even happiness, the maintenance of the mass-marketing machine depends on its ability to fuel our *dis*content. While appearing to satisfy our wants and needs, it must also ensure that those wants and needs are never satisfied. The insistent message to buy *more, more, more* implies that you have to keep doing it or the magic will fade. The whole point of the consumerist game is that you must never be satisfied – just like any other addiction.

Consumerism is seductive, no question; it's also fun to participate in, as long as you're capable of pacing yourself and as long as you occasionally remember to check both your bank balance and your anxiety index because, in the end, it is designed to reinforce the very anxieties it is pretending to allay. Built-in obsolescence is merely the tip of that iceberg.

Nowhere is this insidious paradox more obvious than in our addiction to digital materialism. Information overload – more information, coming at us more rapidly than we can process and interpret it – is a sure way both to distract us *and* raise our anxiety level. If you can't wait to see the responses to your latest social media post, can't bear to be separated from your smartphone, or expect instant responses to an email or a text, then you are setting yourself up for heightened anxiety. FOMO (fear of missing out) is a classic example of modern, self-induced anxiety, fuelled by our recently acquired greed for digital data.

Nostalgia

Another popular response to anxiety is to surrender to the yearnings of nostalgia for a bygone era. In fact, an epidemic of anxiety was bound to create a boom in nostalgia; our prolonged retro craze in fashion and design can be read as a tangible and visible symptom of our general uneasiness.

The older we become (and this process starts, for some people, in their thirties, not their eighties), and the more difficulty we have coping with the rate of change, the more tempting it is to think that everything was better 'back then'. We like to listen to music, wear clothes and buy gadgets that hark back to whatever era we imagine was calmer, saner, slower and generally healthier than the present. Part of the attraction is that the past is familiar territory; terrain we have already traversed. We know we can deal with it because we have already dealt with it, whereas the present and the increasingly uncertain future can seem both unfamiliar and threatening.

Nostalgia is always lurking. Plenty of people in the 1950s hankered after the 1920s, and that was part of an endless series of regressions. No doubt many who lived through the European Enlightenment felt nostalgic for a more certain past where 'God's in his heaven and all's right with the world'.

Over the past 30 years, I've lost count of the number of research respondents who have said things like: 'We're not as trusting as we used to be, back in the days when you could leave your front door open or leave your car unlocked while you went into the service station to pay.' In spite of the fact that crime rates across most categories have been coming down, nostalgia says otherwise.

Ah, the simplicity of it all, when we could ride our bikes everywhere with no helmets and be perfectly safe! When kids could buy fireworks from the local newsagent and let them off whenever they liked! When summer's first dose of sunburn led to the ritual of peeling great sheets of skin off each other's backs! And when I hear people fondly recalling a childhood spent catching tadpoles in the local creek, I do wonder whether there were ever enough creeks to go around.

Some non-churchgoers are even nostalgic for the time when 'most people went to church' (though there never was such a time; in the 1950s, the focus for a lot of today's nostalgia among older Australians, only 44 percent of Australians attended church regularly). Some are nostalgic for a pre-drug society, forgetting, perhaps, that in the days of 6 pm hotel closing, the resultant 'six o'clock swill' amounted to serious abuse of alcohol on a daily basis – today we would call it 'binge drinking' – leading to a lot of public drunkenness and a lot of private misery in homes where the husband and father arrived home drunk and inclined to violence. The 1950s were also populated by many returned service personnel who were dealing with post-traumatic stress disorder, long before that condition was even recognised, let alone treated.

Nor was anxiety absent from any time in our past you'd like to pick on. 'You'll need Aspro some time today' said an infamous ad campaign of the 1960s, reflecting the widespread abuse of analgesics (especially APC powders containing aspirin, phenacetin and caffeine) as a treatment for such things as 'stress headaches' or simply for vague feelings of discontentment and frustration that were common among the stay-at-home housewives of the 1950s and 60s – 'the problem that has no name' exposed by Betty Friedan in her groundbreaking bestseller, *The Feminine Mystique.*

Nostalgia is a harmless enough pursuit, as long as it doesn't prevent us from functioning in the present. If it leads us to prefer the music of our own teens or twenties to the music of today's teens or twenty-somethings, then we are simply part of the inexorable pattern of history. If we like to play our CDs or plug a USB into a piece of equipment that looks like a radio set from the 1940s, why not? If we think, 'They don't make cars like they used to,' then we're right about that – and it's just as well they don't. Thanks largely to improved car design, along with speed cameras, random breath testing and better highway engineering, road deaths have tumbled from 27 to 5 per 100,000 in the past 40 years, though there's been a recent spike, probably due to drivers' mobile phone use.

Nostalgia is as ineffective an antidote to anxiety as consumerism is, and for the same reason: it's a futile attempt to escape from present realities. The best strategy for diminishing our anxiety level is not to pretend we can wind back the clock, nor to wish the world was different, but to find different ways of living in the world as it is.

Stress and anxiety triggers

The contemporary world offers almost unlimited exposure to sources of potential anxiety. Addiction to IT devices – smartphones, tablets, laptops – increases the risk of anxiety and so, paradoxically, does separation from them. A 2010 study by Finnish psychologist Marjut Wallenius measured cortisol levels in school-aged children who had used information/communication technology (ICT) for an average of three hours in a day. The study found that, regardless of the content of the material being watched, the stress response to prolonged use of ICT can persist overnight and still be affecting a child's stress levels the following morning. After reviewing the research into the relationship between screen time and stress, the Canadian Paediatric Society advises that 'no child should be allowed to have a television, computer or video game equipment in his or her bedroom'.

In an *Atlantic* article entitled 'Have smartphones destroyed a generation?' the eminent US psychologist and adolescence researcher Jean M. Twenge concluded unequivocally that 'the more time teens spend looking at screens, the more likely they are to report symptoms of depression'. She also noted that 'significant effects on both mental health and sleep time appear after two or more hours per day on electronic devices'. Twenge, like other researchers, has found that today's adolescents are reluctant to be parted from their smartphones, typically checking them last thing at night and first thing in the morning, and often taking them to bed at night so that they won't 'miss out'. So concerned is Twenge about the impact of smartphones on anxiety levels in children and adolescents, she advises parents not to give a smartphone to a child under the age of fourteen years, and to install an app that limits the phone's use to 90 minutes per day.

In Australia, a partnership between Twitter and ReachOut, an online mental health service for young people, is a sign of how significant social media have become in raising anxiety levels through excessive exposure to all the world's problems – often live and in real time, right there on your smartphone. The ReachOut program aims to give young people strategies for disconnecting from distressing material, rationing their consumption of bad news, and dealing with the effects of exposure to traumatic images – especially video footage featuring the victims of terrorist attacks, natural disasters and similarly disturbing content.

Overstimulation resulting from drug abuse or from an overdose of heavy rock music can leave the revved-up listener's nerve ends jangling. An excess of violent, risk-glorifying video games in adolescence can get the adrenaline rushing too fast and furiously (and, a 2012 longitudinal US study by Jay G. Hull and Ana M. Draghici suggests, will also increase the probability of risky driving and involvement in traffic accidents in adulthood). Mortgage stress, rent stress and credit card stress all act like a drip-feed of the poison that raises our anxiety level, and you can even feed the anxiety monster through an obsessive preoccupation with diet and physical fitness.

The high rate of relationship breakdown and the resulting disruptions are a source of long-term stress and anxiety for many people: *Where did I go wrong? Could I have managed it all better, or differently? Are the children suffering?* Such questions drive a vicious circle of self-doubt, stress and anxiety.

Workplace stress can do it, too. The very modern concept of 'stress leave' is a sign of how easily work can become a mental health hazard, especially when we are relying on it as a source not only of income but also of dignity and a sense of identity and purpose. Some workplace stressors have been around forever: bullying, intimidation, narcissistic or nepotistic bosses, an excessively competitive culture, harassment based on sexism, racism or ageism. But the contemporary workplace has become a more generally stressful environment partly because almost universal access to IT devices means many employees feel as if they are connected to their work 24/7.

Then there's the widespread sense of job insecurity arising from the steady erosion of full-time, permanent work in favour of casual, part-time jobs, and the pressure generated by the constant cry to work both harder and smarter. Absurdly long hours at work combined with the rigours of a big-city commute and the demands of a family can be enough to send anyone's stress levels through the roof, and stress is often just a polite word for anxiety, since the two are so closely connected. Compounding the problem, for many workers, is the gnawing realisation that the next wave of the IT revolution, involving increasingly imaginative and extensive applications of artificial intelligence, will see jobs disappearing at an alarming rate.

Ironically, leaving work can also raise your anxiety level, fed by the phenomenon called 'relevance deprivation syndrome' (a term coined by Gareth Evans, former Australian foreign minister, when he moved to the Opposition benches after thirteen years in government). As the gap continues to widen between the end of our working life and the end of our natural life, the challenge of finding something useful and meaningful to do in retirement becomes more pressing. Caravan trips, ocean cruises and golf are wonderful forms of recreation for many people, but they don't fill the long years of retirement. Ultimately, you have to find ways of defining yourself in retirement that bring you the kind of satisfaction that paid work once provided. In the meantime, this period of coming to terms with 'relevance deprivation' can be very stressful, especially if your work was the main source of your life's meaning and purpose.

Whether you're in work or out of it, the cost of living is an ever-lurking source of potential anxiety – especially when soaring power prices create a significant challenge to the task of balancing the household budget. Since the credit revolution of the 1980s transformed our thinking, we have become increasingly willing to solve our short-term financial worries with borrowed money, thinking of it as 'credit' rather than 'debt' and assuming, vaguely, that it will all work out in the end. Yet a state of prolonged and unplanned indebtedness is almost guaranteed to raise your stress level. For people living in the 20 percent of households with an average annual household income of around $25,000, anxiety generated by cost-of-living pressures can scarcely be imagined by those higher up the income scale.

Many people claim to thrive on moderate levels of stress, but the well-documented effects of stress on the body show why it's often hard to distinguish between stress and anxiety. In stressful situations, the body releases adrenaline to help us cope, but if the stress is prolonged, then so is that increased dose of adrenaline.

This puts strain on the body that can lead to pain, fatigue and mental health issues, especially anxiety. All this is likely to be accompanied by raised blood pressure, muscle tension and the kind of hormonal imbalance that can weaken the immune system and cause sexual dysfunction. Those symptoms can themselves increase feelings of stress and thus perpetuate the stress–anxiety–stress–anxiety cycle. In that way, stress-induced anxiety can feed on itself – a potentially dangerous situation.

A particularly insidious source of heightened stress and anxiety is our failure to forgive someone who has wronged, offended or hurt us. US researchers Loren Toussaint and Everett Worthington have found that forgiving someone is an effective way of reducing your stress level and that failing to forgive – nursing a grudge, harbouring a bitter resentment – has adverse consequences for your mental health. As the researchers put it: 'Carrying this hurt can be a burden to one's social, physical and mental wellbeing. Forgiveness eases this and not surprisingly is linked to improved health and quality of life.'

Another villain in this sad story of unhealthy levels of stress and anxiety is the popular idea that, since we all enjoy being happy, the *pursuit* of happiness is a suitable strategy for living: 'If you're not happy, there's something wrong with you.' But if you fall for the deeply misguided idea that you're entitled to personal happiness as a default condition, then you've almost certainly set yourself up to boost your anxiety level. What could be more stressful than living in perpetual expectation of happiness? If that's your mindset, then you'll have to learn to live with ever-deepening frustration and disappointment as it gradually dawns on you that life isn't like that. Our deepest satisfactions don't come from doing things that make us happy, but from doing things that give meaning and purpose to our lives, some of which, like work and parenting, may involve prolonged episodes of quite distressing *un*happiness. But if we think we're entitled to feel 'up' most of the time – positive, cheerful, appreciated, gratified – then anxiety will stalk us like a mugger.

Given the current tendency to oversell the pursuit of happiness, we shouldn't be surprised at the inexorable rise in the use of so-called recreational drugs, especially among the young. If you've become convinced that you're entitled to happiness and things are not working out that way, then why wouldn't you feel that a pharmaceutical shortcut might be the way to achieve this elusive state?

Dig a little deeper and you'll find that some of the anxiety afflicting so many of us springs from uneasiness about the direction society is heading. Many people worry about Australia's failure to take dramatic action to combat and mitigate the effects of climate change, about our harsh treatment of asylum seekers, our cuts to overseas aid and our protracted military adventures in far-flung places. Many also worry about the income inequality that has produced a gap between rich and poor Australians not seen for 80 years or more, with greater numbers than ever before at the top and bottom of the economic heap and our once-famous economic middle class shrinking. We know that poverty has bad consequences for health, including mental health, and we also know that serious inequality, left unaddressed, builds frustration, resentment, anger and – potentially – violence into the social system, and doesn't history tell us that inequality is a breeding ground for revolution? Many people are made anxious by their own loss of faith in political, religious, commercial and social institutions that were once a source of confidence and reassurance. Some people are even stressed by their perception that *other people aren't as anxious as they should be* about such issues as climate change, inequality, institutional corruption, regional politics, the global rise of extremism, or any other matter of concern to them.

★

We're not just talking here about passing worries that might disturb and distract us, or even those existential questions that occasionally threaten to do our head in. We're talking about the widespread incidence – potentially affecting one in three of us – of a disorder that produces symptoms serious enough, and sustained enough, to cause people to seek professional help, or to take medication, or to discover that they need to develop conscious strategies for keeping their anxiety under control.

This is an epidemic whose effects deplete the emotional resources we need to function at work, to maintain personal relationships, intimate and otherwise, and to lead satisfying lives. Those effects range from the crippling anxiety that leads to uncontrollable panic attacks or episodes of foetal-position withdrawal, through to obsessive-compulsive behaviour (*having* to count your steps when you walk; *having* to check you've locked the door, even after you've already checked, perhaps several times; *having* to wash the tap before you turn it off; *having* to check your phone for messages last thing at night and first thing in the morning, and every spare moment in between), all the way down the scale to the nagging suspicion that no one really loves you (they're just pretending to), or the vague sense that all is not well, that the system is out to 'get' you in some way, or that there's something you should be worrying about, even if you can't identify what it is.

(Some people are in a quite different category from those of us whose anxiety comes in episodes. These are the unfortunate individuals who suffer such permanent, profound, life-limiting anxiety that it seems to be an inherent state – perhaps genetically determined – rather than a response to external pressures. Luckily, we live in a society where, for such people, professional help, including both medication and psychotherapy, is readily accessible. If you're in that state, and you've never sought treatment, start with a visit to your GP.)

Anxiety has become one of the hallmarks of modern Western society. As our consumption of tranquillisers and other medications – legal and illegal – rises ever higher, we need to confront some deep questions about the character, the values and the direction of societies like ours.

The underlying problem:
Loss of social cohesion

When we're looking for explanations of anxiety on such a large scale, rather than specific causes in individual cases, we need to examine the changing nature of society itself. In spite of all those specific factors – ranging from IT addiction to cost-of-living pressures to a nagging sense of job insecurity – that can trigger stress and fuel anxiety, an underlying *climate* of anxiety is generated by the increasing fragmentation of our society, through changes to the structure of families, workplaces, neighbourhoods and communities that have traditionally provided the comfort and security of knowing where we belong. Such fragmentation means that more people than ever before are experiencing periods of social isolation, increasing the risk of loneliness that morphs into feelings of social exclusion, and then into a more extreme sense of alienation. It's fair to say that our anxiety epidemic will be exacerbated by a looming epidemic of loneliness.

You have only to look at the way most humans choose to live – in cities, suburbs, towns and villages – and at our predilection for congregating in groups large and small to realise that the central truth about the human species (like most other species on this planet, by the way) is that we are social beings. Any erosion of social cohesion is therefore potentially damaging for our mental health in two ways.

First, it challenges our very nature as social beings who need communities to nurture, sustain and protect us, and give us a sense of personal identity. If I were truly alone, I would have no need of an identity. In fact, the whole idea of personal identity is meaningless without the context of the people you mix with. You don't look in the mirror to 'find yourself'; you look into the faces of the people who love you, or work with you, or live with you, or are at least prepared to put up with you. So a sense of social isolation diminishes our very sense of who we are.

As Thomas L. Friedman wrote: 'It is so much easier to venture far – not just in distance but also in terms of your willingness to experiment, take risks, and reach out to the other – when you know you're still tethered to a place called home, and to a real community.' What Friedman calls a 'real community' cannot be imagined except in terms of people interacting with each other, face to face, in the same place at the same time. Human presence is the one essential requisite of a 'real' community, and the health of local communities is still the best indicator of the health of a society. Online communities have their own valuable functions to perform as well, but they are communities of a quite different kind, and they make no contribution at all to our sense of social cohesion – indeed, they may well detract from it. (Compare your emotional state after an hour online with your emotional state after an hour spent with a friend or neighbour over coffee.)

The second effect of a loss of social cohesion is that when we feel alone, disengaged or unsupported, we are more vulnerable to all the other factors that might fuel our anxiety. It's harder to deal with any kind of challenge in your personal or working life if you're not supported by caring and compassionate people. Suffering alone is always harder than having a comforting arm around your shoulder or a group of friends to laugh or cry with. If the sense of belonging is fundamental to our mental health, it follows that we are less robust, less able to deal with whatever life throws at us, when we lack that support. So there's a compound effect: social isolation is of itself a risk factor for anxiety, and it increases our vulnerability to other risk factors as well.

Over many years, my own research has consistently identified 'loss of community' as one of the most common concerns among contemporary Australians. That concern is often expressed as a regret that local neighbourhoods are not functioning as well as they once did. 'We don't know our neighbours' has become a cliché of contemporary urban life, and it is never said with pride or pleasure, as if it is an achievement. On the contrary, feeling like a stranger in your own street is bound to fuel your insecurities.

A disturbing piece of research from Edith Cowan University has found that only 35 percent of Australians say they trust their neighbours (and, as we shall see in chapter 4, levels of trust tend to be lowest when a neighbour is from a different ethnic background). Clearly, that could not possibly mean that 65 percent of us have untrustworthy neighbours; what it must mean is that most of us don't know our neighbours well enough to have learnt to trust them.

In our quest to understand the nature and causes of the anxiety epidemic, therefore, the key question is this: *Are* families, neighbourhoods and communities – once a powerful source of the sense of belonging – less stable and less cohesive than they once were? When you look at the evidence, it's hard to argue with the popular perception that they are. (In chapter 3, though, we'll look at some lovely examples of neighbourhoods that are learning how to thrive again.)

Ever since the Industrial Revolution radically changed the way we live and work, we have struggled to adapt to those changes. And while, as a species, we are still – after 250 years – trying to absorb the impact of *that* revolution, we have had many more recent revolutions to cope with: the gender revolution, an economic restructure amounting to revolution, an information technology revolution, and even a revolution in the sense of our cultural identity as Australians.

Many of the changes that have been reshaping our society have also been propelling us in the direction of becoming a more fragmented, more individualistic, more competitive, more aggressive, less cooperative . . . and therefore more anxious society.

You know what those changes are because you've been living through them and, in your own way, contributing to them. But here's a quick reminder of seven of the most significant.

Changing patterns of marriage and divorce

With at least one-third of contemporary marriages likely to end in divorce, the consequent disruption of families, friendship circles and communities means you'd have to put 'less stable marriage' up there among the revolutions that have increased the risk of social fragmentation. Social analysts have been examining this trend for years, but it's a statistical fact about us that can't be ignored because it not only points to a transformation in the way we regard the institution of marriage, but it also taps into a deep well of human misery.

This is not to criticise the divorce rate (as a twice-divorced person, I wouldn't dare). On the contrary, I think we should regard a high divorce rate as a sign that people are demanding more from marriage – taking marriage more seriously – than in previous generations. And young people's tendency to postpone or avoid marriage may be similarly interpreted as evidence of a greater caution, based on a greater seriousness in their approach to marriage.

Divorce can be a very good thing: it releases people from a marriage that has become intolerable or simply pointless, and it may release children from a feeling that they are somehow implicated in their parent's misery, disappointment, anger or sullenness. But let's not kid ourselves; in all but the most civilised cases, the *process* of divorce tears at the social fabric. I'm not talking about the legal process – that's been made easier than ever (though not everyone feels that justice has been done when they walk away from the Family Court). I'm talking about the pain, the tension, the bitterness, the sadness, the anger, the bullying and intimidation, the accusations, the recriminations, the violence (sometimes physical, sometimes emotional), the reckless words spoken that can never be unspoken . . . and the anguish of those who have to stand by and watch it all happen. It's tough for the divorcing couple, tough for their families and tough for their friendship circles, especially if people feel they have to take sides.

And it's tough for the children, if there are any. The demographic fallout is easy to describe: one million Australian children now live with only one of their natural parents, and about half of them are engaged in a regular – mostly weekly or fortnightly – migration from the home of the custodial parent to the home of the non-custodial parent. Disruptive for all concerned, wouldn't you say? A situation crying out for compassion, generosity, patience and a single-minded concern for the wellbeing of any children involved? Of course. Yet these are the very circumstances in which most of us are emotionally crippled by our own pain, remorse, confusion and possibly regret – not a state of mind likely to encourage compassion, generosity, patience and a single-minded concern for the wellbeing of any children involved.

The pain can last for years. It would be amazing if the rate of divorce and other relationship breakdowns – including extended live-in relationships that go unrecorded in the nation's statistics – did *not* fuel the overall level of anxiety. The goal of separation and divorce is to make peace; too often, the reality is that the split provokes an ugly war of attrition, in which children who should be shielded from all this tension are actively recruited in the conflict.

If you've experienced a breakdown in a long-term intimate relationship and escaped such ugliness, be grateful that you and your ex-partner had enough maturity and compassion to treat each other with the respect due to a person you once willingly shared your life with.

Falling birthrate

While we're on the subject of children, we should acknowledge the contribution made by a record low birthrate to the changes in the dynamics of neighbourhoods and communities. Again, this is not to criticise the low birthrate, and certainly not to call for people to start having more children, as politicians do from time to time. The low birthrate in Western societies (many recording a lower rate than Australia) is an inevitable result of at least three factors: the rising education level of women, since better-educated and more affluent women tend to have fewer children than less well-educated and less affluent women, for reasons mostly connected with their very different attitudes to paid employment; the growing awareness of the world's limited resources leading many potential parents to make a rational choice to have fewer children; and the feeling among more affluent young adults that kids would drain their bank account and their energy, and interfere with a very nice lifestyle. (As the average age of mothers at the birth of the first child has crept up into the early thirties, the lifestyle question becomes increasingly significant.)

Why mention children in relation to community fragmentation? Traditionally, children acted like a social lubricant that facilitated the formation and maintenance of neighbourhood networks. A new family moved into the district, the kids met other kids on the school bus or at the park, they started visiting each other's homes to play and gradually the parents got to know each other as well. Sounds a bit twentieth century now, doesn't it?

As we approach the end of the second decade of the 21st century, we are actually producing our smallest-ever generation of children, relative to total population, which means that valuable social lubricant is in shorter supply than ever.

Ah, but we've figured out a way to compensate for the dearth of kids in the neighbourhood: while the birthrate has plummeted, the rate of pet ownership has soared, and we know that many of those dogs and cats are child substitutes, because they are given human names. Forget Fido or Smudge; I recently met a dog called Ian. (No reason why not, of course, and I'm not sure why it seemed such a strange name for a dog. No stranger, I guess, than Wendy, another dog of my acquaintance.) So walking the dog, or taking the dog to the park, has become a new way of making social contact with neighbours. And many people would argue that if dog ownership discourages breeding among humans, that's a good thing for the planet – though, no doubt, there'll soon be a crisis of pet overpopulation.

High-rise housing

Another sure way of breaking down communities is to house people in high-rise apartment blocks where they are remote from the life of the street. Yes, there are some glorious exceptions – I've received invitations from people who, having heard me fulminate against the social and emotional hazards of high-rises, want me to come to their apartment block's Christmas party to see what a close-knit community they have become.

Seductive terms like 'vertical villages' notwithstanding, the general picture is depressing. Shove people into a high-rise residential setting – anything above four or five storeys – and see them begin to obsess about privacy, security and the need to avoid eye contact in the lift or the carpark. See them install multiple locks on their doors. See their balconies remain deserted, because they feel too high up, or too exposed, to be safe. See their attempts to keep a struggling potplant alive, as if to say, 'Look, I really am in touch with nature.' No wonder the pet rock craze coincided with the explosion of high-rise apartment living – a little bit of 'nature' on your mantelpiece or kitchen bench, with zero maintenance.

It's unfashionable to talk about how humans are 'supposed' to live, but nothing in our evolutionary history has prepared us for high-rise living. And yet, in the world's most populous cities, it's now simply the way things are. The potentially horrendous social and environmental effects can be somewhat mitigated by imaginative architects and sympathetic developers who are prepared to make serious attempts to integrate recreational areas, gardens, cafes and coffee bars into the fabric of the tower. It can be done – even some old high-rise blocks in New York are getting a new lease of life courtesy of some imaginative interior re-engineering. Thriving commercial activity at street level helps, by increasing opportunities for those incidental social encounters that help make a neighbourhood function like a community. The provision of recreational parks and passive open space around high-rise developments can also minimise their negative effects.

But, broadly speaking, if you want to make humans anxious and neurotic, pack them into high-density housing. It's not the only reason why psychiatrists and psychoanalysts are run off their feet in places like New York and Buenos Aires, but it must be one factor. In that respect, as in many others, we're a bit like the lab rats that go quietly bonkers when their population density reaches the point at which they can no longer sustain the dynamics of communal living.

As many parts of Europe (and some of the older inner suburbs of Australia) have shown, medium-density, low-rise housing works very well – even better, perhaps, than the strung-out house-and-garden suburbs that were designed for a very different way of life from the one we now have. In fact, given the way we live, a suburb consisting of traditional quarter-acre blocks may potentially increase personal anxiety by increasing the risk of social isolation.

This points to the crucial role urban planners play in the social and, therefore, the moral and emotional health of our neighbourhoods and communities. The way we live owes more to the quality of urban design than to the urgings of ethicists or preachers.

Two-income households

The rise of the two-income household is partly a cause and partly a symptom of a more anxious society. It's a cause to the extent that, as a reflection of the increasing busyness of the age, people in households where both partners are working have less time and energy to devote to the life of the neighbourhood. It's a symptom in that it reflects the belief that two incomes are required to achieve the level of material comfort that is now associated with middle-class prosperity. I offer no judgement about any of this, but only suggest that we do need to recognise the personal and social consequences.

Increasing mobility

Our increasing mobility also has an obvious impact on the stability and cohesiveness of local neighbourhoods and communities – mobility, that is, in the sense of moving house more frequently than previously (we now do it, on average, once every six years), as well as our increasing reliance on the private car for transport to and from home. Waving at a neighbour's car is not quite the same thing as having a chat at the bus stop or on the footpath.

The IT revolution

While all that has been going on, the IT revolution has led us to confuse data transmission with communication, altered our perceptions of privacy and identity and – above all – made it easier than ever to remain apart from each other. (More on that in chapter 5.)

Shrinking households

Many of the factors listed above exert massive pressure on individual lives, but the one social change that most graphically symbolises our potential loss of social cohesion is the phenomenon of our shrinking households. The average Australian household now contains 2.5 persons (heading for an estimated low of 2.2 persons), and the single-person household is our fastest-growing household type, already accounting for one household in four, and projected to increase to about one household in three by 2030. Living alone doesn't equate to loneliness – for many solo householders it actually equates to freedom and independence – but it increases the risk. Given that we are herd animals who typically used to live in 'domestic herds' of five, six or seven people (often spanning three generations), the current size of our households means that we have to look elsewhere for herds to join – even if we have to resort to grazing with the herd in a food court.

How an anxiety epidemic affects us all

Because some level of anxiety is part of being human, most of us learn to cope with it, as we cope with occasional bursts of melancholia, failure, disappointment, or a common cold. But when it reaches the epic, epidemic proportions it now has, this is something quite different from the normal occurrence of anxiety in individuals. Anxiety (often twinned with either depression or obesity or both) has become so widespread, its effects are having a visible impact on the kind of society we are becoming.

Quite apart from the rather desperate embrace of consumerism and nostalgia already mentioned, a society under this kind of stress is likely to display three clear symptoms:

- a heightened and unrealistic yearning for *certainty*, often expressed in the flight to the black-and-white simplicities of fundamentalism (and not only in religion);

- an obsession with *security* and *control*, expressed in a willingness to accept more rules and regulations, more surveillance, and more bars on our windows;

- a retreat into a cocoon of *self-absorption*.

The yearning for certainty

When we're feeling anxious, we're more likely to embrace a set of beliefs or convictions that seem to offer the certainty of knowing we're right; that we have *the* answer; that we know *the* secret.

In the religious context, fundamentalism is the label we've given to such beliefs. The term was first applied to certain evangelical Christians who, disturbed by trends in liberal theology and by what they perceived as an increase in moral degeneracy in the early years of the twentieth century, published a series of pamphlets under the general title *The Fundamentals*. The name stuck. Today, it is still applied to some branches of evangelical Christianity, but also to followers of more rigid or conservative versions of Islam, Judaism, or any other religious group committed to their own narrow and strict interpretation of scripture.

The appeal of religious fundamentalism to people suffering from anxiety is obvious: it promises to ease their emotional and existential pain via a complete set of doctrines – dogma – that replace doubt with certainty. Not surprisingly, given society's present state of heightened anxiety, fundamentalism has thrived while other more liberal expressions of the religious impulse have faltered.

But fundamentalism thrives in anti-theism as well, courtesy of writers like Richard Dawkins, whose single-minded attack on one rather outmoded and highly conservative branch of theology is designed to convince his readers that *all* religious faith is delusional. In the realm of his own expertise as a scientist, Dawkins would never allow himself to adopt such a prejudiced position; his biology is better than his theology.

Some environmentalists have turned into fundamentalists, and so have some climate change deniers. Some militant feminists (especially those who believe there's only 'one true way' to be a feminist), some literary critics, some politicians, some architects . . . fundamentalism pops up wherever people are having trouble accommodating doubt, uncertainty, or the awful possibility that they might be even a bit wrong. Rigidity and a refusal even to entertain alternative views are hallmarks of the fundamentalist.

You can find fundamentalism everywhere, once you recognise it as a symptom of the anxiety of the age. Fitness fanatics, food faddists and diet propagandists, morals campaigners, opponents of sugary soft drinks, the marketing of bottled water or the use of plastic shopping bags . . . they all share the same driving passion for their cause. Many of those causes are worthy, of course, and these zealots do the rest of us a huge favour by bringing such issues to our attention. But their relentless, take-no-prisoners approach is often a response to their own deep-seated restlessness.

In her 2017 bestseller *First, We Make the Beast Beautiful*, Sarah Wilson recounts the story of her own unending struggle with generalised anxiety disorder that has several times threatened to derail her media career. In her parallel career as a ferocious anti-sugar campaigner (her *I Quit Sugar* books are runaway bestsellers), Wilson has convinced many thousands of her readers to give up sugar, or at least encouraged them to think seriously about reducing their consumption of it. This may well be a case of persistent, debilitating personal anxiety being channelled into crusading zeal. Such connections are not uncommon.

An obsession with security and control

A second symptom of the anxiety epidemic is our society's increasing willingness to accept the imposition of ever more draconian rules and regulations – especially those that seem to offer the promise of improved security (however that might be defined). Paradoxically, our sense of *insecurity* is only likely to be heightened by the installation of triple bolts on our doors and bars on our windows, since they constantly remind us of our fears and their symbolism reinforces the sense of danger and threat. Even as we accept the idea that more surveillance is probably good for national security, the surveillance itself can become a source of yet more anxiety.

When we are feeling anxious and insecure, we are less trustful of each other, less likely to smile at people we pass in the street, less willing to offer help to strangers in need or distress, less open to appeals to show more compassion towards refugees and others on the margins of our society. The inner voice of anxiety warns us against 'getting involved'. And we are more likely to disapprove of other people's behaviour, to become less tolerant and even to edge back towards wowserism – a point where religious fundamentalism and a general desire for a greater sense of control can intersect.

In this kind of mood, we're prepared to hand ever-stronger powers to police; to exaggerate the likely impact of terrorism; to obsess about 'border protection' as a symbol of our security more generally. It's the epidemic of anxiety that partly explains why so many people silently acquiesce in the treatment of asylum seekers, whether in offshore detention centres or in the community. We'd have to be feeling a bit spooked to put up with that sort of stuff being done in our name.

A society suffering from an epidemic of anxiety is more vulnerable to political leaders' attempts to play on our fears in order to secure our support for all sorts of measures we might otherwise resist – especially those that infringe our civil liberties in the name of tighter security. And it's no secret that when we are feeling frightened or nervous, politicians' grip on power becomes more secure; governments have always tended to benefit from fear in the populace. Just look at the four big spikes in former prime minister John Howard's popularity: the Port Arthur massacre, the Bali bombings, the 9/11 attack in the US and Australia's participation in the invasion of Iraq.

Politicians and parties that trade on such fears are more likely to receive oxygen when anxieties are running high, so it serves their interests to promote anxiety. It's hard to believe that political motives would ever outweigh a concern for the common good – let alone a nation's security – but that often seems to be the way. Hitler was successful in reinforcing Germans' suspicion of the Jews, elevating it to a ferocious anti-Semitism that bolstered his own position. Margaret Thatcher's 1982 decision to engage with Argentina in a war over ownership of the Falkland Islands was widely recognised as having been driven by her own domestic political agenda. In 2017, when Malcolm Turnbull's Coalition government had been trailing Labor in the polls for many months, it was not hard to guess the prime minister's motives for exaggerating the terms of the ANZUS treaty to suggest, in a grave tone, that Australia would automatically be at war with North Korea if that country launched an attack on the US – a view quickly challenged by an assortment of diplomatic, legal and military experts.

In her 2007 book *The Shock Doctrine*, Naomi Klein has documented many cases where governments have systematically exploited the public's disorientation following a shock – especially a war, a terrorist attack or even a natural disaster – to push through measures that serve their own or their corporate supporters' interests.

When we are being fed propaganda (*Stop the boats!*) that seeks to foment fear and anxiety, we would do well to ask: what is the *real* motive here? Politicians love nothing more than an 'enemy' as a focus for our fears – once it was communism, now it is terrorism.

The retreat into self-absorption

Possibly the most graphic of all the effects of an epidemic of anxiety is the emergence of a powerful Me culture. At one level, the Me culture appears as nothing more than a heightened sense of personal entitlement and an exaggerated concern with personal comfort and personal appearance (including both the boom in cosmetic surgery and the closely related tattoo craze). At another level, though, as I have already suggested, it can be read as a sign of disengagement from political and social issues and a corresponding desire to escape into our own comfort zone – both physical and digital. The so-called echo chamber effect of social media appeals to us precisely because it shortens our horizon and narrows our focus.

You could say that people taking pictures of the meal they are about to eat so they can post it on Facebook is simply cute and quirky – an entirely harmless little game. You could say that running up record levels of household debt, mainly via credit cards, is a sign that consumers have learnt the important lesson that debt sounds better when you call it 'credit' and that living on borrowed money makes more sense than saving – isn't that what rich people do, after all? You could say that QPL syndrome – that quest for the perfect latte or the perfect designer dog – is a sign of the pleasantly sophisticated society we've become.

You *could* say all that and, in other circumstances, you might be right. But when you know that all this coexists with high levels of stress and anxiety; that up to one-third of us will experience mental health problems in our lifetime; that 20 percent of young Australians will have had at least one episode of clinical depression (not just 'feeling blue', but depression as a mental disorder) before the age of 25; that two-thirds of us are overweight and obesity is now a public health issue; that binge drinking and drug abuse are on the rise; that, in epidemic proportions, we can't bear to be disconnected from our smartphones . . . doesn't it strike you as highly probable that all those cute little signs of self-absorption are actually danger signals?

For an individual, anxiety is always debilitating and sometimes disabling. For a society facing an epidemic of anxiety affecting millions of people all at once, it's like the enemy within our walls: sapping our energy, reducing our motivation to engage with the community beyond our own tight little circle (or the network of online contacts we may call 'friends', though they exist for us only in cyberspace, and may not even be who they say they are).

Unlike most of the factors that threaten our social cohesion, anxiety exists within us, rather than between us, and yet, by increasing our tendency to self-absorption, it has the potential to isolate us from each other. Anxious people are more likely to become obsessive about their own personal comfort and well-being, their own personal rights and entitlements, and their own personal priorities. Correspondingly, they are likely to become less concerned about the rights, the needs, the priorities or the wellbeing of others, and less trusting of them. Anxiety leads us to confuse self-indulgence with 'control': I can't control the big picture stuff, so I'll concentrate on the stuff I can control – that old QPL syndrome again.

Am I painting too grim a picture? Not at all. We need to understand the true dimensions of the problem, and its true implications, if we are ever to address it.

We can address it, of course, but that won't involve holding back the tsunami of change that threatens to engulf us. The way to alleviate our anxieties is *not* to pretend that disruption and uncertainty are avoidable; *not* to disengage from the real world; *not* to refuse to face the future – which is, after all, at least as promising as it is threatening, and even quite an exciting prospect if you are equipped to deal with it. Getting our anxieties under control might require some radical life surgery, so we must first decide if it's worth it.

Given what we know about the effects of social fragmentation on our levels of anxiety, we'd be crazy to go on living – and teaching our kids to live – as we are now. We're not going to turn the clock back; we're not going to junk the technology; we're not going to stop enjoying the fleeting pleasures of consumerism (for pleasures they are); we're not going to give up the pursuit of material prosperity for a life of poverty in a monastic cell somewhere. Of course we're not. But is easing back a possibility? Rethinking our priorities, slowing down, disconnecting from technology *sometimes* (such as when we're eating a meal in the company of family or friends, or heading for bed), *noticing* what is happening to our children as a result of the toxic blend of their excessive screen time and our excessive busyness . . . in other words, being a little more observant, a little more moderate, a little more restrained, a little better prepared for the future.

Too much to ask?

Australia is a wonderful country, but the statistics tell us it's also a sick society: overanxious, overweight, overmedicated and financially overstretched. May I remind you that one-third of us are likely to be affected by mental illness at some time in our life. One in three. In any one year, according to *beyondblue*, two million Australian adults will experience an anxiety disorder and one million will be engaged in the silent battle against depression. Each year, between 65,000 and 70,000 Australians attempt suicide.

A sick society needs healing, and a good starting point for that process might be to face the truth about what we're doing to ourselves, our kids, and the society we are responsible for building.

I've already acknowledged that anxiety has always been with us, one way or another (though not usually in today's proportions). We therefore have a very long history of dealing with it, and several strategies have proven effective in helping to minimise the anxiety arising both from our existential, cosmic fears and from the pressure, the uncertainty and the essential unpredictability of daily living.

Here are the top four.

The magical power of faith

The first is faith, religious or otherwise. Placing our faith in something greater than ourselves – something grand, inspiring and enduring – can give us the same sense of security mariners associate with being close to the 'mother ship'; it can enlarge our perspective and give us a kind of borrowed strength. Research conducted by Martin Seligman, the pioneering leader of the positive psychology movement, has led him to conclude that faith in something larger than the self is the one absolutely essential prerequisite for a sense of meaning in life – and the larger the entity, the more meaning people can derive from it. Seligman does not promote religion; he has written that the 'something greater than the self' might be the family, or the nation, or an institution – though he also notes that faith in those things is waning. Faith in leaders, especially in Australia, is also on the wane.

For most of human history – and for most people living on the planet today – the God of religion has supplied that 'something greater'. But in many Western societies like ours (such as North America, Scandinavia, the UK and parts of Western Europe), where traditional religious faith and observance are in steady decline, the vacuum created by the absence of religion must be filled by something else.

Even if we reject traditional notions of an external, supernatural God, we might yet be able to place our faith in the inherent goodness of humankind, or in the spirit of loving-kindness within and among us – an echo of the psychoanalyst Carl Jung's idea of 'the God within' – or in the power of a good idea to change the world. Some monarchists, especially in places like the UK, place their faith in the monarchy itself. Others put their faith in democracy. Indeed, some leaders have such faith in their preferred version of democracy, they feel entitled to try to impose it on other countries.

We might place our faith in the inspiring ideals of truth, beauty, peace and justice, or we might look beyond all that to Earth itself, or to 'the universe'. We might engage with some kind of non-religious spirituality – perhaps via the practise of a secularised adaptation of Hindu yoga or Buddhist meditation – that provides a discipline and a context for enriching the sense of meaning and purpose in our lives.

For some people, a cause – clean energy, environmental puri-fication, world peace, or the therapeutic benefits of mindfulness or honey or fasting – can act like a kind of god by providing such a clear focus that the cause becomes the 'thing greater than yourself'. And, certainly, if you invest your faith, your time, your energy in the promotion of your chosen cause, this will enrich your sense of your own life's meaning and purpose and that may well keep your anxieties at bay. However, personal observation leads me to suspect that the emotional (spiritual?) benefits of passionate devotion to a cause may be somewhat diminished when the focus is entirely negative – anti-capitalism, anti-socialism, anti-liberalism, anti-Semitism, anti-Islam, anti-*all*-religion, anti-homosexuality, anti-alcohol, anti-gambling, anti-sugar, anti-red meat, anti-vaccination (though anti-slavery and anti-corruption are obvious counter examples). Causes rooted in a desire to stop other people being who they are, or believing what they believe, or doing something they enjoy or want to do, are bound to take their toll in frustration, and even rage, among those promoting them. Crusaders can live heroic, noble lives, but they can also become martyrs to their own zeal.

In a material world, some people put their faith in the free market via a quasi-mystical belief in the laws of supply and demand, or in some bizarre economic equivalent of the 'survival of the fittest', leading to the idea of prosperity as the mark of a successful life. In most Western countries, about one-third of people claim to believe in astrology, placing their faith in their horoscope to unlock the mysteries of human life – their own and other people's. ('Astrology can't be true,' said one of my research respondents, 'except that my husband is a textbook Aries.')

Whether it's any of those things, or the twelve steps of Alcoholics Anonymous or the practise of formal religion, the underlying truth here is that when we place our faith in a 'higher being', a 'higher ideal' or a 'higher purpose', our anxieties are likely to be at least partly allayed. Research into the correlation between religious faith and mental illness strongly suggests that people with religious faith are less likely to suffer from anxiety and depression, and are likely to bounce back more quickly from depressive episodes, than those with no faith in anything beyond themselves. As Seligman puts it: 'The self is a very poor site for meaning.'

It sounds simplistic, but the available research (summarised in *Handbook of Religion and Health*, by Harold G. Koenig et al.) is compelling. It suggests that if you were to predict the likely effects on a society of declining religious faith and practice, one of those effects would be a rise in the level of anxiety and depression. And, yes, there's a downside: many people have in the past been spooked *by* their religion; religion can certainly raise our anxiety level when it's all about sin, judgement, revenge and punishment, rather than grace, peace and love.

In a society like Australia, where 52 percent of the population still identify as Christian but only 15 percent attend church once a month or more often (though it rises to 25 percent at Easter and even higher at Christmas), either religion must recast itself in ways that will increase its relevance to a broader section of society, or substitutes must be found for the benefits of religion. That's a challenge for the churches and other organisations that promote faith in a higher power; it's also a challenge for society at large. In a post-religious society, what context might parents use for teaching their children about the value of faith? What might non-religious cultural institutions have to say about ideas and ideals worth placing our faith in? Where should we look for the sense of a 'higher purpose' that might unite us as a society and revive our faith in idealism?

Or should we be content to muddle along, faithless and pragmatic – and increasingly anxious – to the end?

The secret power of community

Much of the research into the health benefits of religious faith and practice is actually reporting on *two* influential factors, not just one: people who engage in the rituals and other practices of their religion, like those who practise the disciplines of non-religious spirituality, are typically doing so in a communal setting. The benefits of membership of a faith community are only partly related to faith; they also flow from group membership itself – the powerful sense of belonging to, and being accepted by, a community of like-minded people who, at their best, will be characterised by mutual support, kindness and respect.

Which brings us to the second great anxiety-reducer: engage-ment with a human community. A family, a neighbourhood, a workgroup, a friendship circle, members of a sporting or social club, a faith community, a book club, a drinking group, a writing group, a painting group, a theatre group, an adult education class, a choir, a garden club . . . any kind of community has the potential to ease the anxieties of those who belong to it.

Think of it as a series of propositions based on probability, not certainty. *If* we are socially isolated, *then* our anxiety level will probably go up. *If* we are relying on information technology to connect us, at the expense of face-to-face contact – especially if we also resist engagement with our local neighbourhood – *then* we are more likely to feel anxious. *If* we overdo the very important need for solitude at the expense of our equally important need for social contact and personal relationships, *then* we will be prey to the fears and doubts that haunt people who spend too much time in their own company.

This is why the most devastating punishment we can inflict on a prisoner is solitary confinement. It's why being 'sent to Coventry' by people who refuse to speak to you or even acknowledge you evokes such abject feelings of desolation, well beyond mere rejection. Most of the desires that drive us (apart from basic bodily survival needs) are social desires: the desire to be taken seriously, the desire to connect, the desire to belong, the desire to be useful, the desire for love.

Belonging to a community of any kind has two big psychological advantages for most of us: first, we feel we are not alone – others are there to call on when we need help; second, the dynamics of a group usually exert pressure on us to conform to its mores and values. 'Hey,' you may say, 'that doesn't sound like an advantage,' and yet, although it does sound stifling, it is actually one of the ways we are saved from doing reckless and stupid things, and perhaps even inspired to lift our game. A key benefit of membership of a social species is that we are shaped and influenced by those around us. That can be bad, of course, if we've chosen to link ourselves to a gang of rogues, renegades, layabouts, rebels-without-a-cause . . . or terrorists. But it's mostly good. 'It takes a village to raise a child' is a wise African proverb that doesn't only apply to children; we are all formed and even disciplined – as well as potentially inspired, enlarged and motivated – by the energy of the groups we belong to. That's one of the reasons why many parents are keen to have their children participate in team sports: any tendency to brattishness and egomania is generally stamped out more quickly through the experience of playing as part of a team than it is, say, in young tennis players.

The Australian actor and writer Ailsa Piper (author of *Sinning Across Spain*) has noted that when she writes in company with a small group of friends, her own performance is lifted: 'There is such value in a community because of the debt we feel we owe to it. I absolutely feel I must aim higher and work harder when I'm with those women, because I don't want to let the group down, even when the only group activity is silent solidarity.'

So is the sense of belonging to a community enough, on its own, to relieve our anxieties? Does it work just because being part of a herd or a tribe is natural for us? Do we feel better simply because we're bending to the pressure of our genetic destiny?

I think not. I accept that cooperation is in our DNA, and that we are, by our very nature, social beings, but not every community will make you feel welcome. All of us can point to experiences where being part of a group actually heightened our anxieties; where petty bickering, gossip, backbiting and ego struggles actually brought out the worst in us. All of us know someone who can't bear to spend too much time with their family. All of us know people who have left a neighbourhood, or a town, because they felt suffocated, rather than comforted, by the prospect of being absorbed into that particular culture.

So the power lies not merely in community itself, to the extent that any old community will do. Not at all. The *secret* power lies in something that happens to us when we become part of a healthy, supportive community. While the benefits of social engagement are practically self-evident, there's a less obvious benefit as well: belonging to a community keeps us in touch with people who might need us, and nothing relieves anxiety like a focus on someone else's needs. When we belong to a community characterised by mutual care and respect, that experience will develop our capacity for compassion towards others. And it is *the exercise of compassion* – not merely the experience of belonging – that is the great antidote to anxiety.

Here's a specific example of how that works. Compassionate people are more likely to forgive those who have wronged, hurt or offended them, and the act of forgiveness, as we have learnt from the work of Toussaint and Worthington, is a great stress-reducer both for the forgiver and the forgiven. They argue, for example, that the capacity for ready forgiveness is the most significant feature of a good marriage, since forgiveness – born of compassion – is how damaged emotional bonds are repaired. As in a marriage, so in a family, a neighbourhood, a workplace – even a nation.

It may sound harsh, but anxiety thrives on self-absorption, and bearing a vengeful grudge is a classic form of self-absorption. As we have already seen, the habit of forgiveness – like the habit of compassion itself – is one of life's great stress-busters.

This is not to criticise those trapped in the coils of anxiety, since our most crippling anxieties often spring from causes way beyond the control or understanding of the person experiencing them – especially if the anxiety is the result of early childhood deprivation or neglect or, conversely, a childhood spent trying to live up to the unrealistic expectations of an overly ambitious parent. But wherever the anxiety comes from, nothing relieves it like the focus on someone else's concerns rather than your own. In *First, We Make the Beast Beautiful*, Sarah Wilson notes that at times when she was focused on someone else's needs, and when she was pregnant, her anxieties melted away – as of course they would. Knowing that someone else is depending on us is a great steadier of the emotions.

Ideally, our capacity for compassion – our disposition to be compassionate – is nurtured in us as children by our own family. This is what lies behind the oft-quoted (and generally misinterpreted) proverb: Charity begins at home. Like all the best proverbs, it conveys deep wisdom – in this case, that children need to be taught the lessons of kindness, charity and compassion while they are young and within the security of their own home. Then, as they spread their wings, those lessons will stick: from being a member of a compassionate family, they are likely to become compassionate adults.

Not all of us grow up in ideal families where the habit of compassion is nurtured. Most of us are damaged, however unwittingly, by our parents, and most of us damage our children, equally unwittingly. The nature of the damage varies from case to case, but the deepest wounds are inflicted by a parent's failure to teach, by example, the lesson of compassion. Compassion always carries the implied message of unconditional acceptance; of taking someone else seriously. When compassion is withheld, or dispensed selectively, that message is achingly absent.

Children growing up in emotionally deprived, neglectful or abusive family or institutional settings – or who have become anxious through some other less obvious cause – often experience difficulty in later life both with forming intimate relationships and with maintaining 'normal' social relations that rely on the exercise of some degree of compassion. Such people may struggle all their lives to cope with their unresolved anxiety, even if they become accomplished in some field of endeavour – often involving a heightened imagination – that compensates for the lack of formative attachments that would encourage compassion.

In *Solitude*, the British psychiatrist Anthony Storr discusses writers and other creative artists who found ways of compensating for this type of deprivation in childhood. Beatrix Potter did it by focusing all her attention on tiny animals, drawing them and making up stories about them until, at the age of 47, she formed a permanent intimate relationship, married, and stopped publishing. Storr comments: 'She is not the only example of a writer whose interest in imaginative invention seems to have declined in similar fashion.' It's not that love drives out creativity; rather, where the creativity is a compensation for the lack of love and compassion in a life, the arrival of love reduces or eliminates the need to live more in the imagination than in the world of interpersonal relationships.

P.G. Wodehouse retreated almost entirely into the fictitious world of his novels. Wodehouse, Storr notes, was not ill-treated but simply 'passed from hand to hand' in childhood, and so he created an imaginative world in which 'there is no violence, no hatred, no sex, and no deep feeling'. Rudyard Kipling also lacked the emotional support and stability of a family home, was bullied at school and virtually tortured by a foster carer, and suffered all his life from insomnia and digestive ailments. His escape, like Potter's and Wodehouse's, was into the intensely private and imaginative world of writing.

Storr is careful to note that difficulties in forming relationships can't always be attributed to adverse circumstances in childhood. Nevertheless, it remains generally true that a childhood in which compassion is not displayed, encouraged and nurtured is likely to provoke the kind of anxiety associated with difficulties in forming close attachments. It's not merely the lack of a sense of connection to a family or other social group that is the problem; it's the lack of development of the habit of compassion.

A friend who spent most of her childhood in boarding school once told me that she had attended a school reunion at which it emerged that all the girls in her year who married boys who had also attended boarding school had been divorced. Her take on it was that none of them had acquired the emotional resources to cope with the demands of marriage and, with both partners equally 'deprived' in this way, the marriages never had a hope. That is nothing more than one anecdote, of course (though I've heard many other people raise the same issue, especially in the case of children sent to English boarding schools at a very early age), and it certainly does not amount to a general criticism of modern boarding schools. But it does point to the particular challenge institutions face when they try to compensate for a child's loss of the emotional support of a reasonably secure, loving family.

I repeat: compassion – not just belonging – is the great antidote to anxiety.

Compassion will release us from the trap of self-absorption. Compassion will encourage our tolerance of difference, our disposition to be kind and non-judgemental, our willingness to respond to the needs of the other members of our group and, indeed, to those outside it, since the habit of compassion will naturally assert itself when we are confronted by a stranger in need, just as much as a friend.

One of our greatest Australians, H.C. 'Nugget' Coombs (the leader of the reconstruction program following the Second World War, architect and founding governor of the Reserve Bank, inaugural chair of the Australian Council for the Arts and the Council for Aboriginal Affairs) said as he approached his own retirement: 'Retirement should be active, purposeful leisure shaped by the thought of others' need.'

I'm not suggesting that a lack of engagement with a local neighbourhood is an inevitable source of anxiety for everyone, but the risk is great. When we lose sight of our role as members of a community – especially our role as neighbours – this is bound to erode the habit of compassion and make us less responsive to others' need. After all, it's easier not to respond to someone's need if you have managed to avoid eye contact with them in the street.

This is how the health of the community suffers, and when the health of the community suffers, we all suffer.

We don't act compassionately in order to make ourselves feel better; that would be a travesty of the whole idea of compassion. Still, it's no accident that compassionate people, people for whom kindness is a way of life, typically (though not universally) report high levels of life satisfaction – often expressed as 'peace'– and low levels of anxiety.

The lack of compassion is a health hazard. If we lose sight of our true nature as members of a community and focus too much on our own wants, our own entitlements and our own gratifications, with little regard for the needs and wellbeing of others, there will be some inevitable erosion of our capacity for compassion and a corresponding threat to our mental health.

The restorative power of nature

A third traditional source of relief from anxiety comes from the experience of being connected to nature – gardening, bushwalking, strolling in a park, walking the dog, climbing a tree, tending a garden, swimming in the sea or sailing on it, picnicking in a tranquil and beautiful setting, playing games that take you outdoors and into a natural environment.

How does that help? Because we humans are part of the natural world, our stress levels are likely to rise when our access to nature is restricted. Being in touch with 'the earth' turns out to be important for us. We instinctively know that 'grass time' – running on it, rolling in it, throwing and catching a ball across it – is vital for the health and wellbeing of children. We hardly need research to tell us that if kids are cooped up indoors for too long, glued to a screen rather than engaging directly with the natural world (to say nothing of interacting with each other), they are likely to suffer. But adults are no different. We, too, need our 'grass time' (no drug jokes, please), our park time, our garden time, our beach time, or our mountain time. Going for a walk or a run is good for us in many ways; chief among them is that we are in touch with trees, flowers, birds, the sky, the grass, the weather. We see nature, we smell nature, we touch nature, and the therapeutic benefits in stress reduction and a widely reported 'clearing of the head' are very reliable.

Running on a treadmill at a gym or swimming in an enclosed pool don't offer the same therapeutic benefits, even if your muscles and respiratory system are still getting a good workout and, perhaps, your performance is being revved up by a suitably motivational music track. Pounding pavement or turf with audio buds stuck in your ear and a podcast demanding your attention has been shown to enhance your absorption of the material you are listening to, but it may diminish the effectiveness of the exercise itself by disrupting the feedback loop between muscles and brain.

What if your reason for exercising outdoors was to get your stress level down not only by working up a sweat but also by getting more closely in touch with nature? Isn't listening to that podcast going to limit the sensitivity of your response to the breeze or the rain on your skin? Won't you be less likely to notice the colour and movement of trees, to 'smell the roses', to attend to the subtle changes in the texture of the ground you're crossing, to hear the birds sing or to see them forage, to be *in* nature? If the purpose of getting out into 'nature' is anxiety-reduction, wouldn't the material playing in your ears and occupying your mind be a major distraction from the benefits of all those natural experiences?

The term 'nature deficit disorder' was first used by Richard Louv in his 2005 book *Last Child in the Woods*, in which he presented the results of his extensive field research into the negative effects on children of spending too much time indoors, being supervised, or 'protected', or else overstimulated by electronic devices. The lack of free play time in a natural environment appeared to increase children's anxiety and represented a threat to their mental health and wellbeing, quite apart from the obvious connection between outdoor exercise and general physical health and fitness.

Nature deficit disorder is not a recognised medical disorder; it doesn't appear in any doctors' manuals, though some US psychologists are now identifying 'nature deprivation syndrome' in anxious children, particularly those with short attention spans. Many other research projects have confirmed Louv's hypothesis (to say nothing of most parents' hunch) that restricting children's access to nature has a negative effect. A University of Illinois study showed that outdoor exercise can help to reduce attention deficit disorder (ADD) in children, and other studies have pointed to the benefits of incorporating some outdoor experience in the teaching of a wide range of subjects.

But do you really need to be convinced by research? Doesn't it make sense that, as humans, we are viscerally connected to the natural world that sustains our very life, and so we are likely to suffer when that connection is restricted? Wouldn't you expect that not only anxiety but also obesity and reduced attention span would all be exacerbated by a significant reduction in time spent playing and relaxing in a natural environment?

And while you're rethinking the question on behalf of your children, don't forget to rethink it on your own account as well. If you're running or walking *and* playing a podcast, your fitness and your learning may both benefit, but what if you're passing up the therapeutic stress/anxiety-reduction benefits of intimate, direct connection with the natural world?

The therapeutic power of creative self-expression

Though most of us manage to ignore this fourth strategy for reducing stress and anxiety, perhaps claiming we're too busy for such trivial pursuits, participation in the creative and performing arts is a brilliantly effective stress-reducer and anxiety-reliever. (It also has the great advantage of making us feel better without having to burden our friends with our tales of woe, and sometimes without having to seek professional help – though there are many occasions when a bit of professional help can help break the anxiety cycle and calm you down.)

People who sing in a choir, for instance, typically report that this is one of the most therapeutic things they've ever done – it's good for your breathing, your posture, your mental acuity, and for building trust within the group. They will tell you that the experience of using only your voice to make music in company with others is uniquely thrilling. That's why the most ancient and primitive rituals often incorporate group chanting and singing, and it's why the singing of hymns is often the most uplifting part of a church service. (If you were ever told that you can't sing, the person who told you that was wrong: you don't have to have a wonderful voice to sing, and any competent teacher can help you learn to hit the right note.)

Singing, dancing, painting, photography, sculpture, pottery, writing poetry or stories, acting . . . participation in any of the creative and performance arts adds a significant dimension to your life and can make a big contribution to your mental health.

Which is not to suggest that people who make a living from the creative or performance arts are mentally healthier than the rest of us. Oh, no. Many creative artists are notoriously neurotic, socially awkward, narcissistic and emotionally troubled. You wouldn't have wanted to live with Beethoven, let me tell you. Nor Van Gogh. When creativity or performance is your job, then you need some other form of relaxation to relieve the stress and anxiety resulting from that kind of job. (Maybe Beethoven should have played touch footy. Or chess. On the other hand, it might have been his neuroticism that fuelled his creativity. It often is.)

But when you are engaged with creativity and/or performance as a relief or escape – or simply a change – from the demands of your daily grind, *that's* when the magic kicks in.

Reality check. Okay, then: we place our faith in something greater than ourselves; we engage with a community – a neighbourhood, a workgroup, a friendship circle, an extended family – that gives us a sense of belonging; we gradually develop the habit of compassion; we factor in more 'nature time'; maybe we even join a choir or learn to paint . . . *terrific!* In those ways, we have increased the probability that our anxiety level will fall. But there are no guarantees – especially if you're one of those unfortunate souls who seem to have been born anxious, or if you have never been able to identify and do something about the source of your anxiety.

Sarah Wilson's book about her personal struggle with anxiety listed some features of modern life that she believes are bound to increase our stress levels. Here's a selection:

Working on the fly from laptops.

Weaving in and out of traffic.

Eating on the run.

Walking around with takeaway coffees.

Keeping up with technology updates.

Taking the whole family to Paris and London (for no reason other than everyone else seems to be doing it).

Online grocery shopping on your lunch break.

Wilson points to an excess of *movement* as a primary villain in the anxiety story: crazy cab rides across the city, overnight interstate trips, flying, driving long distances. Though she describes herself as being 'arrogantly attached to many of the factors that make me anxious – the speed, the multitasking, the constant change', she does draw breath for long enough to acknowledge that many pragmatic mothers would say to offspring racing to nowhere on this high-speed treadmill: 'Now, what are you going to do about it?'

Good question. If your level of anxiety is a problem for you, you may have to take serious, perhaps even temporarily painful, remedial action. If your level of debt is stressing you, then reducing it should be your highest short-term priority. If your housing costs are a major source of stress, look at alternatives to the housing you currently own or rent. If you're in an abusive, miserable or tense relationship, either persuade your partner to enter into joint counselling with you or find your own pathway out of the relationship (and, yes, you can terminate a relationship respectfully and with compassion). If your job exerts the pressures of overwork and/or overstimulation on you – too much screentime, too much travel, too much *speed* – then consider looking for different work. There are no prizes for martyrs when the source of your suffering can be identified and dealt with.

If you know that 'the speed, the multitasking, the constant change' are sources of anxiety in your life *and you continue to do them*, then at least there's no mystery about where the constant anxiety comes from.

On the other hand, if your anxiety comes from a deep-seated concern about the state of our society, it might be time to join a revolution – or to start one.

The central theme of this chapter has been that when a society is gripped by an epidemic of anxiety and depression, this has an impact not only on the individuals who suffer directly, but on the whole character of the society. In that sense, we are all afflicted.

Silently, insidiously, the effects of anxiety on individuals become societal effects as well, partly because anxious people are less likely to want to engage with those around them. The healing task is therefore a task for all of us, and it begins with a determination to offer comfort, companionship, kindness, compassion, reassurance, support and encouragement – especially by being prepared to be a patient listener – to the people in your own circle of family, friends, neighbours or work colleagues who are obviously suffering and may be acting quite erratically as a result. To help them is to help us all.

Anxiety is usually a symptom of a deeper malaise. When it reaches epidemic proportions, it should alert us to the fact that too many people in our community are struggling to find their bearings in this new and still emerging sociocultural landscape. That sense of disorientation is compounded for anyone already feeling socially isolated and unsupported.

The sense of belonging is the result not only of others' acceptance of us but of our acceptance of them as well. Two-way compassion – treating each other with kindness and respect – is the key. It's also how we get our anxiety level down. Few things are more relaxing than knowing you're doing the right thing by those who need your support, help or friendship, or perhaps simply your acknowledgement of them.

A reflection

On the culture of busyness

A brochure recently arrived in my letterbox from Audible, the Amazon audio-book company. The headline said: 'No time to read? You need Audible.' That was the pitch: Audible's audiobooks are for people who have *no time to read*.

Now, there are many good things to be said about audiobooks. The main one is that you can hear a professional actor adding all the nuances of voice – timbre, tone, accent, rate of speech – to the words that would otherwise sit lifeless on the page. You can also indulge the pleasing illusion that you are being read to, rather as you might have been as a child.

Neither of those benefits is about saving time. In fact, if you have 'no time to read', then you would certainly not have time to sit – or lie down – and listen. It takes less time to read a book than to have one read to you, since our rate of speech when we read aloud is far slower than when we read silently to ourselves.

But Audible is not promoting the pleasure of listening as an alternative to the pleasure of reading. This is about saving time; it's about lives so consumed by busyness that we need to listen to audiobooks *while we're doing something else.*

It can be done, of course: you can listen to them while driving, though if there's a challenging situation on the road, you'll miss a chunk of the story, since the eye always trumps the ear; you can listen via earplugs while you're walking or running, though this will dilute the pleasure of being outdoors; you can play them while you're cooking a meal, ironing or weeding the garden, though there are therapeutic benefits from giving single-minded attention to such activities, believe it or not, that are diminished by distractions.

Audiobooks seem, on the surface, to be a very efficient way of squeezing books into an already overcrowded life. But whatever happened to the sheer, unalloyed pleasure of reading that can only be achieved when reading – or even listening – is *not* combined with doing something else? Do these people who have 'no time to read' have no time for other pleasures either? Perhaps they also find sex a bit too time-consuming, especially when a partner demands all that tedious foreplay. Or do they halve the pleasure of both by combining sex with audiobooks?

Audible's campaign strikes me as being like the canary in the mine, warning us there's a poison in the air. That poison is called 'busyness'.

'How are y'going, Bob? *Busy?*'

'Nah, not really. Just, you know, coasting.'

Imagine Bob admitting such a thing. Not busy? Poor bugger must be on his last legs. He doesn't look old enough to have retired, but if he has, surely he knows it's de rigueur to say: 'I'm so busy I don't know how I ever found the time to go to work.' Maybe he's been retrenched. Why can't he just *pretend* to be busy?

(The recently retired father of a friend had a better strategy than Bob's. When asked what he was doing since he gave up work, he would reply, 'I'm a human being, not a human doing.')

No matter how we try to dress it up, disguising it as a virtue or a badge to be worn with pride, relentless busyness is a health hazard – yet another contributor to our epidemic of stress and anxiety. For too many of us, holidays have been compressed into 'short breaks', the pleasure of walking or running in the open air has been swapped for a quick burst at the gym, the therapeutic joy of aimlessness has been overwhelmed by the need for everything to have both a purpose and an outcome.

A sane person would regard excessive or sustained busyness as a warning signal. No time to read? No time to walk? No time to play? No time to nurture a neglected relationship over a cup of coffee? Surely there's something awry in a life like that, yet too many of us are inhabiting a mad world where *not* to be busy is seen as an admission of failure, and where the most dangerous propaganda of all – *time is money* – can convince you that you really can't afford to spend 'unproductive' time with friends, let alone find time for simple pleasures.

There are many reasons why we might allow busyness to rule our lives. An employer might be making unreasonable demands on our time, and we might fear losing the job if we aren't prepared to shoulder the whole burden being laid on us. If we're self-employed, we might fear that the work will dry up if we don't accept whatever is available. If we're juggling the demands of a full-time job with the demands of a family – perhaps involving ageing parents *and* dependent children – we might feel there is simply no alternative; that we have become martyred to our busyness.

Or we might be inefficient. (Strange how rarely we assume that a busy person might be inefficient; the culture of busyness inhibits the discussion of such possibilities.)

Or we might *want* the work to expand to fill the available time so we'll *seem* busy because we know everyone equates busyness with importance.

Or we might be using our busyness as a cocoon of self-protection, shielding us from other responsibilities we'd rather not confront: an unhappy home life, a partner who has become a source of more pain than pleasure, or the prospect of watching yet another school concert, play or soccer game in which our offspring are involved.

Busyness – whether real or confected – creates a sense of entitlement: if you can claim to be busy, then you can scale your priorities accordingly, and who's going to argue with you? Busyness is the greatest of all excuses. In this culture of busyness, we don't pity those who are busy, or blame them for letting their lives spin out of control. On the contrary, we praise their busyness, we admire it, we respect it, tiptoeing quietly around it so as not to add to the burden already being borne by the Busy One. 'Don't disturb Mummy – she's busy.' 'Daddy is still at work – he's busy.' No other explanation required.

One of the ironies of the IT revolution now engulfing us is that we are so busy receiving and sending messages to each other, there's not enough time to reflect, ponder and interpret thoughtfully, which is why texts and emails so often result in misunderstandings, unintended slights, or humour (especially irony) being mistaken for insensitivity. In fact, we're *so* busy, we are devising a new, abbreviated form of written language, to save time (btw, wtf, tx, asap, lol, cul8r); we have embraced Twitter, bowing to its demand that we say everything in 280 characters or less; we have become scanners, rather than readers, of anything longer than a short paragraph. I was amused to receive an email recently from a young person seeking career advice that included in the subject line: 'Warning – long email'.

There are three obvious effects of our addiction to busyness. First, we are becoming a sleep-deprived society in which people increasingly complain of fatigue, and a shortage of sleep is now a significant public health issue.

The second effect is more insidious: we are becoming afraid of stillness, solitude, inactivity. In fact, 'I'm bored' has become the ultimate cry of despair of the rising generation of digital natives who are so accustomed to constant stimulation that, when things go quiet or they are temporarily unplugged, they feel threatened by the silence.

It's not only children who are afflicted by the fear of boredom. When a few minutes spent sitting on a bus or train can't be endured without a screen to gaze into, or an hour or two – let alone a day – of 'nothing to do' feels like a threat rather than a blessing, we know we are being devoured by the busyness monster.

The third effect of our relentless busyness is the most disturbing of all: it can both distract us and insulate us from the needs of the people around us. Busyness 'decompassions' us.

As I write this, the media are reporting that an elderly man died in his Sydney home, but no one had noticed that anything was amiss. His wife – frail, blind and dependent on her husband as her carer – subsequently died of starvation. When the police suggested that we all need to reach out more to our neighbours, to keep in touch with people in our street, to look out for signs of anyone in trouble, there was surprising pushback from people claiming that they were too busy to notice such things.

Isn't that the dark side of the culture of busyness? Not just too busy to help; too busy even to notice that help was needed.

Next time someone asks you if you're busy, see how they respond if you say that you're trying very hard to be less busy and more efficient. Better still, try to reorganise your life just enough to make this answer so close to the truth that, if you decide to buy an audiobook, you'll be motivated by the pleasure of listening rather than the need to do something else at the same time.

3

Who's afraid of diversity?

The first concern ... should not be to create an Australian culture, but a cultured Australia.

Simon Leys, *The Hall of Uselessness*

Early in 2017, Miranda Devine, a columnist for the *Daily Telegraph*, NewsCorp's Sydney tabloid, declared that 'diversity is the weaponisation of political correctness, and it's going to kill us all'. Devine's is not some isolated voice crying in the wilderness; her sustained fury on the subject of cultural diversity would draw strong support from xenophobes, racists, and others who have failed to grasp one of the central facts about life on earth: across all biosystems, including ours, diversity is a source of strength. Generally speaking, mongrels are hardier than purebreds.

That's not to say that we find it easy to deal with an unexpected increase in the diversity of our local neighbourhood. Human nature being what it is, we are naturally wary of 'otherness', and our wariness increases with the degree of difference – especially in terms of ethnicity and religion. In his 2010 book *Disconnected*,

Andrew Leigh drew on a wide range of research to conclude that as ethnic diversity increases in a community, the level of trust falls.

That's not as disturbing as it may first appear; it simply reinforces the point that we are least trustful when we are most wary. Given the long-term advantages to any society of increasing its cultural diversity, the challenge is not to embrace some fantasy of homogeneity such as 'racial purity', but to find ways of bridging the culture gap between 'us' and 'them' as quickly and respectfully as possible. Learning to trust people who are different from us is a greater challenge than learning to trust people who are like us, and the rewards for our society are correspondingly greater. (And, by the way, haven't you sometimes been let down by people who are just like you?)

In Australia, the topic of diversity is usually cloaked in the garb of 'multiculturalism'. The word has gone out of fashion both here and elsewhere around the globe, but why? It would be nice to think it's because politicians and others who now eschew the word have finally heeded the wisdom of Pierre Ryckmans, the late Belgian-born Australian writer, critic and Chinese scholar. Writing under the pen name Simon Leys, Ryckmans declared in an essay on provincialism that 'culture is born out of exchanges and thrives on differences. The death of culture lies in self-centredness, self-sufficiency and isolation.'

Béla Bartók, the Hungarian composer and ethnomusicologist who died in 1945, would have agreed with that assessment. Bartók spent much of his early musical life collecting and adapting folk music, mainly from Hungary, Slovakia, Romania and Bulgaria. In the process, he discovered that the richest and most engaging folk tunes came from border regions – rather like cultural fault lines – where different ethnic groups intersected, leading him to become a firm believer in the value of cultural diversity. In the same vein, as mentioned in chapter 1, the British philosopher A.C. Grayling identifies the cultural collisions resulting from the large-scale displacement and relocation of people following the Thirty Years War as one of the contributing factors to the European Enlightenment.

In a 2017 essay for the *London Review of Books*, British writer Julian Barnes endorsed Ryckmans's view that the essence of culture lies in difference, and also gave us Ryckmans's opinion of multiculturalism: '"National culture" is a self-contradiction and "multiculturalism" a pleonasm.' (To save you looking it up, as I had to do, a pleonasm is a redundancy of expression – the use of a superfluous word or phrase.) Leys/Ryckmans's point was that any robust society is essentially multicultural; that culture is by definition 'multi'; that diversity is what *makes* culture.

So perhaps those politicians, journalists and social commentators who now avoid the term have simply decided that 'multiculturalism' is indeed a pleonasm, though I've never heard them put it quite like that. What I have heard, or at least inferred, is more sinister: they have seemed to suggest that we no longer want to celebrate diversity in our culture, because we would prefer that people from different ethnic, religious or cultural backgrounds be integrated into the Australian way of life.

Well, of course they should. That's why they came here – to do precisely that. That's the aim of almost anyone who migrates, either freely or as a refugee: they seek a better life in another country and their whole purpose is to enter into that 'better life' by becoming a participant in the life and culture of that country.

Yeah, yeah; not everyone. There are deranged exceptions: people who move to a country with malevolent intent, perhaps wanting to spread fear and disquiet through acts of terrorism or to undermine its values through propaganda; people who settle somewhere precisely because they disapprove of its culture and have a missionary's zeal to change it; people who thought life would be better elsewhere and then find it isn't, and spend the rest of their lives grizzling about how things were better where they came from. (When they return home for a visit, they usually find either it's not as wonderful as they had fondly recalled/imagined it to be, or that things have changed there, too. Malcontents, basically.)

Overwhelmingly, people come here to join in – yes, to integrate – which is not the same as saying they come here to lose their sense of who they are, or where they have come from, or what they have been through, or to suddenly take on a transformative mantle of Australianness, whatever that might mean. And many migrants retain a strong sense of pride in the culture of their birthplace, or in the values they hold (about marriage and the family, for instance) or in their religious beliefs. Integration is not assimilation; nor is it a case of 'them' merely becoming replicas of 'us'. It's more complicated than that, luckily. Just like Bartók's border-region folk music, both sides benefit from the cultural enrichment produced by the intersection and gradual blending of host and immigrant. After all, our sense of personal identity – like culture itself – is a construct that can only emerge from our relationship with our social environment.

What's touching, from the perspective of the host community, is that these people have chosen ours, out of all the societies on earth they might have chosen. But wanting to be part of us doesn't stop them being themselves, too. They never cease being who they were – their roots never change – even as they gradually acquire an identity that's inevitably more complex, more nuanced, than it was. Some of them are understandably bewildered by this transformation in themselves.

Our entire history since 1788 has been about the process of intersection and blending of cultures. If we imagine the first non-Indigenous settlers were a relatively homogeneous bunch, we should think again: culturally, convicts were very different from free settlers and soldiers, officers from other ranks, petty crooks from hardened criminals, the English convicts from the Irish,

French, Americans and Africans who were also on board. In fact, more than 60 nationalities were represented in the First Fleet.

When they landed in the bay that became known as Farm Cove, they had set foot on a continent already populated by more than 400 Indigenous nations, so cultural diversity was alive and well here long before the arrival of Europeans. And we might as well acknowledge, right here, that the arrival of the First Fleet ushered in 200 years of moral blindness towards Indigenous people that is only now being seriously addressed. For too long, the heart of our nation has been hardened towards its First Peoples, partly because moral and emotional disengagement is an effective way of avoiding the burden of our national shame.

Many Australians who claim to be resistant to diversity cling to the rosy notion that we have historically sprung from an essentially Anglo-Celtic heritage. Okay, what does that mean? What comes to mind when you try to imagine an 'essential' Anglo-Celt? Are you thinking of a man or a woman? A London banker or a Cornish fishmonger (who could scarcely understand each other if they tried to communicate). An Irish Catholic nun or a Scottish weaver? A silversmith from Sheffield or an academic from Cambridge? A poet from Kent or a coalminer from South Wales?

The UK has always been one of the most multicultural places on earth, and that was before the mass migration of people from its former colonies in India, Pakistan and the West Indies, and the later waves from countries in the European Union. The population of London is increasingly diverse: 44 percent are members of black or other ethnic minority groups. (That's nothing, by the way, compared with New York's 67 percent.)

And Australia? As of the 2016 census, 33 percent of us were born overseas: about eight million, out of a total population of 24 million. And 45 percent of us have at least one parent born overseas. In Sydney, our largest city, 43 percent of the population was born overseas. Just pause and process that: almost half the population of Sydney was not born in Australia, which puts Sydney ahead of that famous 'melting pot', New York, where 35 percent of the city's population was born outside the US.

One of our leading demographers, Bernard Salt, argues persuasively that Australia is the world's most successful immigrant nation. Our 33 percent born overseas stands well clear of Canada's 22 percent, Germany's 15 percent and Britain's 13 percent. (Saudi Arabia, with 32 percent of its population born overseas, looks like a contender for the world championship, but Salt points out that 'Saudi Arabia's foreign-born residents are guest workers who do not have the same sovereign rights as migrants'.)

Salt makes this crucial point about the way Australia absorbs its immigrants: 'It's about both cultures growing together over time, fusing in a very Australian way, where we take bits of each culture and create something that suits our values.' While acknowledging that there are bound to be some ethnicity-based tensions and occasional abhorrent acts of racism, Salt's conclusion is that 'this nation should be proud of the fact that we have achieved something that no other nation has achieved or attempted'. And what is that? 'The delivery of sustained economic prosperity combined with a generous immigration program over generations.'

Journalist and political commentator George Megalogenis, in books like *Australia's Second Chance*, has long argued that we are at our best – economically, culturally, socially – when our immigration levels are high. He warns that to break that link between immigration and socioeconomic health would be a disastrous error that failed to take account of history's lessons.

These are strong, evidence-based arguments and they raise the question of why we have been so spectacularly successful at building such a harmonious society out of such diverse racial, ethnic and cultural ingredients. The answer might be as simple as this: it might have worked so well here precisely because of the extent of our diversity. Our population now includes such a huge number of ethnic groups, representing about 180 different birthplaces across the globe, that we don't experience the tensions that typically occur when there are fewer, larger groups.

Attitudes evolve in response to new experiences and so, as you would expect, our attitudes towards immigration, and towards immigrants themselves, have been maturing as the reality of our increasingly diverse society sinks in. In *Reinventing Australia* (1993), I was reporting on attitudes towards immigration that were markedly more edgy, and more hostile, than they are today. That was only 25 years ago, and the idea of 'official' multiculturalism had already been around for twenty years, yet the conventional wisdom was still dominated by an enduring attachment to assimilation as the thing immigrants were expected to do, and assimilation effectively meant homogenisation. (Some of that thinking persists even today, of course, in pockets of prejudice.) There was a simmering resentment of the idea that ethnic subcultures might want to preserve their cultural traditions, even while becoming integrated into Australian society – as if migrants should 'give all that up' if they wanted to be accepted as 'New Australians', a term introduced in the 1950s but still popular with many people into the early 1990s.

In 1993, it was possible to write the following passage about the typical attitudes of the host community, especially those who were at least second- or third-generation Australians:

[Their] attitudes towards immigration, even when benign, have generally been egocentric and one-sided: they have been conscious of their own difficulties in accommodating people who are racially and culturally different from themselves, but they have rarely spent much time contemplating the difficulties faced by immigrants in trying to comprehend and adapt to the

Australian culture. The typical Australian view is that migrants have, by definition, committed themselves to a process of adaptation and that it is they who should be making the primary effort to adjust: there is little currency for the idea that because Australia actively sought its migrants, local communities might therefore have a responsibility to help them adapt.

In effect, the traditional Australians attitude towards migrants is that they should become as invisible as possible, as quickly as possible.

Back then, people often imagined a kind of contest between the ethnic, racial or cultural identity that immigrants – including 'Poms' – brought with them, and the new-found Australian identity they were expected to adopt.

Clearly, there's been a significant shift in our attitudes to immigration since then, but it has taken us a long time to achieve today's greater acceptance of ethnic diversity. The pace of acceptance will pick up as more of us experience small, personal instances of the richness of multiculturalism such as these . . ..

A father previously hostile to 'Asians' learns that his daughter has fallen in love with a Vietnamese medical student whose parents were refugees. Over time, the father learns to respect his daughter's boyfriend, then to accept him, and finally to embrace him with unexpected pride. Social events involving both families turn out to be warmer and more hilarious than he had imagined they would be.

A family of fundamentalist Christians – mother, father and two teenage boys – are horrified to discover that their new neighbours, a young married couple, are devout Muslims. They have long conflated 'Islam' with 'extremism' and are wary of having anything to do with these people, even though they occasionally smile and wave to each other when not to do so would appear rude. The sons are warned to keep their distance. Then the mother is diagnosed with aggressive breast cancer. During the protracted, debilitating period of surgery and subsequent chemotherapy, several members of the family's church bring meals and offer to help with shopping, but the two young Muslims become daily visitors. Before and after work each day, they drop in to see how the household is getting on, to offer companionship and support to the mother, picking flowers from their own garden and putting them in bowls, helping the boys with maths homework (the wife is an accountant) and driving them to and from various events, mainly associated with their school or church, when the father is busy at work. The bond of neighbourliness gradually strengthens and when, after two months, the mother is sufficiently recovered, the Christian family find themselves responding with pleasure when they are invited into the Muslims' home to share a meal. The subject of religion is avoided, except that when the young couple discover that their neighbour's 'second religion' is golf, they ask if he might be prepared to introduce them to the game, and he begins by giving them some putting lessons in their own backyard. 'You wouldn't believe how beautiful their back garden is,' he says to his wife after the first lesson. 'Puts ours to shame.'

The parents of a boy in high school become concerned when they notice a steady increase in the number of Asian – mostly Chinese – students in the school. They start making tight little remarks to other 'Anglo' parents about playing 'spot the Aussie' at sporting and other school events. Their son becomes particularly friendly with an Australian-born Chinese boy in his soccer team, and they begin visiting each other's homes. After one visit, the father remarks to his wife that, when the boys are out of sight, you can hardly tell their voices apart – they sound equally 'Australian'. On another occasion, he asks his son how he feels about the large number of Asian pupils in the school. His son looks puzzled for a moment, and then shrugs: 'Most of them were born here, Dad. But so what if they weren't? What's the point of the question? You only want me to hang out with the Iraqis?'

The small-town advantage

Simon Leys echoed the point made by many cultural analysts and historians: that we are often culturally richer when we live in smaller communities where diversity has more immediate meaning for us than in a huge metropolis. In big cities, the sheer size of the place encourages people to congregate within their own subculture, rarely interacting with those from other subcultures. This is why people in large cities are always exclaiming, 'It's a small world!': the slice of the city they inhabit is probably both small *and* homogeneous, comprising people with similar ethnic, educational, religious or other backgrounds, at a similar socioeconomic level.

According to the Argentine writer Jorge Luis Borges (as quoted by Julian Barnes in the *London Review of Books*), 'the writer who is born in a big country is always in danger of believing that the culture of his native country encompasses all his needs. Paradoxically, he therefore runs the risk of becoming provincial.' It's an idea that seems counterintuitive, though the US may strike you as a good example of Borges's point. The experience of many people bears it out – and the point seems to apply to big cities as much as to big countries: big-city dwellers can easily become more parochial than those in diverse smaller communities, because although their city seems so culturally rich and diverse, they don't actually brush up against much diversity in their daily transactions or personal relationships. In diverse smaller communities, by contrast, the diversity is right there, and you must deal with it.

Bernard Salt points out that the Victorian town of Horsham, which he describes as seeming rather 'white bread' from a distance, actually contains great diversity, starting with the fact that 10 percent of its population of 20,000 was born overseas – a minority far more visible than it would be in a larger city. Leys noted that Goethe had lived in Weimar, 'a town somewhat smaller than Queanbeyan', but had managed to keep up with English,

French and even Chinese literary developments. Like Borges, Leys concluded that 'cosmopolitanism is more easily achieved in a provincial setting, whereas life in a metropolis can insidiously result in a form of provincialism'.

It's so easy to believe otherwise, and yet there have been plenty of famous examples of writers who have felt compelled to leave a big city to work in more provincial settings: J.D. Salinger, of *Catcher in the Rye* fame, left New York for the woods of New Hampshire (from where he wrote about almost nothing but New York). James Joyce had to leave Ireland to write about Dublin from a distance. Our own David Malouf did some of his most beautiful work under the influence of the time he spent in Tuscany. There were many reasons for those and countless other writers and artists to flee big cities, but one of them may well have been that they recognised the danger of believing, as Borges put it, the culture of their native country (or city) could encompass all their needs.

That doesn't, of course, mean that we can't appreciate and learn from the cultural diversity of our big cities, but it does mean that we probably experience it more richly in small, manageable pockets — in the 'urban villages' of inner-city Melbourne or Sydney, for example, or in suburbs that have undergone cultural transformation under the influence of immigration, urban renewal or other factors that have rendered them less homogeneous — perhaps mixing wealthier with poorer, older with younger, childless couples and singles with families, public housing with private. Cultural diversity comes in many forms.

The many dimensions of diversity

When people resist — or even fear — the idea of multiculturalism, it's usually because they think of it as having only one dimension: multi-ethnicity, perhaps, or multi-faith. Think again about that word 'multiculturalism' – or, if you prefer to avoid using that word, think more generally about the inherent diversity of any culture, and the great diversity of ours.

I'm drafting this chapter in July 2017, when the prime minister of Australia is Malcolm Turnbull and the deputy prime minister is Barnaby Joyce. How's that for cultural diversity? Though leaders of the same political coalition, they could hardly be more different in style, background and cultural formation. There is Turnbull, the suave, urbane lawyer-cum-merchant banker, investor and property owner, exuding confidence and socioeconomic superiority in everything from his house to his suits to his rounded vowels. In the infamous words of Tony Abbott's former chief of staff Peta Credlin, he is 'Mr Harbourside Mansion'.

Barnaby Joyce, by contrast, keeps his vowels as flat as possible, in order to reinforce the impression that he is a country boy through and through – as, indeed, he is: he grew up on a sheep and cattle property in the New England district of New South Wales. Though a graduate of the University of New England, Joyce always presents himself as rather homespun, rather rustic, rather unsophisticated – a person prouder of his rugby career than his academic credentials. Farmers and small-business people are his natural social milieu, whereas we associate Turnbull with rich and powerful bankers and boardroom lizards; he looks uncomfortable out of a suit and off pavement. (This is an inaccurate perception, since Turnbull owns a farm and is said to be a competent horseman, but that would come as a surprise to most voters.) Barnaby Joyce has always been widely known as 'Barnaby' even by those who don't like his politics, and his manner has often seemed to imply that he's just removed a stalk of paspalum from his mouth before fronting the camera or microphone.

The opponents of one would call him a 'silvertail'; opponents of the other would call him a 'hick'. Though they are both white, middle-aged, precociously ambitious males, you'd certainly never mistake one for the other, would you? Nor would you expect them to agree about everything, given their differences in background. And such a partnership is probably very good for the health of the Coalition . . . just as cultural diversity is for the health of a school community, a workplace, a neighbourhood or a football team. In *The Diversity Bonus*, Scott E. Page argues that diversity has been a crucial ingredient in the most successful management teams operating in the knowledge economy – even though, as I've already acknowledged, ethnic diversity can initially pose a challenge to our capacity for trust and mutual respect.

'WASP' was an acronym in vogue back when we were still coming to terms with the idea of diversity. Standing for 'White Anglo-Saxon Protestant', it was intended to convey the characteristics of most Australians at the time – the so-called mainstream. In fact, it's a label for an extraordinarily diverse group of people who, in many respects, have little in common with each other beyond the colour of their skin and the name of the religion to which they ascribe. Take that word 'Protestant'. Have you ever been in a room with a stern, Bible-brandishing fundamentalist, a mild-mannered liberal and an exuberant Pentecostalist? They are like the cultural equivalent of three distinct tectonic plates, constantly threatening to collide and erupt. Indeed, they might as well represent different religions, so disparate are their beliefs and practices. WASP is one of those labels – rather like 'British' – that identifies a demographic category, but conceals the many interesting and important nuances within that category.

Multiculturalism implies that we will more or less cheerfully absorb all shades of Protestantism, plus Catholicism (Roman and Anglo), plus entirely different religions, from Baha'i to Hinduism, into one multi-faceted culture. The cultural diversity project is far from being only, or even mainly, about ethnic diversity. In a multicultural society we willingly incorporate a rich diversity of ethnic backgrounds, of course, but, equally, we accommodate a rich diversity of personal aspirations (economic and otherwise), sexual orientation, religious faith or the lack of it, recreational and lifestyle preferences (including the widely divergent lifestyles of urban and rural dwellers), fashion sense, tastes and preferences in the arts – from music to movies – to say nothing of different household and family structures, and widely different intellectual endowments and physical abilities.

The embrace of cultural diversity means we each enjoy the freedom – which we extend equally to others – to lead our own kind of life (within the law), raise our children in our own way, go on the kind of holidays we prefer, play our favourite music, worship different gods or none, play different games, do different jobs, spend our money differently. And – here's the rub – we accept this about ourselves and each other, because we know that the peaceful and harmonious society and the robust local neighbourhoods we want to live in depend on each of us learning to accept and appreciate the value of those differences, including those that don't happen to appeal to us.

In other words, diversity – and only diversity – teaches us both tolerance and compassion towards 'otherness'. Diversity also teaches us humility, as we come to acknowledge that ours is not the only way to live, and not necessarily the best way, either. To take some simple examples: the Mediterranean diet is being adopted by Australians with no family ties to Mediterranean culture; yoga is popular among people with no background in Hindu religion; meditation and mindfulness training are experiencing runaway popularity with people who have no particular interest in exploring Buddhist philosophy. Those are all healthy signs of the impact of cultural diversity.

The essence of multiculturalism – the essence of culture itself – is that we are all both influenced and enriched by this intersection with difference. We are all involved in the cultural exchanges that build and strengthen the society we live in.

Those persistent 'generation gaps'

No discussion of the ways we intersect with difference would be complete without mentioning generational diversity – a source of tension, bewilderment and mutual suspicion that impinges on practically all of us and does more than most other forms of diversity to challenge our cultural complacency.

If you accept the common practice of defining generations in roughly fifteen-year chunks, then the three dominant generations in contemporary Australian culture are: baby boomers, the postwar generation born between the late 1940s and early 1960s; generation X, born between the early 1960s and late 1970s; and millennials, the smart new label for the old 'gen Y', born between the late 1970s and the mid 1990s. It would be hard to imagine three more different cohorts of Australians, not because they set out to be different from each other, but because the accelerating rate of social, cultural, economic and technological change through the second half of the twentieth century created radically different contexts for the formation of those three generations.

Forgive the gross generalisations, but broadly, this is how they each were shaped . . .

Baby boomers rode an upward escalator of postwar prosperity and learnt to expect more of the same. *And* they lived with the tensions of the Cold War and the ever-present threat that it would turn hot. So terms like 'nuclear holocaust' and 'mutually assured destruction' (MAD) were not only part of their lexicon but were lodged deep in their psyche. Their generational challenge was to reconcile the rosy prospect of endless prosperity with the equally likely prospect of nuclear war and mass annihilation. How did they do it? They embraced instant gratification as their generational ethos. Their generational catchcry became: *We're not here for a long time; we're here for a good time.* They became famously short-term planners and poor savers (so poor, in fact, that Paul Keating had to invent compulsory superannuation to give them a nudge and set a better example to following generations). They also became impatient iconoclasts and protesters – not only about the Vietnam War, but also about the place of women as second-class citizens in society, about the patriarchal culture and punitive ethos of religion (they led the stampede out of churchgoing), and about the broader right of young people to be taken seriously. Their sheer size – the largest generation of children, relative to total population, we had ever seen – gave them a loud voice and a huge footprint. They expected to be seen *and* heard.

The oldest boomers turned 70 in 2016. Like the rest of their cohort, they have come to see themselves as the Forever Young generation, believing that they look younger, feel younger and are fitter, healthier and more stylish than their own parents had been at the same age. (Generally speaking, they're right about all that.) Stretch denim was invented for them, so their generational uniform – jeans – could cope with their changing shape as they aged.

To their own amazement, they survived. Annihilation didn't happen. But they had to learn to cope with the fallout from some radical social revolutions. New laws allowed them to become our most divorced generation in history (though their children may outdo them); economic upheavals made them our most retrenched and unemployed generation since the Great Depression; and the women's movement liberated many women from the shackles of the attitudes and values they had inherited from their own mothers and grandmothers, while leaving many men bewildered by the assault on the attitudes and values they had inherited from their fathers and grandfathers.

The boomers also had to rise to the early challenges posed by the information and communications technology revolution, and to acknowledge, more or less painfully, that their world (including, ultimately, their own children and grandchildren) was being profoundly and sometimes mysteriously reshaped by that revolution. Being the children of the postwar period, their attitudes to cultural diversity were shaped by the influx of 'reffos', 'dagoes' and 'wogs', and the adjustment to a more liberal view of cultural diversity has been harder for many of them than for the generations who have followed them.

Generation X, largely shaped by the cultural influences of the 1970s and 80s, might as well have been a different breed from that shaped by the 1950s and 60s. Think ABBA versus The Beatles. They were like slipstreamers, neatly tucked in behind the revolutionary boomers, with much of the hard yakka of social change and reform having been done for them – or, at least, the process being well underway. The anti-Vietnam war protests had borne fruit, the threat of military conscription had passed, and the Whitlam era was upon them. Feminism was no longer a new and heady (or scary) concept: Germaine Greer's *The Female Eunuch* had been published before most of them were born. Gender equality was an established part of their thinking, even though there were still many pockets of male chauvinism in the ranks of gen X, under the lingering influence of their own fathers.

Think of them also as lifestylers: they took that word 'lifestyle' and made it their own. They were settling into a sense of a newly confident Australia – more culturally mature, more ethnically diverse than ever – yet they had not been seduced by the prospect of endless economic prosperity nor spooked by the threat of nuclear war. All that had passed by the time they reached early adulthood.

The label 'gen X' was coined to symbolise the mysterious, indefinable X factor that so sharply distinguished them from the boomers. They were set for the long haul, and wanted to make the most of it, but they were never gripped by the same generational impatience as the boomers.

★

And so to the millennials. Mostly the offspring of boomer parents, the millennials are at least as different from gen X as that generation was from the boomers. Their cultural formation through adolescence and early adulthood has been influenced by the upheavals of the 1990s and the first decade of this new millennium. The resulting differences between them and their own parents have been a more or less inevitable source of strain and tension.

Older generations throughout history have criticised younger generations for not cheerfully adopting the values and following the conventions of their elders, but the attacks on the ethos and values of the millennials, including attacks from their own parents as well as their employers, have been quite extraordinary. Lazy, self-indulgent, expecting everything to be handed to them on a plate, no respect for their elders, impatient . . . most egregious of all, some boomers have taken to calling them the 'Me generation', when that was the very label created for the young boomers by their own appalled elders.

Demographer Bernard Salt, himself a boomer and long-standing critic of the millennials, wrote a newspaper column in which he accused them of not being able to afford to buy their own homes because they squander their money on 'smashed avocado' breakfasts, eaten out, instead of saving. So entrenched are the prejudices against millennials that the phrase 'smashed avocados' quickly passed into the lexicon as shorthand for the stock-standard accusations against them. It was amusing, it was unfair and it was, of course, absurd.

In fact, millennials have grown up with far more uncertainty, instability and unpredictability than gen X, and a different kind of uncertainty from that faced by the boomers. For the millennials, *everything* is uncertain: the prospect of stable work, affordable housing, questions about a commitment to marriage and parenthood (they are, after all, the offspring of our most-divorced generation of parents), and their engagement with the ever-changing world of technology, where, as 'digital natives', they have appropriated the new social media in ways that both mystify and worry their elders. As a result of all this, millennials appear to take unpredictability in their stride while being deeply affected by the knowledge that nothing stands still. For them, the next thing, whatever it is – job, partner, updated technology – is just over the horizon.

What has all this taught them? Their catchcry – *Keep your options open* – couldn't be more different from their parents' at the same stage. Though both generations were motivated by a sense of uncertainty, one was based on the prospect of obliteration and the other on less existential anxieties. Millennials have become, quite understandably, the 'wait-and-see' generation, happy to hang loose, withholding commitment until the last possible moment. 'Let's see what happens' is a line that might infuriate their parents, but it neatly sums up their caution about commitment, learnt from their own experience. They are marrying later (if at all), having children later (if at all), and buying real estate later (if at all) – not because they are squandering their savings on smashed avocados but because of their keep-your-options-open philosophy.

When boomers, and even gen X-ers, took some pleasure at prospect of the global financial crisis of 2008 having a 'corrective' or 'sobering' effect on millennials, they had failed to realise that this was probably the generation best equipped to cope with global uncertainty; uncertainty is the very air they breathe.

And what of the post-millennial generation, born since the mid 1990s? Given our determinedly low birthrate, this is the smallest generation, relative to total population, we have ever produced.

In the US, they are sometimes referred to as 'snowflakes', an unkind, pejorative label, though you can see where it might have come from. Many members of the rising generation are the product of overprotective parenting (often as overcompensation for absent parenting), and of a childhood that was filled with praise, reward, and the promise of endless praise and reward to come: *You're wonderful! You can do anything!* These are the children who were being saved from disappointment and failure, and who, in the process, were being given a seriously unrealistic expectation of what life would be like. I'd hate to see a label like 'snowflake' catch on, since it implies fragility and lack of resilience, though it's true that many post-millennials are in for a painful reality check as they hit young adulthood and the challenges of serious study, intimate relationships and the world of work. Before rushing to judge them, their parents and grandparents might need to reflect on what made them the way they are.

For Jean M. Twenge, the US adolescence researcher quoted in chapter 2, the 'smartphone effect' has been so influential on the formation of post-millennials that she has dubbed them the iGen. She makes the point that they not only see the world differently but that, thanks to the smartphone revolution, they are spending their time differently from previous generations – in particular, spending more time alone in the privacy of the bedroom sending and receiving incessant messages on their smartphone and often, Twenge says, distressed by feeling left out of whatever others in their circle might be doing. She notes that they are less keen to learn to drive, less keen to start dating and generally less keen to be independent than previous generations have been at this stage of their adolescence. According to Twenge: '18-year-olds now act more like 15-year-olds used to, and 15-year-olds more like 13-year-olds. Childhood now stretches well into high school.' The silver lining is a reduction in teen pregnancy rates.

Considering their very different formative influences, and the resulting differences in their attitudes, values, aspirations and behaviour, it's no wonder that generational differences seem even starker and more challenging than many of the ethnic, religious or other cultural differences we point to more readily.

Generational intersections are challenging partly because we don't always appreciate that they are just like any other cultural collision. Perhaps they seem even more mystifying than some other dimensions of diversity precisely because they occur between us and people – such as our own offspring – whom we expect to be just like us.

But, as with any other aspect of diversity, we all have much to learn from the generations other than our own – the older from the younger just as much as the younger from the older. (And, by the way, talking to people younger than you is a useful way of stimulating brain plasticity, so there's a personal benefit as well as an enrichment of society, though I do worry when I hear parents trying to act and look as if they are members of their children's generation. Where will their children go when they need a parent rather than an older adult in the house who likes to 'hang out' with them and borrow their clothes?)

So . . . more understanding, please, boomers! After all, you created the circumstances that shaped the generations that have followed you. And, millennials, please stop bleating about how older generations are holding you up, getting in your way and failing to take you seriously enough. Of course they are! That's what older generations always do, except that this time you have a bigger than normal culture gap to contend with, so you look even more alien to them than young people generally do to their elders. Plus there's the fact that your parents are members of a huge cohort that became accustomed to getting its own way, and will live longer than any previous generation in our history. Under their influence, watch aged care become our number one priority.

The challenge is clear for the members of any generation dealing with the members of any other generation: Listen! Learn! Adapt! Accept! And that's the same challenge, obviously, as the one we face when we are dealing with any people who seem significantly different from us, for whatever reason.

It's our exposure to difference, and the challenge of accepting difference, that fuels our moral as well as our cultural development. Learning to accept people who are unlike us, learning to get along with neighbours we wouldn't necessarily have chosen . . . such learnings are fundamental to our growth towards moral maturity. Moral muscle is formed by developing the art of compassion, respect and tolerance towards those who are quite unlike us, including those we don't like much. And that's the kind of muscle we need if we are to build communities that are both diverse and cohesive.

Bigotry is fun (unfortunately)

Twenty-five years ago, the issue was how we would come to terms with the fact that 'Australian identity' was virtually indefinable because of our increasingly diverse culture. We were starting to cotton on to the idea that we were actually defined by our diversity.

Today, we get that idea, almost universally, so the pockets of racism, xenophobia and trenchant resistance to the idea of diversity represent a rather sad little rearguard action – a throwback to a time when we didn't yet grasp what a towering achievement our unique brand of harmony-in-diversity really is. Or perhaps those lingering prejudices represent a hankering after a time when there seemed to be less diversity because our many cultural differences were concealed beneath the veneer of a somewhat less ethnically diverse population.

I suspect what we're actually seeing is nothing more than a fresh outbreak – from a small but vocal minority – of the latent racism and xenophobia that lie within all of us. No one likes to be branded a racist, or to be accused of prejudice of any kind. Yet our innate sense of tribalism cannot be denied, and racism, like most other prejudices, is no more than an expression of that primitive urge to bond with our own herd and to keep our distance from that other herd.

Who among us hasn't felt an ugly little tug of racism at the hem of virtue's cloak of tolerance? Who hasn't experienced a flicker of sympathy for the idea that those who are different from us – racially, ethnically, socially, economically, sexually, culturally, intellectually, religiously – are also inferior? And who hasn't been comforted, ever so fleetingly, by feelings of hostility towards an out-group?

Teenage gangs are an expression of that primitive tribalism. So are the football fanatics who attack the supporters of rival teams. Old money versus new money is tribalism at its most genteel, and the varieties of religious belief or the philosophical nuances of political factions have a long, inglorious history of sparking tribal conflict.

That darker side of our nature poses an ever-present threat to the creation and maintenance of a civil society. This is one of those impulses, like the disposition to violence, that, over the millennia, we've learnt to control, most of the time, but it requires constant vigilance.

The problem is that when we let the dark stuff bubble to the surface – when we throw a punch or utter a racial slur or mock a person's ethnicity or their religious faith – it actually feels good. It gives us an adrenaline rush precisely because we know we've stepped into dangerous territory; we experience it as a form of liberation that can make us feel powerful, brave, and strong. Once we're in that mood, it's easy to attack 'political correctness' as though it is an unacceptably harsh shackle; as though freedom of speech should be utterly unrestricted – part of our entitlement as citizens in a free country – and the notion of respect for others should exert no limiting or restraining force on us.

'We should be free to mock anyone's religious beliefs!' I once heard an enthusiastic participant in a Sky News panel discussion declare, and found myself disagreeing with her as profoundly as it would be possible to disagree with anyone about anything. In a liberal, multicultural, civil society we are absolutely at liberty to critique each other's tastes and preferences in everything from religious faith and practice to politics or literature. What we're *not* free to do – because the principle of mutual respect forbids it – is to *mock* each other's beliefs, values or practices.

Once we've broken free of the notion of mutual respect, though, we tend to keep on doing it. Because it feels good, we become repeat offenders, serially rude, increasingly disrespectful towards those we don't like or don't agree with, and happy to be characterised as rebels or larrikins or outsiders. We might even manage to convince ourselves that, in our bigotry and intolerance, we've done something heroic, something exemplary, rather than something culturally insensitive and potentially destructive of the social fabric.

Writing in the *British Journal of Social Psychology*, Michael Billig reported that bigotry is not based on 'a cognitive appraisal of social reality' but is the expression of an intensely emotional state that can be fomented and reinforced by 'hate talk'. Billig also demonstrated that bigots enjoy their bigotry, partly because of the pleasure associated with doing something that is forbidden.

As Billig put it: 'Dehumanising the other can be enjoyable, as the bigot is freed from the constraints of respect, tolerance and reasonableness. Thus one should not expect extreme racist propaganda to be devoid of humour and mockery.' This is the great hazard of bigotry: bigots derive pleasure from their hatred and mockery of others, and feed off each other's pleasure.

A much-publicised example of that occurred in 2017, when a group calling itself the Q Society held a fundraising dinner in Sydney, addressed by such luminaries as cartoonist Larry Pickering, the former Liberal MP turned Sky News presenter Ross Cameron, and crime fiction author Gabrielle Lord. Pickering was reported as saying: 'Let's be honest, I can't stand Muslims. If they are in the same street as me, I start shaking.' Later he added: 'They are not all bad, they do chuck pillow-biters off buildings.'

Cameron allegedly attacked homosexuals throughout his speech, describing the NSW division of the Liberal Party as 'basically a gay club'. (He later apologised to any gay people who were hurt by his remarks.)

A good time was had by all, apparently – as you would expect, in the light of Billig's conclusions. Intolerance and bigotry, whether directed at ethnic, religious, sexual or any other minority, feeds on itself.

The implication is clear: if we believe in the importance of tolerance, compassion and mutual respect – the cardinal virtues of a culturally diverse society – then we must stand up for those things, mainly by example.

How does it feel to be 'other'?

It's easy for people who have never been migrants or refugees to overlook just how difficult the process of integration can be, or how wide the divide between 'them' and 'us' can appear.

Many migrants speak of the problem of rootlessness – the feeling that they have been uprooted from the culture of their birthplace, yet have never managed to sink equivalent roots into the culture of their new home. In the contemporary world of social media, the pain of rootlessness might even be sharpened by an immigrant's ability to stay in close touch with the community left behind and to allow that to slow the process of integration with the new community.

Their children won't feel rootless to the same extent, or possibly won't feel it at all: whether they were born here or arrived as young children, there's plenty of time for them to become acculturated (the cultural equivalent of becoming acclimatised) through their exposure to Australia's particular brand of multiculturalism at school, in the neighbourhood and, later, at work. For many of them, the process of integration is completed when they marry – perhaps someone from a birthplace different from theirs, or someone from the host community; Australians are world champions at ethnic intermarriage, which is another reason why we're world champions at cultural diversity.

Here's an extract from an email I received in 2017, edited to preserve the anonymity of the author:

> I have many Australian friends, all educated people, but somehow in their eyes I remain Argentinian, and I feel different. I could honestly say that I suffer from 'otherness'. I think the culture that surrounds our formative years is indelible from our psyche. I feel I was shaped by my mother tongue . . . [even though] I also happen to know French and Indonesian [as well as English].
>
> I get edgy when I hear politicians talking about migrants needing to 'integrate'. This is the theory, but experience is different. One can learn another language but one's mother tongue is somehow richer. And I'm not saying Spanish is richer than other languages . . . it could be Arabic to a Kuwaiti or to an Egyptian, French to an Algerian etc.
>
> Of course anyone who migrates to Australia should [learn to] speak English, but that is not to say they will feel 'at home'.

The fact that someone chooses to come here, settle here and even raise children here by no means guarantees that they will feel 'Australian'. Part of our responsibility as the host nation is to acknowledge the struggle that many migrants go through in their attempts to integrate; their goodwill – and ours – might not always be enough to overcome the sense of otherness.

Here's another story, from a research respondent who migrated to Australia from the country then known as Yugoslavia:

When I came here I was determined to get my children to be as Australian as possible. We always talk English at home – although they are allowed to speak to their grandparents on the phone in their own language. I cook Australian meals. We go to the local Anglican church. They are turning into real little Aussies. I've told them there's only one way I don't want them to be like Australians – when they pass someone in the street, I want them to smile and say hello, and Australians don't do that.

Ouch.

The sense of otherness is not confined to immigrants. Many people who were born here feel 'other' because of an unsympathetic response from family or friends to their sexual orientation, or their ambition to live a life very different from the one lived by their family, or because they feel stifled by the mores of a particular school or church community. Some feel 'other' because they have a disability; others because of an irresistible urge to write or dance or paint or sing or act, rather than 'go into law' as their parents had wished. Some report feeling like aliens in their own poorly educated family because of the impact of higher education on their own outlook on life.

For some Indigenous Australians, especially children, the problem is neither rootlessness nor otherness, but a sense of 'two-ness': a fractured identity that arises from being in two cultures at once, and finding it hard to forge meaningful links between them.

When we celebrate our cultural diversity, we need to remember that many people struggle to fit in, and some pay a very high emotional price for the richness they add to our culture, simply by being perceived as 'different'. Most of us are required to make far more modest contributions towards the diversity project: a little more warmth in our welcome of strangers, a little more compassion towards those who are struggling to adapt to us, a little more acceptance of 'otherness', occasional small compromises in the interests of greater harmony . . . not too much to ask, really, is it?

When confronted by difference, the question is not, 'How can we make them be more like us?' In a civil society, the questions are, 'What can we learn from them?' and 'How can we respond to their needs?' and, in particular, 'How can we show them that they are both welcome in our community and valued for who they are?'

Insularity and the desire for homogeneity breed prejudice, intolerance and fear. Look at Nazi Germany; look at South Africa's apartheid era; look at the US South before the civil rights movement; look at history's appalling rollcall of so-called ethnic cleansings. That's where fear of diversity leads us.

Our social cohesion is not threatened by diversity, in spite of its many short-term challenges to our complacency. Unless we choose to exist in tightly bound little communities of like-mindedness – including the echo chambers of social media – we are all the beneficiaries of diversity. Difference stimulates thinking; thinking stimulates wisdom; wisdom leads us, inevitably, to an understanding of the fact that peace and harmony are impossible without an under-lying commitment to social inclusion, driven by compassion.

Early spring. Late afternoon. I was walking down Parramatta Road from Sydney University towards Broadway and Central Station. An old man sat on a low wall near the traffic lights at City Road, holding a battered guitar and smoking. An upturned hat sat hopefully on the pavement in front of him, with a few coins in it. A group of three young students arrived at the corner and stood, waiting for the lights to change. One of them went over to the man with the guitar, threw a dollar into his hat and said, 'Not playing today, mate? Not singing?'

'It's way out of tune. Can't get the bugger to come right,' said the man, sounding dispirited. 'And I'm feeling a bit crook, to be honest.' The temperature was dropping and his pullover was threadbare. I had the uneasy sense that he might be sleeping rough – perhaps in the adjacent park.

'I can do it for you, mate,' said the student.

'Do you know how to tune a guitar?'

'Sure I do,' said the student. 'I play too, you know.'

Warily, the man held out the instrument.

The student (I'm assuming he was a student) sat down on the wall beside him and began carefully tuning the strings. The lights changed, and his friends waved goodbye and crossed the road.

There's nothing uniquely Australian about a young person helping an old person out of a spot of bother. There's nothing uniquely Australian about the intersection of hope and despair on a street corner. There's nothing uniquely Australian about unlikely connections being made via music.

What made it seem like an Australian moment was the nature of the divides that were being so casually, so effortlessly bridged by these two: generational, educational and ethnic. The old man was Aboriginal and the young student was Chinese.

A reflection

On choosing our words carefully

On Anzac Day 2017, Muslim youth leader and former ABC presenter Yassmin Abdel-Magied posted a message on Facebook that caused an instant and widespread uproar. The message read: 'Lest. We. Forget. (Manus, Nauru, Syria, Palestine . . .)'

In response to the reaction, Abdel-Magied withdrew the post, saying it had been brought to her attention that the message was disrespectful, for which she unreservedly apologised. She replaced the original post with the simple message: 'Lest we forget.'

Many questions arise. *Was* it disrespectful, and if so, to whom? Was it inappropriate to use Anzac Day as the moment to make a point about Australia's treatment of asylum seekers and its deeply mysterious and confusing military adventures in Syria? (Palestine seems like the odd one out, since we are not directly engaged in the Palestinians' struggle with Israel.)

A bit of context. It's true that the phrase 'Lest we forget' is traditionally reserved for remembrance of the fallen in battle. But it's also true that the character of Anzac Day has evolved over the years; it was in some disrepute in the 1960s when, in the thick of the anti-war demonstrations focused on Vietnam, it was deemed a vehicle for the inappropriate glorification of war. Support for it has waxed and waned ever since. There's no denying that, for many Australians, its solemnity comes about as close to a religious occasion as they ever get. 'Solemnity', of course, refers to the morning of Anzac Day, especially its many dawn services. But Anzac Day has a curiously schizophrenic quality – by the afternoon, the mood has swung from solemnity to party mode, with alcohol and two-up its twin motifs.

The other thing about the evolution of Anzac Day is that, for many people, its focus is shifting from an exclusive recollection of the sacrifice and heroism of those who have served on our behalf in theatres of war, to a deep and equally solemn consideration of what we have done with the peace that has been so hard-won for us.

In that context, it is perfectly appropriate to wonder how those who died to protect our freedom and way of life might react to what is being done in our name on Manus and Nauru, and in Syria. I suspect that many of those who made the supreme sacrifice, were they still with us, might see Abdel-Magied's point. Did they die so we would be free to imprison and torture asylum seekers who have committed no crime by throwing themselves on our mercy? Was their heroism designed to encourage our participation in the disastrous invasion of Iraq, or the destruction of much of Syria's ancient civilisation, along with countless lives, in a conflict where it's unclear to many of us whose allies are whose or why we are involved at all?

The recent surge of support for Anzac Day among young Australians with no family connections to it suggests that the day is becoming a time for reflection not only on the extent of the sacrifices made on our behalf, but on the nature of sacrifice itself. If Abdel-Magied's message was designed to stimulate such reflection, then I certainly got it. Others saw it differently.

Abdel-Magied insulted no one; she did not overstep the bounds of common decency; she did not set out to offend. I suspect she was merely trying to say something like this: while we're remembering the horrors of war, let's also ponder the moral obligations of those who are enjoying the peace.

Nevertheless, many people were apparently offended, presumably because they felt the juxtaposition of commemoration with provocation was inappropriate. But it would be scandalous if any part of the hostility provoked by her Facebook post was linked to her ethnicity, religion, generation or gender.

Needless to say, I'm all for freedom of speech. Who isn't? But we don't mean *total* freedom of speech, do we? We mean freedom of speech, up to a point. Where that point is, precisely, is unclear. I'm generally against censorship, for instance, but strongly in favour of the protection of children. I support people's right to express themselves, but I'm against racism, sexism, ageism or any slights or insults based on where a person came from or what they believe, just as I'm against bullying – including verbal bullying – intimidation and humiliation of *anyone*. In my personal Utopia, I'd like us all to strike the proper balance between the freedom to speak our mind and the need to show respect towards others, whoever they may be.

If we want a civil society, we have to put limits on freedom of speech; it's as simple as that. Civility, kindness and respect for others should ideally evolve naturally within us as part of our maturation – influenced by parental example, formal education and peer pressure – but when our passions are aroused and we become angry, frustrated or offended, the shackles of self-restraint are sometimes loosened and we may need some external pressure to restrain us. We are all capable of racist, sexist and other prejudiced thoughts, but if we are to be even half civilised, we must learn to keep that stuff on the leash. 'Educative' laws have their place in this process.

That means I'm in favour of section 18C of the Racial Discrimination Act, which prohibits language that offends people on the basis of race, colour and national or ethnic origin. But I'm also uncomfortable with those who try to twist legitimate criticism of someone's behaviour by falsely interpreting it as a racist or religious slur. If a Jew behaves badly and is criticised for it, that's not a case of anti-Semitism; if he or she is criticised *for being a Jew*, or if the bad behaviour is attributed to the person's Jewishness, that is clearly anti-Semitic.

I once sat on a committee where a woman attacked another member's contribution on the grounds that it was 'typical of a male'. When I suggested we should consider the proposition only on the basis of its content, not the gender of its author, my objection was brushed aside on the grounds that I would say that, being another man.

It's very easy – and quite good fun – to slip into these little prejudices based on stereotypes. 'Oh, isn't that just like a woman!' 'Ah, but of course he's Irish.' 'He's so aggressive – but, then, he's a man.' 'A good Catholic girl would never say a thing like that.' Fun, perhaps, but deeply unfair and potentially dangerous to the harmonious operation of a civil society. Civility demands that, out of respect for each other – to say nothing of respect for the truth – we should try to avoid generalisations that only serve to reinforce prejudices.

Unfortunately, we seem to be moving in the opposite direction. In fact, we are living in the Age of the Reckless Generalisation, where instant theories about anything can be magicked out of the air by anyone, and where everyone's opinion is to be regarded as having equal status to everyone else's, regardless of qualifications or expertise. Social media fuel the trend: messages all look equally valid when they're sitting there on the screen. It's also easier to be reckless when you're anonymous, or when you know there are no consequences likely to flow from saying whatever you feel like saying on the spur of the moment. And you're less likely to choose your words carefully if your real purpose is not to communicate but only to draw attention to yourself.

It's become fashionable for wild statements or subjective assessments to be accompanied by airy references to 'what the research says' and yet, in the present era, people are rarely asked to cite the specific research, let alone offer any assurances about its reliability or validity. In the Age of the Reckless Generalisation, it would be churlish to demand such rigour.

In fact, the daily drip-feed of ever more 'research' only makes the situation worse. Not every research project is rigorous; not every research project has value; not every research project can stand up to scrutiny. You can't, for instance, talk about statistics having integrity if they are based on a self-selected panel of people completing an online survey, without the researchers having any certain knowledge of who the respondents were, and without any of the statistical 'randomness' required in the selection of respondents for a legitimate sample survey. And you can't draw any quantitative conclusions – such as 'most people said' – from qualitative data. A newspaper report in mid 2017 referred to 'the unanimous view of undecided voters' based on nothing more substantial than the views expressed by undecided voters in two 'focus groups' in Sydney and two in Melbourne. (Don't get me started on 'focus groups' – a fashionable but highly suspect version of a valuable and well-proven qualitative research technique.)

If this is, as people are now fond of saying, the 'post-truth' era, then we have no one but ourselves to blame. It's our own impatience for easy answers and instant explanations, our gullibility, our willingness to overinvest our faith in the latest leader, the latest guru or the latest plausible celebrity that causes us to swallow fake news and fake research – not that people are falsifying or distorting their research findings (as far as I know) to make a good story, but research that lacks scientific rigour is, in its own way, 'fake'. And if we ourselves don't choose our words with care, respecting both the truth and each other, then we are complicit in the whole mad game.

4

Beware: Overshare!

The freedom to choose what I reveal about myself and what I keep private is one of our core freedoms.

Elizabeth Coombs, Chair, UN task force on
'Privacy and Personality'

The internet has wrought a cultural revolution that has transformed both our personal and working lives. How's that for a massive understatement?

It's not all wonderful, of course; the worldwide web has perhaps inevitably cast its own evil shadow in the form of the dark web, cyberspace's equivalent of the criminal underworld. But the ever-expanding world of information technology has created new channels for cheap, instant contact with people across the globe; given us astonishingly easy access to the world's store of information and entertainment; provided stay-at-home comfort for shopping and banking; brought far-flung families and friends together in ways that, for sheer speed and convenience, have broken the boundaries of pre-revolutionary mail and telephone calls; alleviated feelings of loneliness and isolation for people homebound through illness, frailty or social awkwardness; transformed the lives of people with brain damage or other forms of cognitive impairment whose smartphones act as a supplementary brain; brightened all our lives with devices that are so extraordinarily clever, reliable, convenient and companionable that many of us have become addicted to them, and some of us almost seem more attached to them than to each other, even sleeping with a smartphone under our pillow.

And yet, when I hear people say such things as: 'Facebook has brought me closer to people far away, but it's made me lazy about seeing my friends,' and, 'I often feel lonely when I'm online,' I wonder whether we are talking about a revolution whose primary effect might be to undermine social cohesion – the very opposite of how it looks on the surface.

It's a paradox. Technology connects us like never before, but makes it easier than ever to stay apart from each other. And although we're all in favour of sharing, we are now discovering that there is such a thing as *oversharing* – not just the relentless flow of data we send each other via our devices, but the torrents of data our devices are sending to unknown others (let's call them 'UOs'), mostly without our knowledge or permission.

The IT revolution has created in us such a voracious appetite for data and a correspondingly voracious appetite among data-providers for more data *about us*, we are now facing a major upheaval in our attitudes to privacy. We might resist the whole idea of big data, with its Orwellian overtones of Big Brother, yet we willingly feed the data monster with more and more information about ourselves. Facebook and Alphabet/Google already know far more about you and me than any government agency does, including not only our history of internet browsing but our every credit card transaction as well. And that's because we've told them – perhaps unwittingly – everything they want to know.

Question: Why do they want to know all that information about us? Next question: What will they do with it? The answer to both questions has a dollar sign in it: social media giants like Facebook – the owner of WhatsApp, Instagram and Messenger, and the fifth most valuable company in the world – might say they are in the business of connecting people, which is how users feel about it, but that is incidental to their real purpose, which is to offer commercial advertisers unprecedentedly accurate targeting of potential customers. The British writer John Lanchester suggests we think of Facebook as a company that is basically in the surveillance business.

Whether we like it or not, we now know that the security of digital data is impossible to guarantee and, perhaps in response, we have become increasingly reckless about the protection of private information. When we look back on this phase of the IT revolution, we may well rue the amount of data we were prepared to toss into the bottomless pit of cyberspace as if it were so much e-garbage. Perhaps we are consciously choosing to do this; perhaps not. Yet almost every day, we hear fresh revelations about the erosion of our freedom to choose what we will reveal about ourselves. Here are just three that have stayed with me:

- *The Australian* newspaper has reported that a patent granted to Facebook in the US will allow lenders to use the credit history of an applicant's circle of Facebook friends when deciding whether or not to grant a loan. I repeat: not just the credit history of the applicant, but of the applicant's circle of friends. (Be careful who you hang out with on Facebook if you're in the market for a loan in the future.)

- A widely reported hacking scandal exposed the identity of millions of users of the infamous Ashley Madison online dating service for people already in relationships. What really struck me as ironic was that people who were reckless about protecting their own privacy were outraged when they fell victim to hackers who treat *everyone's* privacy with contempt.

- The infamous '#PlaneBreakUp' social media phenomenon that arose from a female passenger on a flight out of New York using her mobile phone to live-tweet a raging argument between a man and a woman before take-off. The argument, though apparently ferocious enough to have seemed terminal, was resolved in a boozy and very physical make-up session after take-off – again fully documented. The material went viral, of course.

Notice that all those examples refer to involuntary and unauthorised data sharing. No doubt you have your own privacy-invasion stories, but step back from the clatter of daily news reportage for a moment and ponder some bigger questions. What is this thing called privacy and how does it relate to social cohesion? Will we be more or less trustful of each other in a world where data flows seem unrestricted? Does our present recklessness with personal data signal a radical shift in our attitudes to privacy? What will be the long-term effects of all this oversharing – what do we gain or lose, as individuals and as a society, when we tighten or loosen our grip on personal information about ourselves?

The privacy–media link

Our attitudes to privacy are inevitably shaped by the culture we live in. That culture, in turn, is strongly influenced by the character of our dominant modes of communication. The history of the link between media and privacy is long and complicated, but here's the short version . . .

Before the invention of the printing press in the fifteenth century by William Caxton in England and Johannes Gutenberg in Germany, our forebears lived in a culture in which literacy was confined to an academic and ecclesiastical elite. Most people lived in villages and small towns where they communicated with each other via the spoken word, complemented by the unspoken messages conveyed via body language. Conversational communication, as we know, tends to be more emotionally charged, less precise and formal, more subjective and more personal in character than communication via the written word, since the spoken message and the speaker are indivisible.

A pre-literate culture is also characterised by open sharing of information. Apart from intimate communication within family groups, the privacy of information is not an issue: what one person knows, the whole community knows. (Throughout history, different languages and regional dialects have evolved to ensure that this openly shared information didn't spread beyond *our* village or *our* tribe.)

Enter the printing press. If you're looking for an IT revolution to rival the internet in its impact on society, look no further than this. It may have taken 500 years to reach its full flowering, and few could have foreseen at the time the scale of the cultural upheaval to come, but the invention of the printing press marked the dawn of a new communication culture in which the written word would come to displace the spoken word as the 'gold standard' of communication. People still spoke to each other in their ordinary daily interactions, of course, but the printed word gradually came to be regarded as the highest form of language and the basis of serious education, partly because it had such a long tradition of being associated with the elites.

As more and more European readers and writers learnt to submit themselves to the rigorously rational, linear form of print – one word after the other, left to right across the page, line by line down the page – our habits of thought and our view of the world were subtly influenced by the character of the medium itself. We learnt to say rational-sounding things like, 'Let me see it in black and white,' as if the written word had some inherent authority lacking in mere speech. We warned each other against 'reading between the lines'.

The social and cultural consequences of such a revolutionary shift in the way we communicate were profound. For a start, the advent of mass literacy – combined with capitalism and the rise of consumerism – gradually encouraged a new emphasis on individualism, since both reading and writing are solitary, private activities, whereas speaking and listening involve social interaction. It also separated the intellectual life of 'the word' from the social life of the community. And it heightened our sense of privacy: written messages can't be overheard, and no one likes having someone else reading over their shoulder.

During the first half of the twentieth century, print tightened its grip on our culture as compulsory education brought us closer to mass literacy than we had ever been. By the second half of the century, that grip had begun to loosen as television threw out a challenge to the primacy of the printed word. A kind of counter-revolution was set in motion that began edging us back towards our pre-literate, spoken-word cultural origins. Courtesy of TV, mass communication now took the words off the page and put them back in the mouths of people saying them: the subtlety, the nuances of speech, facial expression and body language were restored, on a magic screen, right there in our living room.

The TV executives who invented canned laughter knew that TV had the potential to simulate some of the features of the old pre-literate village culture: 'Laugh along with the laughter track,' they were saying, in effect, 'so you'll feel like one of the crowd.' In the second half of the twentieth century, TV became a kind of electronic campfire where millions of people gathered to watch the same material at the same time, and then to discuss it at work or school the next day.

This was the leading edge of a revolution that would ultimately bring us the social media of the 21st century. That term 'social media' is highly appropriate: it points to the shift away from media as vehicles for transmitting professionally produced program content to a more informal sharing of information – just like the old tribal and village cultures, except now our networks were potentially global, and consisted mainly of strangers. In information-sharing terms, we're *all* in the global village.

Is the value we place on privacy diminishing?

As in the pre-literate culture from which we evolved, the privacy of information is coming to seem less important in the digitally connected world we now inhabit. The emphasis, once again, is on sharing, belonging, being part of the group. Fear of missing out (popularly known as FOMO) has become a major driver of our addiction to our IT devices, and even the traditional idea of personal identity is challenged by the phenomenon of multiple online identities and by the impossibility of knowing whether online 'friends' are who they say they are.

In such a culture – leaving all political considerations aside – figures like Julian Assange and Edward Snowden have become folk heroes to many people for opening up previously private, 'officially secret' information. Their specific motivations are submerged beneath a general impression that their actions are merely part of an unstoppable trend towards everything being 'out there'.

So did we enact the 2014 Australian Privacy Principles in the nick of time for a rising generation of 'digital natives' who couldn't care less about privacy or the security of personal data – whether financial transactions, health records or personal messages to Facebook friends?

Not exactly. Research from the Office of the Australian Information Commissioner (OAIC) published in 2013 and 2017 has shown that we are becoming increasingly concerned about online privacy: about 80 percent of us are particularly uneasy about our internet activity being monitored. And yet, over-whelmingly, we continue to engage with the very websites and social media platforms where we believe such monitoring is taking place. Almost 80 percent of us say we don't want data given to a business organisation to be shared with another, though we know this is constantly happening. (As usual, attitudinal change is lagging behind behavioural change.) A mere 12 percent of us say we trust social media and 25 percent regret having posted some material on social media; 83 percent of us believe privacy risks are greater when we are dealing with an organisation online. Yet both social media usage and e-commerce patronage continue to explode, and most of us don't use basic privacy protections that are available to us: 65 percent of us don't bother reading privacy policies, and 50 percent of us never clear our browsing history.

We may not *like* the idea of our smartphone revealing our whereabouts and potentially a great deal more to the phone company and, in turn, to UOs – advertisers, retailers, banks, insurance companies, government agencies – but that doesn't restrain most of us from the ever-increasing use of our phone. When we hear that our smartphone may be 'listening to us', we're already conditioned by the revolution to accept that that may well be true but, again, we trade off the risk of privacy invasion for the convenience of the device.

Some of us don't like knowing that our travel card reveals when and where we hopped on or off a bus or train. We are spooked by the idea that a smart TV could transmit our domestic conversations, as well as our viewing tastes and preferences, to the manufacturer . . . and thence to UOs. And we certainly don't like the idea that a log of all our phone calls and text messages is now recorded. (In the US, it appears, even the content of those conversations may be recorded as well.) We don't like knowing that our personal web-browsing history is permanently stored and accessible . . . to whom, exactly?

We don't like any of that, but we live with it and are coming to accept it, perhaps seeing it as the price we have to pay for all that near-miraculous and highly seductive technology, and for the convenience and stimulation it has brought into our lives. Another finding from the OAIC's 2017 research is that 63 percent of people now believe *social media usage is a public activity*, presumably because they've already adapted to the idea that so-called private messages, once launched into cyberspace, could end up anywhere. We now know that digital data is never really secure if someone wants it badly enough for their own commercial or other purposes.

Does all this mean that we no longer value privacy as much as we say we do? And are we only saying we do as an echo, a vestige, of the attitudes and values of a bygone communication culture? Are we resigning ourselves to a massive loss of privacy and deciding that, on balance, we're okay with that?

It's hard to predict where this will take us, because we are still in the thick of the revolution, but there are some signs of resistance to a free-for-all incursion into our personal privacy. In various parts of the world, for instance, new laws have been enacted that respond to privacy concerns on behalf of young users of the internet, giving those users the right to erasure – 'the right to be forgotten'. The laws are aimed at protecting young people who may be haunted by youthful indiscretions at a time of life when many of us self-reveal before we self-reflect (though that tendency doesn't always stop at adolescence).

A rather unexpected 'overshare' concern emerged from a survey of teenagers in eight EU countries. The Global Social Media Impact Study, conducted by anthropologists at University College London, reported that European teenagers were typically unconcerned about how information about them is used commercially or as part of surveillance practices by security agencies, yet they had a very different concern about Facebook privacy that had caused them to abandon the site in droves: *their parents were on it*. It's not just the risk of oversharing with parents: for teenagers, sharing a social media site with younger children is terminally uncool.

But the bigger picture is that we are adapting, and one source of encouragement has come from an unexpected source: reality TV.

'Reality' TV: Softening us up for surveillance

It all seems innocent enough: put a few people in a 'Big Brother house', keep the TV cameras running and see what happens. Or film people going on a first date, or getting *Married at First Sight* – a program described by its producers as 'a groundbreaking social experiment'. Hey – why not get couples to meet in a beach hideaway somewhere, have them naked from the start, and see where *that* leads? (Sorry, the Dutch have already done that.) Better still, get them to undress each other as soon as they meet, and then hop straight into bed. Originating in Italy, spreading to the UK and now here, *Undressed* is a so-called reality TV program that does just that: a pair of strangers meet, undress each other down to their underwear, sit or lie on a bed and respond to questions or instructions that appear on a screen, designed to accelerate the getting-to-know-you process. After 30 minutes, they are asked whether they would like to spend more time together. Naturally, the producers describe this, too, as 'a social experiment'.

To some extent, such programs *are* social experiments – or, at least, a showbiz version of social experiments, a bit like stage hypnotism. But who are the experimental subjects – the participants or the viewers? At one level, it could be fascinating to see two strangers undressing each other and then having a D&M in a TV studio designed to look like an intimate setting. At the same time, let's be frank, such programs *pose* as social experimentation because it gives them more legitimacy than if the pitch was simply to 'come and look at this pair undressing each other and chatting in their undies'. Rather than true social experiments, reality TV shows are no more than a series of tightly structured, internationally franchised products devised by media strategists who have realised that if you put ordinary people (i.e. not professional actors) into unusual situations, the results can be entertaining for viewers.

Not all reality TV goes for the salacious or scandalous. Some programs place the cameras in a seemingly safe, even wholesome, environment – a kitchen – and create 'reality' out of a cooking contest. As David Dale, one of our most astute culture-watchers, has said of such hugely popular programs as *MasterChef* and *My Kitchen Rules*:

> These programs function as soap operas. The producers have turned what looks like a talent quest into a melodrama. They use an exhaustive audition process to choose a cast of characters who will go through a classic 'journey' – heroes, villains, jesters, mentors, neurotics, tricksters, motherly types, sexy types, mystery men. By editing and cutting hundreds of hours of film, the producers become storytellers. We let ourselves become addicted because the cooking element suggests we are learning to be better people. But it's really about the drama.

It's also about the cameras that turn ordinary people into TV celebrities, and about the fact that such programs blend fantasy with reality, especially when, as in *Big Brother*, viewers are invited to participate by 'voting' for people to be eliminated from the show. *Undressed* may well stimulate sexual fantasies – what *would* it be like to undress someone you've only just met? (The answer, obviously, is that there'd be a lot of nervous laughter, as on a fully clothed first date.) But the most pleasing fantasy for reality TV viewers is that it could be them right there on the screen.

After all, the thing that makes TV series or films popular is that they provide a vehicle for the clarification, reinforcement or affirmation of our own sense of identity and our own values through our psychological responses – positive and negative – to the characters and situations being portrayed: *Yep – that's how it is for me, too.* Or: *I would never have got myself into a situation like that.*

Reality TV goes one step further, by showcasing amateurs – people even more like us than actors pretending to be like us – who seem to bring the glamour of the screen within the reach of all of us. *Anyone* could do that – even me. *Anyone* can be fascinating to watch – even me. *Anyone* can be a media star – even me. Part of the fantasy is that this would be the easiest possible pathway to celebrity: we wouldn't have to go to drama school; we wouldn't have to learn our lines; we wouldn't have to *act*. We'd just have to be ourselves, but a version of ourselves ramped up to the level of stardom.

In a society increasingly saturated by media – both mass and social – it was perhaps inevitable that we would come to regard mediated information as being in some strange way superior to the flesh-and-blood, three-dimensional variety. (You might have heard the story about the mother who was wheeling her baby in a pram through a park when she was stopped by a passer-by. 'What a beautiful baby,' said the stranger, leaning over the pram. 'That's nothing,' said the mother, 'you should see his photo.') This is simply a continuation of the process begun by the printing press that led to the evolution of 'typographic man' – the literate person described earlier, who is conditioned by an enchantment with literacy to privilege the rational above the emotional and to look for logical patterns, even where there are none.

But in the new era of 'reality' media – whether on TV or in our own social media posts – something is going on that transcends the process of communication. This is an era of such torrential information sharing, the reality TV craze is merely a small part of a much larger cultural movement that has already challenged our traditional ideas about privacy.

In *1984*, George Orwell's dark tale of totalitarianism, the fact that Big Brother was watching you was a source of terror; now it has become the basis for light entertainment. Reality media have been conditioning us, however unintentionally, to accept and even to welcome the idea of a camera being trained on us – whether our own or someone else's. Once we accept that it's fun to post information about ourselves on social media, the distinction between sharing and surveillance begins to blur.

The more willingly we give away information about our move-ments, our social networks, our purchasing patterns, our taste in music, fashion, books or food, and the more we engage with the pleasing fantasy – fed by reality TV – that having cameras on us is harmless fun, the less we are likely to worry about governmental or commercial incursions into our privacy. The freedom to choose what we will reveal and what we will conceal about ourselves was once regarded as one of our most basic freedoms; perhaps, in the era of overshare, such a freedom seems more quaint than precious.

Our devices are oversharing, too

Those driverless cars we are expecting to see in the near future won't just be clean, efficient and safe. They will also be intensely knowledgeable about us. Our travel habits, our time of departure and arrival for every trip, our favourite destinations, the frequency of our overriding of the automatic process, our radio, podcast and other listening habits, the number of passengers we carry and perhaps the conversations we have with them, too. They'll be able to establish if we were gazing at our smartphone when we should have been attending to the road, whether we ate, drank or smoked while we travelled . . . and all that data could be transmitted to central locations for storage. The stated purpose of such storage would be to analyse the data in the service of improved safety and continuous product development. But what else might it be used for?

People with pacemakers know that part of the deal is that the machine will transmit continuous data to a central medical computer where it will be stored and analysed, and from which your cardiologist can retrieve it. It will perhaps be able to alert the doctor if something seems amiss, before you're even aware of it. But stored data is accessible data, so we need to know that when we agree to have the pacemaker installed, we are also agreeing to a record of our heart's performance being available to UOs. There doesn't seem to be anything particularly disturbing about that; we constantly make trade-offs between privacy and convenience or, in this case, privacy and a life-saving device.

The privacy question only arises if one of those 'unknown others' turns out to be someone you'd prefer did not have access to the state of your heart – your medical insurance company, perhaps, or, if you're up to something nefarious, the police. There's a landmark US case, reported by Jedidiah Bracy on the International Association of Privacy Professionals' blog, in which Ross Compton, a resident of Middletown, Ohio, was arrested on suspicion of having burnt his house down in order to claim the insurance. In developing their case against him, the police obtained a warrant for all the electronic data produced by his pacemaker – heart rate, pacer demand and cardiac rhythms before, during and after the time of the fire. That data demonstrated that the suspect could not have quickly packed some bags and thrown them out of his window before escaping through the window himself, as he had claimed to have done. In spite of the accused's attempt to have his pacemaker data kept private, the judge ruled that it was admissible evidence.

In exploring the privacy implications of the case, Bracy concludes: 'I can choose to not use my smartphone, or employ alternative privacy-enhancing features like Signal or Tor. The same alternative isn't true for a pacemaker or other life-saving medical technology.'

No doubt most of us would think the privacy trade-off was worth it, but as medical and other systems become more highly interactive and 'willing' to share our data, we need to know what's at stake. As Bracy says: 'We've known for years that hackers can access insulin pumps and connected vehicles. But there hasn't been much talk about government access to data generated from these devices.'

You might think a 'sex toy' like a vibrator would not involve any invasion of your privacy, but a particular product marketed in the US was controlled by a smartphone app that also recorded the details of the devices' usage – frequency, time and duration of use, and selected vibration settings. As Charlie Osborne reported on the business technology news website ZDNet, two women launched a class action against the Canadian company concerned, won the case, and the company was obliged to pay four million Canadian dollars in compensation, and undertake to destroy all the personal information stored.

We know about those 'smart' TV sets with the potential to spy on us, but how about Barbie dolls? In 2015, Samuel Gibbs reported in *The Guardian* that there was growing concern over Mattel's 'Hello Barbie' doll that can have 'conversations' with its child owner based on voice recognition technology like Apple's Siri. The worry, of course, was that recordings of a child could be sent to third-party companies (those UOs, again) for processing, 'potentially revealing his or her intimate thoughts and details'. But 'Hello Barbie' did not arrest flagging sales of the Barbie doll, so perhaps this can be partly interpreted as an expression of parental concern about the privacy implications of an interactive doll.

Such developments are merely harbingers of what lies ahead as we surrender more and more of our privacy to the so-called Internet of Things – a network of devices that share data with each other, often without our knowledge and potentially against our will. That friendly robot, bot or pod parked in your living room will be an unflagging source of stimulation, entertainment, conversation, comfort and companionship . . . and an incorrigible e-gossip, transmitting your every word, your every sigh, to a central database and then, quite likely, to those notorious UOs, some of whom will respond with offers for the various products and services that could make your recently confessed dreams come true. (That's only a minor variation on what's already happening on YouTube and Google.)

Perhaps it doesn't matter, but perhaps it does, when you consider the impact on our culture of an ever more sophisticated assault on our privacy and the implications of that for our sense of trust, not just in the machines, but in each other.

Erosion of privacy; erosion of trust

We all know what we gain from the wonderful new world of IT, but what do we lose? What risks do we run when we surrender to the seductions of the new technology (including, as part of the deal, its capacity for surveillance), and willingly adapt to a world where we are steadily removing human presence from more and more of our encounters and transactions?

Some of the risks have already become apparent:

- the erosion of trust between citizens and their government, because citizens are increasingly being asked to place their trust in machines, systems and algorithms, rather than people, and because enough cases have already been reported of accidental online publication of personal information for trust in the security of government agencies' data-storage practices to be provisional, at best;

- the erosion of trust between consumers and corporations, for precisely the same reasons: even the most enthusiastic users of online purchasing facilities occasionally wonder just how secure their credit card details are – to say nothing of their purchasing history – once they are 'out there';

- the erosion of trust between each other: the research finding (reported in chapter 2) that only 35 percent of Australians trust their neighbours arises partly from the fact that there is less pressure on us to engage with the local neighbourhood when we feel utterly absorbed by online connections (even though nosy neighbours can't compete with digital surveillance for the scope of its snooping!);

- an erosion of the sense of personal identity, partly because screen time is eating into the time we might otherwise spend interacting with face-to-face groups (our primary source of personal identity), and partly because digital impulses on the screen all look the same, so the online presentation of our personal style, personality and character is a diminished and homogenised version of us;

- the substantial loss of control over that very significant freedom identified by former NSW Privacy Commissioner Elizabeth Coombs: the freedom to choose what we will reveal about ourselves and what we will keep private. In a 2017 paper co-authored with Sean McLaughlan, Coombs points out that in Australia 'the right to privacy is not recognised in the Constitution, not enshrined in a Bill of Rights, and there is no common law tradition for protection against serious invasions of privacy'. Accordingly, 'all privacy protection depends upon legislation'.

For society at large, that all adds up to a sense of powerlessness in the face of the secret world of big data and data sharing between unknown parties, a heightened sense of insecurity, and a greater vulnerability to fear – the kind of fear that erodes our faith in the integrity of democracy itself, by posing the unnerving question: 'Who can you trust?'

I recently stood on a platform at Wynyard railway station in Sydney, watching the row of CCTV cameras rotating on their stands on the other side of the tracks, continuously filming us all as we waited for our train, and I recalled the words of Hitler's master propagandist, Joseph Goebbels: *If you have nothing to hide, you have nothing to fear.*

Is that the best we can do for a moral principle to guide us through the complexities of the emerging assault on our privacy, with all its (possibly unintentional) consequences for the wellbeing of our society? I hope not.

The revolution is unstoppable, so we shall have to consider how to mitigate or minimise the negative effects of oversharing. When, as policymakers, marketing strategists or information technology professionals, we know that something we are planning to do would have the effect of eroding the level of mutual trust between the members of our society, shouldn't we be thinking very carefully before we take any steps towards implementation?

The IT revolution poses a threat to our social cohesion, simply through the erosion of trust, if for no other reason – though there are plenty of other reasons for concern, mainly based on the effects of our love affair with screens at the expense of time we might otherwise spend with each other.

In 1993, I wrote a research report called 'Living with Technology' that included these reflections on people's fears about the future impact of IT on their lives: 'We may become dependent on machines and unable to function when they fail; we may allow ourselves to be seduced by machines that will dominate us; we may divide ourselves into information-rich and information-poor.' Twenty-five years later, the fears are very similar but the stakes are higher.

Signs of the culture shift are everywhere

When we are caught up in a revolution as significant as the invention of the printing press, radio, TV or the internet, it's not just our media-related behaviour that changes. We change in other ways, too.

Eaten out recently? If so, you will have noticed the trend towards people treating public space like private space. And I'm not just talking about the audible, animated chatter on mobile phones in public places – coffee shops, restaurants, queues, trains, buses, the footpath, retail stores – that's become an urban cliché, though it is remarkable that we generally manage to restrain ourselves from joining in: 'Hey! That sounds awesome – tell them we had a great time in Bali, too.' No, we let all that wash over us. Oversharing is the new black, and it includes the unintentional sharing of highly personal information with total strangers by people on their phones who appear oblivious to the proximity of others. Oversharing, whether accidental or deliberate, is one of the consequences of the emerging media culture in which almost everyone seems prepared to tell almost everyone else almost everything.

The blurring of public and private in the digital world carries over into more general behaviour in the non-digital world, as well. If privacy has become less of an issue online, then it was bound to become less of an issue offline. Back to the restaurant: groups of diners are increasingly inclined to treat restaurant space as if it's indistinguishable from their dining room at home. There's loud chatter – in fact, voices are actually raised to be heard above all the other people also treating the restaurant like the barbecue area in their backyard – laughter, shouting across the table, raucous renditions of 'Happy Birthday'. I'm no curmudgeon, and the conversations you can't help overhearing are often quite engrossing, especially if social research is your thing. I'm merely observing that as we blur the distinction between public and private space, this may be another symptom of the diminishing importance of privacy – or, at least, a symptom of our increasing disregard for the importance of that distinction. A young woman sitting opposite a friend of mine on a suburban train recently offered further evidence of this convergence of public and private space: rummaging in her handbag, she withdrew an aerosol can, undid the top few buttons of her shirt and proceeded to squirt a generous dose of deodorant into each armpit.

The so-called sharing economy can be read as another symptom of the culture shift. Its most positive and remarkable example is Wikipedia – the online encyclopaedia created by and for 'the people', freely accessible to all, with no commercial payoff for anyone. That's one of those cases where the innovation is so brilliant and the technology so efficient, you want to punch the air and say: *Yes!*

But not all manifestations of the sharing economy are so pure. The commercial world has, inevitably, harnessed the appeal of the 'sharing economy'. The GoGet car-sharing franchise, the Airbnb online marketplace for accommodation and Uber's taxi service can all be read as signs that we are less precious than we used to be about personal, private ownership and personal, private space. But let's not get too misty-eyed about the commercial face of the sharing economy: this is not some spontaneous movement of people keen to share their cars or houses with each other, the way we share knowledge on Wikipedia. The owners of these enterprises are set to make vast profits out of our willingness to go outside the mainstream economy in the name of 'sharing'. To the users of Airbnb, it seems kind of quaint, kind of innocent (and kind of cheap, too) . . . but it doesn't look such a good idea if you're a hotelier who is losing business to an operation that neither owns nor leases any of the accommodation it provides, collects no GST, has no superannuation or other employer-type obligations to the property providers who actually supply its services (because they're not employees), and has few of the overheads of a conventional accommodation provider.

Corporate giant Uber's alternative to traditional taxis has attracted predictable outrage from the established taxi industry and appears controversial in several ways, ranging from the remuneration of its drivers to its differential pricing policy (sometimes called 'surge pricing' or, more euphemistically, 'dynamic pricing'). But more general questions have also been raised about the use organisations like Uber could make of personal data obtained from their customers' smartphones. Accusations have been made, for instance, about a price spike for women booking a car late at night, especially if their phone battery is low and they are therefore, presumably, feeling vulnerable. Whether such accusations have been well-founded or not, the idea that any service provider *could* exploit a customer based on unauthorised access to data stored in that customer's smartphone is now regarded as perfectly plausible. Spooky, but plausible.

Naive, community-based organisations run by public-spirited amateurs Uber and Airbnb are not! They represent a new heavily branded business model whose assets – cars and houses – are supplied by the service providers themselves. Both companies sustain market capitalisation in the double-digit billions and have highly sophisticated PR machines to help deal with the demands of government regulators and the objections of traditional operators.

Nevertheless, they and their growing band of imitators have successfully tapped into our enthusiasm for the *idea* of the sharing economy, and I think we can interpret that idea itself as another sign of a significant shift in our attitudes to privacy wrought primarily by the digital revolution.

But information sharing is the big one. So much sharing online; so much sharing offline; so much more sharing even in the mainstream mass media. As someone recently remarked to me of radio, TV and podcasts: 'Everyone is interviewing everyone.' He had a point. The booming market for interview programs, and their podcast spin-offs, is a sign of our insatiable appetite for people's sharing of their personal 'journeys'. If we are indeed on a societal journey towards a more tribal, open, oral culture, then these are some of the early signs of progress in that direction.

At least, I *hope* it's progress. How ironic it would be if we knew the life stories of all those strangers crowding the podcast market, yet remained ignorant of the rich history of the people in our own street or apartment block. *Everyone's* story is interesting; everyone walks with shadows; everyone has a history. If we converted some of our podcast time to 'neighbour time', we would know that. We would also discover that the eye contact of face-to-face conversation engages our empathy in a way that overheard conversations can never do. Even if we are moved to tears by someone's personal revelations to a media interviewer, that is a qualitatively different experience from the interaction with someone who is there, right beside you, in the kind of setting where we make ourselves emotionally vulnerable to each other as part of the gift of listening.

The relationship between oversharing and privacy is a bit chicken-and-egg. When we jump on board with the oversharers, our attitudes to privacy are bound to change in response to the changes in our behaviour: privacy comes to seem less important to us. Then, when privacy becomes less of an issue, we are even more likely to overshare. Soon we are drawn into a kind of perpetual confessional, assuming that everyone in cyberspace is as interested in our insomnia, our travel plans or our renovations – cosmetic or domestic – as we are. In this emerging climate, where even photographing the meal you're about to eat and sharing it with an ever-widening circle of Facebook friends has become commonplace, it's easy to forget how discriminating, how restrained, we once were about what we shared with anyone beyond our nearest and dearest, and how significant and enriching the act of sharing was. More and more, the babble of cyberspace is spilling into what we used to call our personal space.

What will happen next?

Perhaps all this oversharing – voluntary and involuntary – is a sign that we are indeed returning to the more open ways of an oral, village-style communication culture, becoming, paradoxically, more undiscriminating and visceral in our message-exchanging behaviour even as the technology that connects us becomes more sophisticated.

But the present transitional situation is a little more complicated than that. It's as if we're caught between two cultures. We are still a print culture as well as an increasingly oral and e-culture. We still base our school curriculum largely on the printed word. We still place a high value on literacy. Though printed newspapers are dying, we are still reading text recognisable as 'newspapers' online, and we still buy millions of books every year – and e-readers show no sign of totally replacing the printed version, except perhaps in light fiction.

While the communication culture appears to be moving in a more oral/tribal direction, the essential nature of reading and writing is still private, and even the composition of a text or tweet is usually done alone. The ebb and flow of conversational interaction is approximated, but not matched, by digital data transfer, even at high speeds.

Still, the world of communication is changing so rapidly that concepts like privacy and identity and even communication itself are bound to change, too. While some of us are still inclined to laugh at the sight of two people sitting together at a restaurant table, both engrossed in their smartphones, thumbs racing, this has become an urban cliché precisely because it's a symbol of the revolution. Some people do actually prefer texting to face-to-face talking; we might think that's sad, or dangerous, or plain crazy, but it's part of the present reality. We joke that those two diners might be texting each other, but the idea is not at all inconceivable: they might have correctly assumed that eavesdroppers in the immediate vicinity can't overhear texts the way they might overhear private remarks, especially if those remarks are intensely intimate, or consist of indiscreet observations about the people at the next table (though who else might ultimately have access to those texts is a separate question).

We might object when someone in our family or friendship circle disengages from dinner table conversation to bend their head reverentially over their smartphone, but that's part of the present reality, too, and will remain so until the rules of etiquette catch up with the technology. Notice how, in a cinema, we are all enjoined, before the main feature starts, not only to turn off our mobile phones but also to refrain from talking to each other. Once upon a time, we knew not to disturb other people by talking in the cinema, but TV taught us to talk uninhibitedly during programs, and the mobile phone has taught us to talk uninhibitedly anywhere at all, so now we have to unlearn those lessons, at least in cinemas and concert halls. Although we may think our sense of identity and our personal security (emotional as well as physical) depend on having uninterrupted access to our smartphone, it turns out there are social situations that demand we disconnect.

Will literacy die out in the digital age? Unlikely, but what *is* likely is that literate elites will once again emerge, though they might not be regarded as 'elite' by anyone but themselves. All the personal and historical data once stored by ancient elites via the written word (information about lineage, for instance, or wealth, or the outcome of battles) is now stored electronically, so the old association between literacy and social superiority is gone.

Though basic reading skill will be required well into the future – at least until emoticons, emoji and more complex pictographic symbols evolve into some future version of hieroglyphics – the art of handwriting is likely to drop out of most people's skillset, to be replaced by the use of keyboards and touchpads of all shapes and sizes. That's hardly a prediction: schools are already equipping their pupils for life in a digitised communication culture. Hand-written essays, assignments and examinations will soon be a thing of the past.

And privacy? Who would dare predict the long-term conse-quences of a revolution as radical and rapid as this one? It's clear that the climate, the ambience, the context for the decisions we make in the future about how far to exert our right to choose how much we reveal about ourselves will be pushing us to reveal more than we might wish.

In response, we will finally come to accept that there really is no such thing as secure digital data, and learn to work around that. The great irony here is that as we switch away from face-to-face encounters in more and more of our commercial and personal transactions, we are coming to realise that the only really safe way to say something private and confidential is to meet face to face, in an isolated place, preferably outdoors, leaving all your electronic devices somewhere else, and to speak very quietly . . . and that's assuming the other person isn't wired.

Who knows? The handwritten love letter, delivered by a trusty courier, might even make a comeback in the future, at least among the dwindling number of lovers who can still write.

IT and empathy

In his valedictory address, delivered in Chicago in January 2017, US president Barack Obama said this: 'If you're tired of arguing with strangers on the internet, try talking to one of them in real life.'

Real life? Brave words. To the millions of people who regularly spend hours of every day on the internet via their phones, laptops and tablets, that *is* 'real life'. And yet, like Obama's best lines, it sounded simple – homely, almost – while being laden with deep cultural significance.

We are in danger of falling for the myth that online and offline are merely alternative ways of communicating with each other; that digital data is not all that different from the data we exchange when we are talking in each other's presence; that communication is actually more efficient – and can sometimes be more courageous, too, and more intimate – when done screen to screen.

So what was Obama's point?

'Arguing with strangers' occupies a lot of time on the internet. People are often at their most aggressive, most vicious, most reckless, most unkind, most impatient, most unrestrained and least tolerant when they are interacting with total strangers on the internet. In fact, 'arguing' and 'strangers' often go together. That's not to deny that people also fall in love on the internet, keep in touch with friends and family, have factual questions answered, learn new things, see beautiful pictures, collect jokes . . . and access pornography in industrial quantities. But there's something about *remote* interaction with strangers that has the potential to bring out the worst in us.

It's easier to shout abuse at someone from inside the capsule of your car than it is to confront them in the street, though 'road rage' – one of the ugliest symptoms of the short fuse many urban dwellers are operating on – sometimes spills out of the capsule and into personal confrontation. But, generally speaking, we save our strongest reactions for people who are safely insulated from us, ensconced in their own cars. Can you imagine anything more embarrassing than giving the finger to a motorist who has wronged you by daring to change lanes in front of you or committing some equally heinous offence, only to discover that it was a work colleague, or your partner's mother, at the wheel?

This ability to remain emotionally disengaged from remote strangers is what allows human beings to drop unimaginably destructive bombs on their enemies from a great height, or to control the flight of a deadly drone from a distant console. 'Distance lends enchantment to the view' may apply in many situations, but distance can also be a dangerous neutraliser of our emotions.

Why is there so much ugliness on the internet, so much bullying, so much 'flaming', so much 'trolling'? Why are we so much readier to be unpleasant to each other in the digital world than when we are together? And why is there so much misunderstanding of messages sent via emails, texts, Facebook posts and tweets?

One reason for online recklessness is our lack of emotional vulnerability when we enter the digital world, and a corresponding reduction in our capacity for empathy and compassion. It's true that exposure to online communication can, for many children and adolescents, have negative consequences for wellbeing – heavy screen time being associated in many studies with a drop in self-esteem and an increase in feelings of loneliness – and that being the victim of internet bullying can be a deeply distressing experience, bringing some young people to despair or even suicide. But the victim of online bullying or humiliation does have the option of disconnecting and staying away from the site where the bullying is occurring — and that's harder to do if your bully is in the school playground or lives around the corner. More generally, though, our adventures in cyberspace carry fewer emotional consequences than when we make ourselves emotionally vulnerable to each other in a face-to-face encounter.

The very essence of human communication is vulnerability: being open to another person's point of view, being sympathetic in response to another person's emotional state, being *engaged* in a way that melts the ice of detachment. Emotional vulnerability is the prerequisite for empathy and compassion. You can't fall in love without making yourself vulnerable to potential hurt, disappointment and loss. You give yourself to the beloved in a kind of surrender that precludes keeping your fingers crossed behind your back. Not all encounters are like falling in love, but any serious exchange with another person is going to involve making ourselves vulnerable, to some extent, or the encounter will be meaningless.

When we communicate with each other in person, we run the risk of being changed by the subtle and mysterious process of interpersonal influence that always occurs, at some level, when we interact with another person. At their best, such encounters evoke mutual feelings of empathy. The Australian neuroscientist Fiona Kerr maintains that steady, direct eye contact — 'retinal eye-lock' is her term — is the one absolutely essential factor in producing empathy. Similarly, touching someone on the bare skin of their hand or arm, to say nothing of a foot massage, is not merely a symbol of closeness: skin touch can be like an emotional super-highway to the brain, and is highly likely to generate or enhance feelings of empathy.

All these things involve *being there*. Interactions on the internet are far safer, emotionally, than the interpersonal kind, because we run less risk of being changed. And the lack of opportunity for person-to-person eye contact and touch means we can more easily resist any demands for sympathy or understanding. We can also pretend to be what we're not, without fear of exposure.

And the many misunderstandings that occur in cyberspace? They can be explained by the fact that digital data transfer lacks almost all the ingredients humans need for making sense of each other.

This point is so obvious, it hardly warrants another outing, except that it is fundamental to understanding not only the difference between online and offline communication, but also the difference between an empathic and a non-empathic encounter. When we engage in a face-to-face conversation, especially one involving sustained eye contact, most of the data we are processing is not in the words that are being spoken, but in the way they are being presented to us – those non-verbal messages that include posture, gesture (including touch), eye movement (direct gaze, or glazed, or evasive sideways glances, for instance), facial expressions (or the lack of them), rate of speech, tone of voice, the ambience of the place where we are meeting, the social-emotional context, including any shared personal history we might bring to the encounter.

It's complex, it's subtle, and we usually process it all quite effort- lessly, without thinking consciously about it at all: a raised voice and red face say the speaker is probably angry, even when her words insist she's not. The impression that someone is 'shifty-looking' or 'sincere' or 'distracted' is a crucial piece of the jigsaw when we're trying to interpret the meaning of what they are saying to us. As the Chinese say: never trust a man whose belly stays still when he laughs.

On the internet, all those pieces are missing. Most of them are missing in a phone conversation, too, or even in a handwritten letter – though there are more cues on offer in both those exchanges than in the exchange of homogenised digital data on a screen. This is not to denigrate the exchange of digital data – it has its uses and, in some situations, it's better than a face-to-face encounter, especially where brevity and precision are called for, and where you don't want the intention of your words to be blurred or confused or even contradicted by the sound of your voice, your rate of speech, your posture, your gestures, your facial expression, or by a friendly touch on the arm or a kiss on the cheek. That's why it's so much easier to lie online . . .

If we really are moving towards a more open, sharing society, it might be timely to remind ourselves that, while online communities are wonderful for data sharing, there's more to relationships, and more to communal living, than data sharing. In previous chapters, I have suggested that our very identity is inextricably linked to the groups we belong to, which is why we shrivel up (emotionally, if not physically) unless we are nurtured by the experience of engaging with the lives – and sharing the pain – of those around us.

Routinely placing ourselves in situations where it's easy to keep our emotional distance can't be good for our emotional health and the development of our resilience. Empathy, compassion – *relationships* – need practice, and I'm afraid there's no alternative to practising with another person, right there in front of you (and I don't mean on a screen).

You are probably an enthusiastic user of the internet – as I am – and can't now imagine life without it. The internet is the single most significant symbol of our leap into the brilliant new digital age. It allows us to keep in touch with each other – and with the world's store of information – like never before. And it's a wonderful way of augmenting existing relationships that are built on the solid foundation of personal contact.

But it also has the potential to tempt us to pay less attention to personal contact, to diminish our social skills (especially in the young), and, if some neurologists' fears are well-founded, even to affect the brain development of children. 'Don't give a tablet to a child under three or a mobile phone to a child under twelve' is the sort of advice now emerging from the research into the effects of screen time on the brain and social development of children. Did you know, for instance, that watching TV and playing video games typically raises children's blood pressure, while reading typically lowers it? Or that letting a very young child spend too much time staring at a device screen may slow their development of three-dimensional perception? British neuroscientist Susan Greenfield once proposed that computers should automatically shut down every 30 minutes to give our brains a break – and, perhaps, to encourage us to talk to each other.

Financial Times columnist Lucy Kellaway has described a visit she made to the offices of a very hip media production company. The man showing her around referred to the 'incredible buzz' in the place, but Kellaway could detect no buzz at all. As in most offices she visits these days, she wrote, there was only 'the gentle rattle of computer keyboards'. Kellaway was bemoaning the loss of 'office chat'. In many offices, the day used to start with a brief flurry of chatter as colleagues reconnected personally before hitting their desks. Not so much now. More and more, as Kellaway reports, office chat seems to have been replaced by an appearance of uninterrupted concentration on the screens that now typically sit on office desks, since that's the way we now work – even occasionally sending emails or texts to a person just a desk or two away.

Keeping up the appearance of busyness is more important than ever, now job insecurity has hit epidemic proportions. Even so, as a job-secure young employee in the 1960s, I was once advised by a wise head that, whenever I wandered around the office – as he encouraged me to do if I wanted to know what was going on – I should always carry a piece of paper to make it look as if I was working. Today, it's the uninterrupted focus on the screen that creates this impression.

Intrigued by the new silence in offices, even including open-plan set-ups, Kellaway asked her guide at the production company if anyone ever chatted while they were working. 'Of course they do,' he replied. 'They chat all the time.' When Kellaway commented that she couldn't *hear* any chat, the man laughed and said: 'We do it on Slack' (a social media platform, of course).

Kellaway's piece reminded me of some UK research I read a few years ago, reporting that people who spend most of their working time in front of a screen generally feel less connected, less loyal, to the organisation they work for. As of course they would: one screen looks pretty much like any other, and if you also work in an open-plan, hot-desk office, your emotional moorings might be hard to find.

No one could seriously suggest turning the clock back — especially as even more exciting information technology is lying in wait, ready to enchant us afresh. But we need to recognise the need to keep IT in its rightful place, and unless we're social isolates, that rightful place is definitely secondary to our face-to-face interactions. After all, our most precious resource for coping with the disruptions and upheavals of the age is not technology, nor even 'information', but each other.

At least the revolutionary acceleration of data sharing — voluntary and involuntary — has sharpened our awareness of privacy as an issue. It has forced us to confront the nature of the trade-offs we make between privacy and personal safety/national security, between privacy and convenience, and between the privacy of personal relationships and the online community of oversharers. Perhaps it's time to re-establish the primacy of *human presence* in our communication with each other wherever possible, and to recognise what we are losing — subtlety, the richness of nuance, the possibility of empathy — every time we substitute an online connection for a face-to-face encounter. In her 2017 book *iGen*, Jean M. Twenge recounts many cases where teens have 'discovered' the joy of human presence and personal interaction – an experience that no amount of sharing via social media can approach. She quotes a typical eighteen-year-old who says, 'When you are actually with someone it feels personal and loving. Memories are created through experiences that can't happen on the phone or the computer.' Quite so.

In the early days of the IT revolution, Bill Gates, the founder of Microsoft, said that email was a good way to plan a meeting and to record the outcome of a meeting, but it was no substitute for a meeting. I wonder if he still thinks that.

Perhaps it's time to reaffirm that the freedom to choose what I will reveal about myself and what I will keep private is a freedom worth preserving, not only because it is an important freedom in itself, but also because preserving *that* freedom allows us to enjoy other freedoms as well – like the freedom to wander at will, the freedom to associate with whomever we choose, the freedom to sing, dance, laugh, pray or sleep without having the sense that our every movement, our every encounter is being monitored.

Joseph A. Cammataci, the United Nations Special Rapporteur on Privacy, has recently added another dimension to our understanding of the nature and purpose of privacy. In his 2017 report to the 39th International Conference of Data Protection and Privacy Commissioners, he presents privacy as 'an enabling right as opposed to being an end in itself' and argues that the right to privacy is actually 'an overarching, fundamental right to the free, unhindered development of one's personality'. In other words, the loss of privacy diminishes our right to fulfil our human potential – or, as US psychotherapist Carl Rogers would have put it, to become 'that self which one truly is'.

A reflection

On empathy and education

If there's one area of our lives where we need to be most vigilant about the threat to empathy posed by information technology, it's education. As US president Theodore Roosevelt put it: 'People don't care how much you know until they know how much you care.' And that goes double for students.

Eddie Woo, the maths teacher at Sydney's Cherrybrook Technology High School who has become something of a poster boy for mathematics, quotes Yale professor of child psychiatry James P. Comer when describing his own approach to teaching: 'No significant learning can occur without a significant relationship.' Socrates knew that: his whole approach to teaching was based on the intense personal interaction between teacher and pupil. The founding fathers of the great universities of Oxford and Cambridge knew that, too, when they placed one-to-one tutorials at the very centre of the educational process.

An empathic personal response from a teacher won't merely enhance the quality of a student's learning; it is central to the learning process. So what happens when lecture theatres become so large that the possibility of forging any empathic link between teacher and student is virtually impossible? Answer: universities decide that they might as well put those lectures online, for students to access just as they have always accessed textbooks – individually and privately.

We're looking at a future that's almost here: a future where students will have online access to the best lectures in the world on their chosen subjects. While some academics whose lectures are now being recorded complain that there is a significant loss of flexibility in their ability to update their material, lectures can be edited and rerecorded more easily and frequently than text-books can be updated.

Economics is a factor: when 'model' lectures are available as an online resource, the need to keep building vast lecture theatres will greatly diminish, and so will the demand for academics who can deliver brilliant lectures.

What happens next is the crucial bit. You can't generate empathy between an author and a reader or between online lecturers and the students who access their presentations. So when will the empathy be generated?

The most enlightened universities already know the answer to that: back to the small-group tutorial – and by 'small', I mean no more than seven or eight students in the group. Not as good as the Oxbridge model of one-to-one tutorials, but still small enough for personal relationships between teacher and students to evolve, and for empathy to develop.

When James P. Comer says no significant learning can occur without a significant relationship, he's talking about empathy. But we can go further: no significant relationship can occur without empathy and empathy needs human presence. Yes, many people do have online relationships that never convert into face-to-face personal encounters but, generally speaking, the difference between online and face-to-face relationships can be captured in that one word: empathy.

5

The better world you dream of starts in your street

I have always believed that local history is more important than national history . . . Where life is fully and consciously lived in our own neighbourhood, we are cushioned a little from the impact of great far-off events which should be of only marginal concern to us.

Hubert Butler, 'Beside the Nore'

In the era of the internet and 24-hour news services, Butler's assertion that 'great far-off events should be of only marginal concern to us' seems more than a little challenging. We are immersed, daily, in those far-off events, and it's hard to imagine that, in a globalised world, they should be of only marginal concern to us. Aren't we all supposed to be 'global citizens'?

And yet, what can we do about the situation in Somalia, Yemen, Syria, South Sudan, Afghanistan or Iraq — except, of course, contribute to humanitarian aid programs and offer refuge to people fleeing such places? What can we do about the threat of nuclear warfare? What can we do about terrorist attacks in other parts of the world? And what, for that matter, are we supposed to have done about Brexit or Trump, except 'be informed'?

In his 1796 valedictory address after serving two terms as the first president of the US, George Washington specifically warned America against becoming involved in the internal affairs of foreign countries – advice that many of his successors, and some of our own governments, have chosen to ignore. Yet it is as dangerous for us as individuals as it is for nation-states to assume that we should be 'involved in the internal affairs of foreign countries'. Interested, sure; but not involved in matters that lie beyond our control and of which we have no real understanding. (Test question: Who are the good guys in Syria?)

The concept of 'global citizen' needs to be interpreted very carefully, just as the seductively simple idea of a 'global village' does. Yes, being well informed is a good thing, as long as we are not distracted from the business of living *here* by the flow of news about what's happening elsewhere. Keeping up to date with a US presidential election can be interesting – perhaps even fun, for some – but the outcome is entirely the business of the Americans, not us, even if the result might have an impact, directly or indirectly, on Australian trade or defence matters. Ditto for China's attitude to North Korea, or outbreaks of ISIS-related terrorism in Indonesia. Enormous quantities of time and emotional energy can be expended on keeping in touch with – and becoming agitated by – what's going on in the world. But if we allow our headspace to be filled and our personal anxiety level raised by Butler's 'great far-off events', we risk losing sight of the needs of the people who live next door, literally or metaphorically.

Being insular is pathetic, and the level of our contribution towards international humanitarian aid programs – both as individuals and as a nation – is a good indicator of the health of our conscience. But living as if we are personally caught up in events that are way beyond our reach is equally pathetic. The greenies' slogan 'Think global, act local' has some general relevance to our way of life, not just to environmental issues. To be fully engaged members of contemporary society, we need to be aware of what's happening around the world, and to be generous when financial aid is needed to relieve suffering anywhere. We need to take an intelligent interest in our region, and we certainly need to be aware of unfolding events that could affect us economically, culturally, politically or militarily.

Even within our own country, most of the daily news we receive is about matters that neither impinge on our lives nor are within our control. Even if we're desperately unhappy with our government, we can't exert much leverage between elections, except by contacting our local member. 'Solving the world's problems' over a beer or a cup of coffee can be intensely therapeutic for us, but changes nothing.

None of this is intended to discourage anyone from imbibing their daily dose of local and international news and current affairs. It is simply a plea for perspective, for balance; being a 'news junkie' can unbalance us in the same way as any other addiction. In particular, it's a plea to put *most* of our mental and emotional energy into activities and enterprises – in the local community and at work – where we can personally make a difference, and where our personal contribution is sorely needed.

We're all very accomplished at wringing our hands about 'the state of the nation' or, more broadly, 'the state of the world'. It's not always so easy to acknowledge that the state of the nation actually starts in our street, in the sense that how we choose to live will help to determine the kind of neighbourhood ours will become, and the composite character of all our neighbourhoods determines the kind of society we will become. How responsive we are to the needs of those around us, how ready we are to engage with (rather than ignore) our neighbours, how willing we are to contribute to the life and health of the community, how determined we are to cooperate rather than compete . . . these are hugely influential factors in shaping the state of the nation, because the state of the nation is a reflection of the state of our society and that ultimately depends on the quality of our interactions with each other.

Of course, there is plenty to wring our hands about: our growing disenchantment with institutions, the challenge of homelessness, the plight of asylum seekers, the enduring problem of Indigenous Australians' health and wellbeing, the social implications of our growing inequality of income. We might be concerned to the point of despair about the national failure to facilitate the urgent transition from fossil fuels to a clean and sustainable energy environment. We might be perplexed about our declining educational standards (including our low rate of preschool enrolments), or our failure to provide affordable housing for young first-home seekers.

The list of national concerns is long and, naturally, we expect governments of any political persuasion to address such matters on our behalf. We know that problems on such a large scale are beyond the scope of individuals, or even local communities – though some local communities, frustrated by the lack of a cohesive national energy plan, seem set to take the transition to clean energy into their own hands. That response, in fact, points to one of the unexpected ways in which leaders who disappoint us could actually galvanise us to do things we might otherwise be inclined to leave to 'the government'.

How disappointment in leaders can be good for us

When the nation's mood is sagging and things don't seem to be going well – economically, culturally, militarily, or in some other way – there is always a strong temptation to believe that a different leader could make everything right or, at least, get us back on the right track. From Moses to Hitler, human history is littered with examples of nations who came to believe that a leader would save them, only to discover that they had placed too much faith in a mere mortal, burdened by the same flaws and frailties as the rest of us. Disappointment then sets in, usually followed by disenchantment. The disappointment is simply the result of things not changing in the way, or at the speed, people had hoped for. The disenchantment sometimes arises from the unpleasant realisation that the leader was at least as interested in preserving and enjoying his or her own power as in serving the interests of those he or she was supposed to lead.

In Australia, Kevin Rudd and Malcolm Turnbull have been instructive recent examples of what happens when we emotionally overinvest in leaders: their fall from grace and our ultimate disappointment in them are all the more poignant, for them and for us, because our expectations were so high. The best leaders can both inspire and reassure us by placing us in a narrative we can understand and by offering fair and sensible policy solutions to our social and economic problems – Paul Keating was an outstanding example of that in recent Australian history. But 'charisma' can be overrated; Germany's Angela Merkel is a striking example of a successful leader whose 'oratory' would put you to sleep. And the charismatic Barack Obama turned out to be a less successful US president than was anticipated by those who adored him.

While we hope for leaders who will bring out the best in us, we know that leaders can also bring out the worst in us. Sometimes they do it by reinforcing our darkest impulses and prejudices; sometimes they let us off the moral hook by failing to acknowledge the moral dimension of such issues as treatment of refugees, unprovoked invasion of a foreign country, ways of mitigating the effects of climate change or addressing the impact of income inequality.

Visionary, inspirational *and* successful leaders are in short supply, so you'd think we'd learn to expect less and leave some room for pleasant surprises. Perhaps we *are* learning; as part of the general decline of trust in politics, esteem for Australia's current crop of leaders has plummeted to the point where we don't expect to encounter much vision or inspiration any time soon. And we are not alone in that – the success of Trump, Brexit and Macron can be partially interpreted as a reaction to similar levels of disenchantment in the US, UK and France.

In one way, such disenchantment might be no bad thing. It might encourage us to look at the situation differently and accept more personal responsibility for the way things are. We can't manage the economy, of course, but we can decide to spend and save our own money more wisely, and to be more generous to the needy – the marginalised, the disadvantaged, the brutalised. We can't stop the onrush of technology, but we can decide to be its master, not its servant. And when it comes to the character and the values of our society, it really is up to us. We can have a powerful influence on the state of the various communities we belong to – in the neighbourhood, the workplace, the school, the university, the faith community, the sporting association, the book club or other community organisation. How we contribute to the miniatures of life in our own home, street, suburb or town will ultimately help to determine the big picture.

Next time we find ourselves yearning for more charisma in our leaders, perhaps we should ask ourselves: *Am I hoping, yet again, for a leader to make up for the deficiencies in my own effort to make the world a better place? Am I falling for oldest trap in political and cultural history – the trap of believing that a 'charismatic' leader can save us from ourselves?*

I once heard an American civil rights campaigner voicing her sense of alarm at the number of people who felt the civil rights movement needed 'another Martin Luther King, Jr.'. Her strong conviction was that such a leader was needed to generate the movement's initial momentum but that the later, more mature phase of the movement needed more personal engagement in the cause by individuals working to fight racial and other injustices at the local level.

A friend of mine takes a plastic bag with her whenever she goes walking, to pick up any bits of rubbish she sees littering the footpaths or parks where she walks. A man she occasionally encounters on these walks has criticised her for this: 'You're just encouraging people to leave their rubbish to be picked up by someone else,' he says. Her response: 'I'd rather the place was tidy, so I'm happy to help keep it tidy. And maybe a tidy place will encourage other people to keep it that way, too.' She's not waiting for a leader to change her world.

Social cohesion builds social capital

'Social capital' is a grandiose label for a very simple idea. A society needs financial capital to build houses, roads and railways, public transport, hospitals, schools, universities, libraries, museums, public parks and gardens, and so on. In the same way, a society needs to develop social capital to maintain and nurture its institutions and its way of life through the fostering of harmonious social interactions, transparently honest commercial relationships, productive work-places and cooperative communities – all characterised by mutual support, trust and respect, and a willingness to accept responsibility for the wellbeing of others as well as ourselves.

The health of any society depends on the robustness of its social capital. While it's true that social capital is developed through any relationship based on mutual respect, the critical 'nursery' for the growth and development of social capital is the local neighbourhood. This is where we make our homes, raise our kids and do much of the business of living. It's also where we share 'common ground' like footpaths, roads, parks, shops, libraries, schools, churches. It's where incidental interactions occur between people who, generally speaking, did not choose to live in close proximity with each other but who soon realise that a basic level of cooperation, harmony and reciprocity is going to make life more pleasant for all of us. In short, it's where we learn to become citizens.

The local neighbourhood is a place where neighbours are expected to act like neighbours – not by being each other's best friends, though that occasionally happens, but by recognising that when you buy or rent a house or apartment you are taking your place as a member of a neighbourhood, and moral and social obligations flow from that. It's probably fair to say that our moral formation is not complete until we've learnt how to get along with people who aren't our chosen friends, who may be quite unlike us in ethnicity, religion, musical tastes, child-rearing practices or recreational pursuits, but who nevertheless share our locality.

Not everyone sees being a neighbour as involving that kind of social contract. Some people prefer to live as recluses; some will do everything possible to avoid contact – even eye contact – with their neighbours; some totally reject the idea that, by choosing to live in a particular dwelling, they have any moral or social obligations to the other people who live in that street or apartment block or locality. After all, they may say, I didn't choose to have these people as my neighbours in the way I choose my friends, so why do I owe them anything? My 'community' is my work colleagues, or my friendship circle, or the people I play footy with, or my network of school or university friends, or my Rotary or Probus club, or my church, or the local branch of my political party.

But what is a neighbour? And why does being a good neighbour make such a critical contribution to the development of social capital?

We all know how to act like neighbours when there's a crisis – floods, bushfires, storms or horrific events like the carnage in Melbourne's Bourke Street Mall in 2017, when a motorist drove into a group of pedestrians, killing six and injuring more than 30 others. Of course bystanders rushed to the aid of the injured and dying. People almost always help those in obvious pain and distress – that's the kind of species we belong to. So why does it so often take a crisis to remind us of our responsibility to the other members of our community, including the elderly and the isolated, whose need of help – perhaps in the form of nothing more than a bit of conversation – might not be as immediately obvious as an accident victim's?

If we're serious about building social cohesion, we'd do well to attend to comments like this one from a single mother, recently divorced:

> As a sole parent, I feel invisible. It's as if other families don't think we're a real family. I've found I don't get invited to anything where husbands are present. Even when I've taken the initiative and invited a few couples to dinner, they never reciprocate – except if it's a women-only occasion.

Among the elderly, divorce or bereavement can induce a kind of invisibility that leads to social isolation:

> People were really kind after my wife died, but then they sort of dropped me. I'm never included in events with couples. People say, 'You seem to be getting on well,' without ever acknowledging the effort, the loneliness and the pain of it.

> I was relieved when my husband finally left. He was welcome to the younger model, frankly, and she was welcome to him. But I wasn't prepared for the change in my social life – I'm often left out. Maybe some of my women friends think I'm after their husbands. As if! Luckily, I have a neighbour nearby who is in the same boat as me.

Building social capital doesn't only depend on responding to another person's cry for help. We build social capital and help to preserve social cohesion whenever we acknowledge another person; whenever we smile at a stranger; whenever we undertake volunteer work in the community; whenever we ask the neighbours in for a drink; whenever we greet people we encounter in the street, in a queue, in a lift, or beside us in a bus or train; whenever we join a local organisation or patronise a local coffee shop, library or post office and engage in some personal interaction with the people we see there. Smile. Say hello. That's how we help build social capital; that's how we help build social cohesion.

We have plenty of time to enjoy our solitude and privacy when we're behind the closed door of our home. Once we step outside, though, we have nothing to lose and everything to gain by being the kind of person who encourages, by our own example, the idea that since we're all in this thing together, we might as well acknowledge each other, at least.

Social cohesion is obviously harder to preserve when we are a more mobile, more divorced, more childless, busier, more anxious, more isolated and more IT-mediated society than ever before. But, as we are about to see, it can be done.

How do we promote social cohesion?

Artarmon, on Sydney's lower North Shore, was once a solid, middle-class suburb with leafy streets and solid houses on generous blocks. There are still many houses like that but, increasingly, they are being replaced by apartment blocks, particularly in streets close to the railway station. Where once it was a traditional 'Australian family' suburb, it's now a far more diverse community – ethnically, economically and generationally.

When Peggy (not her real name) moved with her family into an apartment block in Artarmon, she noticed that many of the residents only seemed to know one or two other people in the block, and there was even less contact with the residents of other blocks in their street. A couple of her friends shared Peggy's concern about the lack of social cohesion in their part of the suburb and, inspired by the teachings of their Baha'i faith about the need to promote social harmony, decided to do something about it.

As a first step, Peggy's son and some of his friends undertook a series of service projects: running a safe road-crossing awareness program, cleaning up the local park, creating food and care packages for some local homeless people and spending time talking with them.

As the youth group became more engaged with the life of the district, Peggy and her friends and their families decided that they should do something more ambitious to address the problem of social isolation. They sent a note around to the residents of the apartment blocks in the immediate vicinity, put up notices in local shops, and generally spread the word any way they could that, on a particular Sunday afternoon, there would be a gathering in the local park. Everyone was invited to bring their own food and drink, and use this as an opportunity to get to know their neighbours.

The response was enthusiastic: the first such picnic in the park drew 40 neighbours; the second 55. The most obvious immediate effect was that people who subsequently encountered each other in the car park of their building or in the street or a local shop were more likely to recognise and greet each other.

Regular picnics in the local park are now being requested not only by the local community, but by groups from other parts of the suburb who would like to replicate the model in their own nearby parks. Some people are proposing that the events should be expanded to include other activities: bushcare, games, performances by local groups – singing, dancing, acting – and occasional talks about local issues. Peggy and her friends are happy for the idea to evolve in any way the local residents choose; their aim is simply to ensure that more people feel as if they belong where they live, and that the life of the local community will become more vibrant as a result.

Andrew Leigh, Labor MP for the ACT seat of Fenner in the federal parliament, is an enthusiastic supporter of the idea of building social capital through local community connections. In his book *Disconnected*, he lists ten ways to boost social capital: hold a street party; reclaim the footpaths; use local stores; give to charity; use new technology to build face-to-face connections, not replace them; revive local organisations; give time as a volunteer; contact two politicians; break bread with others; try a new activity – swing dance, lawn bowls, the SES.

It's not all theory. Andrew Leigh and his wife organise a street party every December. When friends look sceptical and assume it must take a lot of planning and effort – road closure, finding a date that suits everyone etc. – Leigh replies that it takes about twenty minutes to get the invitations out to neighbours, and about two hours to actually hold the event with the good old 'BYO' taking care of the food and drink. And no roads need be closed; he holds the party in his own home.

Leigh also notes the potential personal benefit from greater community engagement: new activities and stimulating conversations can maintain brain plasticity and help to keep dementia at bay.

In a post on the website of *The Conversation*, the University of Sydney's Emeritus Professor Simon Chapman, a long-term public health advocate, recalled the impact of street parties in France:

> When I lived in Lyon in 2006, the city encouraged street parties. A note from the organising committee came under our door, inviting us to the small park and to bring a plate of food to share. We went, and met people who became great friends. We found that two doors down was a halfway house for men just out of prison. Several came and joined in. I noticed that, from then on, locals would often chat with them in the street, offer them odd jobs etc.

The French also have an annual *fete de musique* where locals perform in their neighbourhoods in another effort to break down barriers. More than wonderful.

I recently enquired with my local council [in Sydney] about setting up a similar event where I live. Immediately the bureaucracy descended with development applications, insurance demands, Portaloo requirements, the need for security staff and a massive application fee.

And while we're overseas, the concept of the 'social street' based on a closed Facebook group was created by an Italian couple, Laurell Boyers and Federico Bastiani, who moved to Bologna and didn't know a single soul in the neighbourhood. As reported by Gaia Pianigiani in the *New York Times:* 'Mr Bastiani took a chance and posted a flyer along his street, Via Fondazza, explaining that he had created a closed group on Facebook just for the people who lived there. He was merely looking to make new friends.' Within a few days, the group had twenty 'followers' and, by the time Pianigiani wrote her report in 2015, there were 1100.

Walking along Via Fondazza no longer feels to residents like strolling in a big city neighbourhood. Rather, they say, it is more like exploring a small town where everyone knows one another. Boyers comments: 'Now I am obliged to speak to everyone when I leave the house – you have to be careful what you ask for!'

'We live near one another and we help each other. That's it,' one resident told Pianigiani. And the help can range from assembling a piece of Ikea furniture to shopping for a frail elderly resident. A 27-year-old law student, Francesca D'Alonzo, joined the group in 2013 and says it 'has changed the walking in Via Fondazza. We greet each other. We speak. We ask about our lives. We feel we belong here now.'

The idea has spread. In 2015, Pianigiani documented 393 'social streets' in various parts of Europe, Brazil and New Zealand.

In a slightly different form, the idea of harnessing Facebook to forge local connections has landed in Australia, too, courtesy of Amy Churchouse, a former veterinary surgeon who founded the Kensington Good Karma Network in an inner suburb of Melbourne. Her project is a perfect example of Andrew Leigh's principle that we should use new technology to build face-to-face connections, not replace them.

Like the 'social streets' project, the Good Karma Network harnesses Facebook to establish a closed community network, but in this case it is designed as a place where people can go to ask for help of any kind – from the loan of a child's car seat to use during a grandchild's visit to help in locating a lost pet, finding potential friends for a child starting at a new school or identifying the best plumber in the district. The project has quickly spread to many other parts of Melbourne and beyond, where, under Churchouse's guidance and following the Kensington model, people are establishing their own Good Karma Networks (twenty-nine at the time of writing).

Amy Churchouse says she is motivated by her desire to help people work together to solve problems and to realise they can make a difference by being more open-minded and compassionate. She bans 'negativity' and insists the network should never be used for selling or advertising. Beyond that, as the network's moderator, she makes no judgements, letting the flow of requests and responses proceed spontaneously.

Quite apart from the specific help given and received through the Good Karma Network, there have been spin-off effects, most notably in the increase in footpath contact between people who now feel more connected to the neighbourhood because of their participation in the project. The network has also spawned many sub-groups in Kensington, including dog walking, cycling and cooking groups, a babysitting co-op, a movie club, a book club, a garden swap-and-share group, a French conversation group, and many more. Amy Churchouse is also planning a website where inspiring stories of local heroes will be told.

On a national scale, Neighbour Day is held on the last Sunday of March each year. It was founded in Melbourne by Andrew Heslop in 2003, after the remains of a woman were found in her home two years after she had died. Shocked by that tragedy and inspired by a neighbour who mowed the nature strip for everyone in the street, took people's bins in for them and did odd jobs for people in the street – all without overstepping the bounds of 'neighbour' by intruding into people's lives – Andrew Heslop decided to act.

His original idea was a 'check on your neighbour day', but it morphed into Neighbour Day, as a more general encouragement of social contact between neighbours. The organisation of Neighbour Day was taken over by Relationships Australia in 2013.

The Random Acts of Kindness Day, held on 17 February each year, has similar goals. Created in Denver, Colorado, in 1995 and taken up by the Australian Kindness Movement, it is intended to encourage spontaneous gestures of kindness or generosity to complete strangers or, as its promoters say, 'to be the light you want to see in the world'.

In Narrabundah, a suburb of Canberra, I was invited into the home of Jane Smyth to observe an embryonic project in progress: the Women Across Generations discussion group. This is a small group of women (normally between five and seven), who meet once every six weeks for conversation about anything that's on their minds. No agenda is set; no topic is announced in advance.

Reflecting on her motives for starting the group, Jane spoke of her own craving for 'a higher level of conversation' in a non-judgemental atmosphere. But she was also keen to create a situation where younger and older women would have access to each other's wisdom, insights and life experiences. So the wide age range, 45–85, was an integral part of the concept.

Jane convened the first meeting of the group in a tentative spirit, but was heartened by the response of the other women. As the meetings have proceeded, the 'strangers' have inevitably become less strange to each other and their encounters have become increasingly frank, open and beneficial. One member of the group has spoken of her enthusiasm for connecting with 'the deeper thought-life' of other women and the benefit she received from 'exchanging glimpses of those parts of self we are usually too busy or distracted to reveal'.

For the members of the group, this is a quite different experience from a conversation between friends or at a book club or any other conventional social encounter; its uniqueness derives partly from the intergenerational character of the group and partly from the fact that it is determinedly not a lunch, or a 'coffee morning', but an opportunity to focus entirely on conversation.

The discussion I attended as an observer ran for almost two hours and ranged from the hazards of having unrealistic expectations about books recommended by friends to the transformative value of entering the consciousness and experience of another person through reading a novel; despair over the state of federal politics; aspects of parenting; Indigenous issues; recent trends in funeral services; the joys of not being on email; the pace of life as a distraction from giving proper attention to friendships and proper acknowledgement of their value to us; the problem of dealing with continuing discrimination against women and the persistence of a male supremacist attitude among older men; the challenges of social isolation; and much more.

For the participants, these discussions have become a precious means of making new connections and, in the process, feeling more integrated into the community. To Jane Smyth's delight, similar groups are already being planned in other places.

'Tucked between a café and a computer shop on Oxford Street [Sydney], surrounded by the roar of city traffic, there is a little haven of civilised pleasure.' So begins Ali Gripper's story in the *Sydney Morning Herald* about a 'free library' set up in a bookcase outside the office of urban designer Kylie Legge, an avid reader who decided she had to reduce the number of books piled up in her apartment. People are free to borrow the books and either return them or replace them with another title. (This is a lovely example of the *true* sharing economy.)

Legge's bookcase is part of a growing trend, here and overseas, based on the Little Free Library movement begun in Wisconsin by Todd Bol when he set up a free library on his front lawn, housed in a model of a schoolhouse in honour of his schoolteacher mother. As you might expect, such mini-libraries become a magnet for people who don't just want to borrow books, but who are also looking for social interaction. As Bol puts it: 'We have a natural sense of wanting to be connected ... Little Free Libraries open the door to conversations we want to have with each other.'

In Australia, imaginative locations for these little libraries have ranged from disused phone booths to birdcages, billycarts, dolls' houses and microwave ovens, and they are popping up everywhere from the inner city to the bush. Gripper quotes children's book illustrator Mary-Kate Khoo, who set one up on her front lawn in Toowoomba and says it has made everyone in her neighbourhood feel less alone. 'It makes me feel more secure, too,' she says. 'People I've never met now say hello over the fence when they're out walking the dogs and I'm watering the garden, all because of the books.'

There's also one in the front garden of the Neutral Bay Uniting Church in Sydney, alongside the 'free wi-fi' garden, the community garden and the garden exchange, where neighbours drop in to take whatever plants they want and leave some of their own in return.

And you?

You don't know your neighbours? Try knocking on the door and introducing yourself. Become the kind of person who is always alert to the possibility that someone needs your help or attention; the kind of person whose life, in Nugget Coombs's words, is 'shaped by the thought of others' need'.

Join a local book club, or start one; start an informal discussion group like Jane Smyth's; participate in a community garden; play a team game with a local club; become a regular at your local cafe; join a community choir. In other words, engage! Be there!

Perhaps the local dog-walking park is where you're making your connections, chatting to the other owners while the dogs are doing the canine equivalent. Or perhaps it's a U3A class, a gym, a parents' group at a local school, or the congregation at a local church, mosque, temple or synagogue, or regular events at your local library. If you were to put a ping-pong table in your garage, you might be surprised by the number of neighbours of all ages who would enjoy a game. One person I know participates in an annual 'ham syndicate' – a loose network of singles who buy a Christmas ham and share it between them. Another joins a group of professional women from her district who meet once a month for an evening of baking – and talking. A third, after wrestling with questions of faith and spirituality for some years, has formed a discussion group for local people who identify as 'soft agnostics'. And ukulele groups have sprung up everywhere.

In virtually all fictional portrayals of a dystopian future, the breakdown of local communities is central. People use their heavily fortified homes as a refuge from the murderous goings-on in the street, communicating via technology with friends and social networks that exist only in cyberspace and not in the three-dimensional space that surrounds them. Such portrayals in films and books seem as bleak as they do not only because they often feature gang warfare on a grand scale and the breakdown of all the services and activities – from garbage collection to policing – that make for a civilised society, but also because they present us with a picture of what life would be like if we withdrew from our local neighbourhoods, retreated into a terrifying individualism, and lost sight of our true nature as social beings who belong in communities.

Most of us hope to live in a safe neighbourhood characterised by mutual trust and respect – and that is still the experience of millions of Australians. But such communities won't survive unless we understand our role in maintaining them. Think about the kind of neighbourhood you'd like to live in, and then start living as if it's that kind of neighbourhood. Pretty soon that's the kind of neighbourhood it will become.

'Love thy neighbour? You don't know my neighbours!'

It might not be easy to engage with the community in a spirit of compassion, but it's certainly easy to mock. Early in 2017, a speech I gave on this theme was published on the website of *The Conversation*. Among constructive comments like Simon Chapman's, quoted earlier, some cynical messages appeared: 'Yeah. Make scones for the neighbours and be kind to baby dolphins'; 'It's not my fault – it's the fault of our leaders and institutions'; 'You're just an old man who should be tending his tomatoes.'

For the record, I guess I *am* an old man – so old, in fact, that raw tomatoes have been deleted from my diet, and I'm not generous enough to tend them for other people. As for scones and dolphins, I'd be inclined to applaud both strategies and to advise my correspondent that there are still many, many places in Australia where people do welcome new neighbours with modest goodwill offerings – if not homemade scones, then maybe a shop-bought cake or a bag of lemons from their tree. And the person who wants to blame 'leaders and institutions' for the state of the nation would be unmoved, I'm sure, by the thought that the state of the nation might start in his own street.

A caller to a radio program on which I was advocating the idea of getting to know the people next door ridiculed the whole idea on the grounds that *his* neighbours were so appalling, he wouldn't wish to get to know them at all – except, I assume, if a storm blew the roof off his house and he needed some urgent assistance.

For the machinery of social capital to reach its peak performance, it needs the high-octane fuel of compassion – the remarkable human quality that makes sense of the idea that you could act charitably towards someone you don't like, or forgive someone who is clearly in the wrong. If you think of compassion as a discipline rather than an emotion – determined action rather than a response to feelings of affection – you've got the idea.

At its most radical, compassion is a way of life. It becomes an impulse that refuses to be selective in the dispensing of kindness or charity or helpfulness, regardless of the waxing or waning of our feelings of affection, pity or empathy towards individuals in need. Compassion tells us the poor deserve our help because they are poor, regardless of how they became poor; the sick because they are sick, regardless of how they became sick; the disadvantaged, deprived, marginalised and bewildered because they can't help themselves.

But the kind of compassion that builds social cohesion is not reserved for categories like 'marginalised' or 'disadvantaged'. A next-door neighbour might need our help with the shopping because she's feeling a bit unwell. A lost child might need us to stay with him until his parents can be located. An elderly person struggling with an overloaded wheelie bin might need a hand. A lonely person might need us to drop in and say hello occasionally. A stranger at the bus stop might need a listening ear for a few minutes. A single mother might appreciate having her preschooler supervised for an hour or two while she goes to the hairdresser.

Commitment to social cohesion does not deny the importance of solitude, the joy of intimacy with a partner or the deep satisfactions that flow from our relationships with those in our circle of close friends. But part of the value of those nurturing experiences is social, as well as personal: they replenish our resources for the challenging business of being a member of the wider community – a neighbour, a colleague, a citizen.

The key to the discipline of compassion is to expand our interpretation of the ancient injunction to *love your neighbour* not only by redefining what we mean by 'love' to embrace this non-emotional approach, but also by redefining the meaning of 'neighbour' so it is not confined to those within our circle who are like us and whom we agree with, but extends to those who are decidedly unlike us and those we disagree with, as well. It's easy to be kind and compassionate towards those we like, not so easy towards those we don't like, and yet how we respond to those we don't like is the ultimate test of our commitment to the civilising discipline of compassion.

An approach to the neighbourhood based on charity, kindness and respect benefits our own mental health, as well as the health of the community. We build a better society by responding to bad behaviour with good behaviour, to ugliness with beauty, to treachery with integrity, to lies with truth and, above all, by responding generously to each other's needs.

What we don't do, of course, is create Utopia. Humans are still humans. Even in a well-functioning neighbourhood characterised by kindness and mutual respect, there will be tensions and occasional conflicts. A compassionate mindset doesn't protect us from disappointment, nor from the foibles, frailties and vanities that are an integral part of the human condition. But at least the habit of compassion will make us more tolerant of these things in others, even though we are all at risk of remaining blind to them in ourselves. In any case, the knowledge that perfection lies beyond our grasp is no reason to give up. Olympic athletes will never get from the starting line to the finish in no time, but they keep trying to get there quicker than last time.

The IT challenge to the life of the neighbourhood

Writing for the *Archives of Disease in Childhood*, September 2016, Dr Aric Sigman said this:

> In Britain today, children by the age of 10 years have regular access to an average of five different screens at home [including TV, computers, computer game consoles, smartphones, tablets etc.] . . . Children routinely engage in two or more forms of screen viewing at the same time, such as TV and laptop. Viewing is starting earlier in life. Nearly one in three American infants has a TV in their bedroom, and almost half of all infants watch TV or DVDs for nearly 2 hours/day. Across the industrialised world, watching screen media is the main pastime of children. Over the course of childhood, children spend more time watching TV than they spend in school . . .

> Irrespective of the content or educational value of what is being viewed [across all screen types], the sheer *amount* of average daily screen time during discretionary hours after school is increasingly being considered an independent risk factor for disease.

A risk factor for disease? Why would that be? There will be many factors involved in individual cases, but surely there are two obvious common factors. First, there's the loss of exercise and 'grass time' referred to in chapter 2, but there's also the erosion of our capacity for giving and receiving empathy and compassion. All that two-dimensional screen time undermines our true nature as three-dimensional social beings, built for life in a nurturing, supportive and interactive community. If we cut ourselves off from those interactions and substitute face-to-face time with too much screen time, we are bound to pay a high price.

It's easy to get excited about the ever-new world of IT, and perhaps even to embrace the idea that our relationships – both personal and working – are going to be radically different in the future, because they will be mainly mediated through a screen. Perhaps the focus of our trust really will shift from institutions to algorithms. But how much of our biologically determined role as social beings – friends, neighbours, colleagues, customers – are we prepared to give up in favour of our interactions with keyboards and screens? Are we ready to compromise the very thing that most makes us human – the time we spend nurturing our face-to-face relationships – by spending more and more time engaging in electronic data transfer, no matter how rapid, brilliant and efficient it may be? It's not going to be one or the other, of course; the choice is not as stark as that. But unless we cling fiercely to our humanity, we might find it hard to strike the right balance.

In *Who Can You Trust?*, Rachel Botsman tells the story of Tom Steinberg, a British internet activist and strong advocate for the UK staying in the EU who, after the Brexit referendum result became known, was searching through Facebook, trying to find someone who had voted to leave. So effective was the filtering of his Facebook access, so impenetrable was the e-bubble in which he operated, he couldn't actually locate anyone whose opinion differed from his. 'I couldn't find anyone who is happy despite the fact that over half the country is clearly jubilant and despite the fact that I'm actively looking to hear what they are saying.'

Reading that, far from worrying about the echo chamber effect of social media (though that *is* a worry), or the fact that a Facebook algorithm had automatically blocked Steinberg's access to people who disagreed with him, I found myself wondering why he didn't get out more. If he was serious about wanting to interact with – or even just to understand – people who were unlike him, they could probably be found in the local pub, or at a football match, the dog-walking park, on a train, possibly even in the house next door or among work colleagues. (Sociocultural diversity, including some political disagreement, is one of the joys and strengths of any reasonably diverse workplace.) The image of a man sitting at his computer vainly trying to find someone to disagree with rather saddened me, in fact. I was similarly saddened when a friend told me that she knew of a woman in Hobart who, courtesy of Skype, belonged to a book club in suburban Melbourne. Very clever, of course, but why not find a local book club to join, I wondered, where all the richness of personal interaction was not being mediated – and inevitably diminished – through an IT device?

If the better world we all dream of starts in our street, and if we and our children are ignoring the street in favour of the online community, then we are shaping a very different kind of society – one where tolerance, humility, sensitivity, empathy and compassion will be in shorter supply than they are now. We can choose to become that kind of society, but we need to understand what we're choosing, and we need to decide if that's really a world we want our children to inhabit.

Join the dots

There is no magic wand for building a better society. No messianic leader can do it for us; no self-help manual has the answer. The truth is so blindingly simple, it's easy to overlook. Because almost all of us live in villages, towns, suburbs and cities, we are already part of a community, or several communities. We already exist in a circle, or several circles. All that is needed is to join the dots.

You'd like to see a more peaceful world? Then start by making your street, your family, your workplace more peaceful. You're appalled by the idea that lonely people can die in their homes, undetected for days? Make sure there's no one in your street, or your apartment block, experiencing the kind of isolation that would make such a thing possible.

You think we're becoming media-saturated at the expense of personal relationships? Then detach yourself from your IT devices except when you really need to use them. Keep reminding yourself that humans communicate most effectively, most completely, most satisfyingly, when they are making eye contact. If that is not practicable, then remember your voice on a phone line is a more effective transmitter of nuance than any digital message on a screen, even one laden with emojis. (Of course, there are times when you might not want to transmit nuance, or when you might not be prepared to make yourself emotionally vulnerable to someone else: digital media are perfect for such situations.)

You fear that online booksellers will force your local bookshop out of business, and that the community would be poorer for the loss of its bookshop? Patronise the shop and resist the online alternative, at least occasionally.

You're worried about the rise of fundamentalism – in religion, economics, gender politics and elsewhere? Resist the lure of simplistic certainties; learn to live with doubt and uncertainty as part of the price you pay for being a non-rational human, in a world full of other non-rational humans. Hold on to your scepticism about *everything* (everything but compassion; abandon yourself to that).

You despair over homelessness, disadvantage and poverty? Ring up any of the charities trying to alleviate these problems and ask what you can do to help. You think society is suffering from too much busyness, too little courtesy, too little eye contact? Or that loyalty and honesty are things of the past? The best place to tackle these issues is right there in the street where you live.

And don't worry about how you're *feeling* about any of this – whether becoming kinder and more respectful towards other people will make you happy. That's not why you're doing it. If you're looking for something to worry about, worry about whether you gave someone your undivided attention when they needed it; whether you really listened, or just pretended to. Worry about whether you apologised quickly enough – and sincerely enough – when you wronged or offended someone; whether you forgave someone readily enough when they apologised, or even when they didn't; whether you were there when someone – perhaps even a total stranger – needed your encouragement and support.

For most of us, personal relationships are the source of life's meaning: even our sense of personal identity only exists in the context of those relationships. Communication is not only our social currency; it's society's life force. Society is like an electricity grid, humming with energy and potential power, but that power comes from us, as well as to us. When we deny our natural impulse to communicate with each other, we diminish ourselves.

The tragedy of busy, fragmented lives is that we are not always living as if we need each other, though we do. We are not always living as if our own health depends on the health of the communities we belong to, though it does. We are not always living as if we understand that a *good* life is a life lived for others, though that's all it can ever be. How else can you make sense of the idea of a good life? You can't be good on your own; morality is only ever about how we treat other people. Goodness is about responding to other people's need of our kindness, charity, compassion and respect. Tribal wisdom – both ancient and modern – tells us that our commitment to the common good is what gives our lives a sense of meaning, purpose and deep satisfaction. We all know this intuitively for the very good reason that we are all human beings, social to the core.

To lose our sense of flesh-and-blood, face-to-face social cohesion would therefore be to risk losing our sense of humanity. What we need most is not wealth, material comfort, a booming economy, an unceasing flow of information and the latest gadget for accessing it – wonderful though all those things may be. What we most need is what humans have *always* most needed: other people, right there beside us.

PART II
FAULT LINES

A long-standing convention in what is sometimes termed 'polite society' is that three topics should never be discussed: sex, religion and politics. Why? Because those are the three topics where prejudices tend to run most deeply. Sex, religion and politics are the classic 'fault lines' that run through every society, with the potential to cause heated disputes, bitter resentments, ridicule and even hatred, often leading people to conclude, through clenched teeth: 'If you believe *that*, I'm afraid we'll have to agree to disagree' – which usually means: 'We disagree because you're simply wrong.'

These are also three areas of life where compassion has traditionally been in short supply. Women and men have typically been less than respectful of perceived gender differences – whether biologically or culturally based – too readily resorting to sexist stereotypes: *What else would you expect from a man/woman?* Though religion is supposed to foster compassion, people of different faiths – or even members of subgroups of the same faith – often adopt uncharitable attitudes towards each other, to put it mildly. And politics is renowned for the lack of respect – let alone kindness or compassion – shown by political opponents towards each other, at least in public.

Though there are plenty of issues still to be resolved in all three areas – and we'll explore some of them in Part II – sex/gender, religion and politics are three of the most obvious signs of a major culture shift now taking place: the shift towards *convergence*. In fact, of all the labels being applied to this phase of our social evolution, the 'age of convergence' is probably the most apt.

In Australia and in many other parts of the world, this is a time of merging, melding, blending, intersecting and overlapping, all of which is potentially good news for social cohesion and for the health of our communities, though there remain pockets of vehement resistance to the whole idea of convergence. But long-standing fault lines are inexorably shifting, reshaping the cultural landscape in dramatic ways and taking the heat out of some old tensions and rivalries.

We've already seen how convergence works in the media, with online applications and time-shifting of programs redrawing the boundaries of broadcasting, online service providers eating into the free-to-air market, and social media postings challenging the traditional role of journalism.

Now we are seeing it in politics, too, with populism blurring the ideological differences between parties and mainstream politicians wanting to position themselves as 'centrist'.

We are seeing it in the gender revolution, as we edge closer to a true understanding of equality and begin to accept that male/female is not the simple dichotomy we might once have thought it was.

And we are seeing it in religion, with the very concept of 'God' under constant review, a better educated and more sceptical population becoming more interested in the similarities than the differences between the major religions, and the prospect of interfaith dialogue more realistic than it has ever been, notwithstanding the loud protests from extremists and fundamentalists. (How slow we are to learn: Buddhists and Hindus have been sharing temples in Cambodia for centuries.)

We're even seeing a shift in the concept of cultural identity itself, as homogenised global culture seeps into many regional and local cultures and the mass movement of people makes 'nationality' a more problematical – and possibly less interesting – concept than ever before in human history.

Where we're *not* seeing the signs of convergence – indeed, we're seeing the reverse – is in the socioeconomic stratification of our society. As income inequality increases and we continue to institutionalise a wealth class at the top and an underemployed/welfare-dependent class at the bottom, inequality becomes not only a persistent fault line, but a widening one.

At a time when Australia seems to have retreated from its previous commitment to egalitarianism as a social ideal, it is worth recalling that access to world-class public education was once regarded as the key to equality of opportunity, and the most accessible pathway out of poverty and disadvantage. But no more: our education system is no longer world-class and access to top-quality education is no longer universal.

That's why, after we've dealt with the Big Three – sex, religion and politics – the final chapter of Part II examines what's been happening to our schools and, in particular, why educational standards are dropping, why the contest between public and private schooling is being comprehensively lost by the public sector, and why there's so much debate about funding yet so little about the role and purpose of education itself.

6

Gender wars:
A pathway to peace

I was tired of being a woman ...
I was tired of the gender of things.

Anne Sexton, 'Consorting with Angels'

The struggle which is not joyous is the wrong struggle.

Germaine Greer, *The Female Eunuch*

Germaine Greer's assertion that a struggle which is not joyous is the wrong struggle contains deep wisdom. It raises a critical issue for women and men still striving to build a truly gender-equal society 50 years after the rise of second-wave feminism – the so-called women's liberation movement – and the ensuing, sometimes bitter, gender revolution.

Fifty years? Perhaps *that* revolution has run its course and it's time to reconsider its aims, re-evaluate its strategies and focus on an entirely different kind of struggle for a new social order that promotes harmony and humanity, with the assumption of equality –

gender and otherwise — at its very core. This would be a society that had evolved beyond ancient, wearying contests between men who still cling to a male-supremacist view of the world — or, if not of the world, then perhaps of their profession, or their family, or their workplace, or their political party, or their church — and women who still get excited about 'the first female CEO of an AFL club', or 'the state's first female premier', or 'the first female jockey to win the Melbourne Cup', or 'the first public company to have a female chair *and* CEO', as though these are revolutionary changes rather than mere blips.

All such achievements are significant for the women concerned, no doubt, and some of them may claim they got there *in spite* of being a woman, but did any of them want us to think their success was *due to* being a woman? Did any of them want us to regard them as *symbols* of the gender revolution, rather than persons who, in their own right, achieved what they achieved? It's hard for anyone, female or male, to win the Melbourne Cup or run a bank or a government: a fleeting moment of pride at being the first female X, Y or Z is perfectly understandable, but any person of integrity in a position of prominence or influence would want to make the most effective contribution she or he could make, and perform in that role to the best of her or his ability, with gender an absolutely irrelevant factor.

The more we promote the idea that a few women in 'top' positions are symbols of the success of the gender revolution or that women should aspire to such positions in order to promote the interests of other women, the more we perpetuate the old order that enshrined the idea of competition between men and women. Meanwhile, there has been a recent *decrease* in the number of women on corporate boards, a *decrease* in the number of women on the frontbenches of federal parliament, and a continuing income gap between men and women. 'Equal pay for equal work' is one of our society's core values, but there still seem to be too many exceptions.

Women have radically reinvented womanhood

The women's movement has been spectacularly successful in creating a revolution in our understanding of gender issues. Some men still harbour reservations about the whole exercise; some feel vaguely bewildered or threatened by women's new-found confidence. And many women feel as if things haven't moved nearly as quickly, or as far, as they would have liked. But you have only to compare the role and status of women in Australia in the 1950s and 60s with their position today to realise that this has probably been the most significant of all the social revolutions of the twentieth century.

From marriage and parenting to education, employment, sport, the arts and politics, women's place in Australian life is vastly different from 50 years ago. Those were the days when female public servants had to resign from the permanent staff when they married, to make way for 'breadwinners' (i.e. males); when women wanting to travel overseas had to obtain their husband's permission, but there was no equivalent requirement for husbands; when women's wages and superannuation were explicitly and deliberately set lower than men's, just because they were women (get it?); when girls typically left high school at the end of the third year because higher education was, overwhelmingly, a male province, and women were expected to prepare themselves for marriage and full-time motherhood, starting with the accumulation of the contents of a 'glory box'. (Ask your grandmother.) And those were the days when a wife typically drew much of her sense of identity from her husband's persona; when a man was expected to support his wife financially and, in return, to receive uncritical and loyal emotional and domestic support from her.

All that has changed. Most women now participate in the paid workforce for most of their adult lives, with some interruptions for childbearing and rearing. Women have set higher standards for an acceptable marriage/partnership than their mothers and grandmothers would have dared to do, and are more prepared to leave if things don't work out: women, today, are far more likely than men to initiate separation and divorce proceedings. The splitting of domestic roles and responsibilities between men and women has undergone a revolution – though, again, many women would say it still has much, much further to go. Today's fathers typically believe they get more pleasure out of parenting than their own fathers appeared to, because of their greater participation in the life of their children, though some overstretched mothers ruefully wonder whether women are getting *less* pleasure out of parenting than their own mothers did, because of their reduced participation in the life of their children. The special needs of women for protection from domestic violence are more widely acknowledged than ever before. The majority of university students are now female, and there are no separate pay scales for men and women.

And yet there's a sense, especially among leading feminists, that the revolution has stalled. 'Stalled' is the very word used by Elizabeth Proust, chairman (she prefers 'chairman' to 'chair') of the Australian Institute of Company Directors, when she notes the serious lack of progress in getting women onto corporate boards. Even in companies where men pay lip service to the idea of gender diversity, the single 'token woman' is still more common than the modest 30 percent female representation being urged by the AICD.

So what went wrong?

In spite of the evidence of the transformative success of the women's movement, any gender-equality strategy that involved attack and defence was eventually bound to stall, mainly because the persistence of the defence would ultimately dull the effectiveness of the attack. Worse, the risk was always present that gender itself would become a festering issue that would undermine social cohesion rather than promoting it. If we continued to see ourselves as no more than combatants in a struggle, rather than partners in a 'joyous' project, the revolution would inevitably collapse (as it is now in danger of doing) into endless sniping with an occasional skirmish.

The Women's Electoral Lobby celebrated its 45th anniversary in 2017. Forty-five years of encouraging more women to enter parliament is testimony to an impressive blend of endurance and passion. WEL has had plenty of success, certainly, and politics needed such a lobby group to raise awareness of the issue and to generate momentum. Now, with an eye to a new social order, perhaps WEL might consider morphing into something broader – a Candidates-on-Merit Lobby, perhaps, committed to promoting the idea that merit should be the sole factor in the selection of parliamentary candidates, and that gender should no longer even be considered as a factor. (But not yet: there's still one more frontier to conquer – quotas – and we're coming to that. I'm heartily in favour of them, by the way, as a short-term shock to the system.)

International Women's Day is a wonderful occasion for raising awareness of the many places in the world – especially parts of Africa and the Middle East – where women are not treated merely as second-class citizens, as they once were in Australia, but where they endure oppression amounting to slavery. In Australia, though, International Women's Day usually involves rousing calls to keep up the struggle against gender bias and to continue attacking what Eva Cox, one of her generation's most militant gender warriors, calls men's 'macho-designed cultural dominance'.

In 2017, the ABC decided to mark the day by having females present all its programs. From this listener's point of view, it made little discernible difference since most of the programs I watch or listen to on the ABC are already presented by women. But what was the point? Was it to say: *Hey! See! Women can do anything men can do*. Or was it to say: *Hey! See how much better the world would be if women ran the entire show?* Or perhaps it was simply to register that the ABC is pro-feminist – again, unwittingly promoting the idea that there's a contest, and that women are winning, at least within the ABC. Or perhaps it wasn't as pointless as it seemed to many listeners at the time; perhaps it was a serious, symbolic attempt to demonstrate solidarity with the women struggling against oppression and exploitation around the world, though I never heard that made explicit.

The previous year, Cox had delivered a stirring International Women's Day address under the title: 'Feminism has failed and needs a radical rethink'. She asserted that, in Australia, 'women are still very much the second sex, insofar as we are permitted limited share of power and resources in the public sphere, but on macho market terms' and noted that 'the increasing numbers of women allowed to join men in positions of power and influence are mostly prepared to support the status quo, not to increase gender equity'. Which is, of course, true: almost anyone – male or female – who reaches the top of any corporate or professional ladder, or achieves a level of status or fame they have long striven for, is inclined to feel gratitude and respect for the system that got them there, and to see no reason why it should be reformed or reconfigured. After all, they will argue, any system that recognised and rewarded their talent must be a pretty good system. That's a natural response, and it explains why so many men have remained resistant to any radical proposals – such as quotas – for restructuring our corporate boards, our parliamentary frontbenches or the upper echelons of business and the professions to better reflect our supposed commitment to gender equality.

As many feminists have recognised, the changing social and economic context created by the rise of neoliberalism slowed the progress of the gender revolution, partly because it shifted the focus from the collective to the individual. But there was more to the 'failure' of feminism than that. The 1970s slogan 'Women who want equality with men lack ambition' seemed to imply that male dominance should be replaced by female dominance, which understandably made men defensive. Many older men remain defensive to this day – some of them even say they have 'quite enjoyed' their wife going to work because it made the wife 'a more interesting person to live with'. (Seriously.)

As part of her 2016 'radical rethink', Cox urged dropping the term 'women's issues' on the sensible grounds that all issues previously identified in that way are actually broad social issues that affect all of us. And that, surely, is the beginning of wisdom about true gender equality – a way of thinking about the social order that would engage all of us in a more cooperative and less competitive approach. One classic example of putting that principle into practice would be in the case of child care: seeing accessibility to affordable child care as a 'women's issue' has held us back from a serious acknowledgement of the fact that many parents – *parents*, not just *mothers* – need to combine paid work with parenting and require child-care support to make this possible.

Cox also noted the absurdity of the proposition that 'women can't have it all', simply because no one – male or female – can have it all. She points out that men need to be liberated from the straitjacket of gender stereotypes just as women do.

There is plenty of evidence to support the assertion that men have been trapped by gender stereotypes, especially when it comes to mental health. Australian psychologist Steve Biddulph believes that men experience a distinctly male form of shame arising from their inability to deal with humiliation or perceived failure, sometimes resorting to violence as a way of compensating for it. Noting that men have always far outnumbered women in the prison system, Biddulph remarks that 'many men of low status, exacerbated by early life experiences of rejection or exclusion, would subscribe to "death before dishonour"' – a slogan he describes as a pillar of traditional masculinity.

British psychologist Chris Athanasiadis has found that depression in men often goes unnoticed, unadmitted and therefore untreated because the stereotypically stoical attitudes of so many men inhibit them from admitting to symptoms that may cause them to be perceived as 'weak' – even by themselves. Writing in *The Psychologist*, Athanasiadis says that, given this cultural context, men are better able to confront their depression when they are assured that the condition is neither uncommon nor permanent. He finds that whereas women are expected to externalise their symptoms – perhaps by crying or by talking openly about them – even in the 21st century, men, being 'the stronger sex', are still expected to 'stick it out', 'pull up their socks' and 'get on with it' in a way women are not. Such stereotypes are damaging for men, but they are equally damaging for women since they tend to reinforce the notion of male supremacy as the norm.

If it was wrong that the culture ever granted automatic supremacy to men – and it was both wrong and crazy – then if we are serious about creating a new order, we need to shift our focus away from the idea that women can do the stuff men used to do. Of course they can: that's not the issue. When we tell girls that 'girls can do anything!' we are engaging with and perpetuating the old order, because we're making it sound as if girls can do anything *because they're girls* whereas in fact girls and boys can do anything they're capable of doing, *because they're human beings in their own right*.

The issue is this: how can we convert the faltering and increasingly dour struggle for gender equality into something more positive and productive?

What might a more 'joyous' struggle look like?

For a start, let's redefine women and men as partners, not competitors, in the noble project of building a more harmonious and humane society. Here are five possible strategies:

First, *throw off the shackles of 'feminism' and drop the slogans of the gender war*. The new struggle is towards acknowledging and encouraging the contribution to our society that can be made by all individuals considered as *persons*, not as women or men. Paradoxically, the continuing focus on gender is holding up our progress towards equality by perpetuating the idea that there is an inevitable contest between men and women.

> My mother was a feminist and she made her life a misery by trying not just to 'have it all' but to have it all at once. It didn't look to me as if she was liberated. I want to be truly liberated, and that means having the freedom to choose what kind of person I want to be, and to change that whenever I like.

Second, *abandon all talk of 'empowerment'*. The conventional (and absurd) masculine concept of power as a form of control has always lain at the heart of gender inequality, and will remain stubbornly at the heart of any misguided struggle based on the 'sharing' of traditional male power. If the new struggle is to be successful in breaking free of those old connotations of power, it will focus on ways to identify and nurture people's capacity for discharging particular roles and responsibilities, not exercising 'power' by one person imposing their will on others. In the social order we may now wish to aspire to, 'power' itself can be reconceptualised as a *creative* force, not a *controlling* force: the power of love, for example, or compassion, kindness, forgiveness and, in relation to gender equality, the power of cooperation.

Third, *do not tolerate any vestiges of the male-supremacist culture*. This is a message as much for young men as for young women: if you ever encounter surviving pockets of that culture – in a political party, in a church, in a college of medical specialists, in a legal or accounting practice, or in any workplace – call it out. Loudly and persistently. Complain! Produce the proof of unfairness based on inequity. Talk to your boss, your colleagues, your local MP, the media, your trade union, or to anyone who will listen. By going along with it, you legitimise and prolong it. To be compliant is to be complicit. The new struggle should propel us towards the creation of a radically new culture, not some grudging revamp of the old one based on that appallingly cynical male-supremacist slogan: 'Add women and stir.'

Fourth, *do not strive to replace male supremacism with female supremacism*. Everything that has been wrong with cultural domination by males would be equally wrong with cultural domination by females. When women are in a position to influence the selection of employees, for example, this new struggle demands a commitment to equity, not revenge; the outcome we want is a meritocracy, not a feminocracy. While it's understandable that some women might feel like seizing the chance to over-represent women as a way of compensating them for thousands of years of cultural inequality, that would be a travesty of the whole notion of equality – as unjust, inequitable and unfair as the sorry history of males favouring males. A growing number of young women have grasped what the *real* struggle is about:

> I don't want to call myself a feminist, because feminists seem to want to replace a male-dominated culture with a female-dominated one, whereas what I want is true equality. That means cooperation, not competition.

Fifth, *focus only on personal qualities, not on gender*. If we are serious about creating a new social order based on gender equality, then we must insist that, in every setting where gender is *not* an issue – commerce, industry, politics, the professions, the public service – we focus exclusively on the attributes we want in a leader, a teacher, a company director, a professional partner, a manager, an employee, a minister of religion, a parliamentarian. Would even one of those attributes – even one of those qualities – *ever* relate to gender? I doubt it.

The time is ripe for gender convergence

History is on our side. This is the right time to be moving away from a step-by-step approach to righting the wrongs of gender inequality in the workplace and elsewhere, and to accept that a blurring of traditional gender differences is part of a broader cultural movement that has powerful momentum.

The rise of the LGBTIQ movement (lesbian, gay, bisexual, transgender, intersex, queer) is a symptom, not a cause, of our growing awareness of the futility of rigid gender stereotyping and of a return to a very old idea: that we are all located on a gender continuum and, even in purely cultural terms, the most 'masculine' of us also contain 'feminine' characteristics, and vice versa, or we wouldn't be fully human.

In the arts, there's a current fashion for gender-swapping to make precisely that point. In 2017, Bell Shakespeare staged a production of *Richard III* with Kate Mulvany in the title role. Her performance was universally hailed as brilliant, though she was undeniably and inescapably a woman acting as a man and the audience (at least in the performance I saw) couldn't restrain a titter at those moments when the king made some reference to his masculinity. But it was a graphic way of reminding us that we are too easily trapped in gender stereotypes; we too easily forget that treachery, disloyalty, promiscuity and aggression are not the exclusive province of males – as Australian psychologist Cordelia Fine has shown in her book *Testosterone Rex*.

There's been a long history of gender swapping on the stage – the traditional pantomime always had a male 'dame' and a female 'principal boy' – and Shakespeare was very fond of confusing everyone by disguising his characters' gender identity. There's likely to be more of that kind of thing in future, simply to remind us that gender is not as clear-cut a concept as we might imagine it to be.

It's not just a matter of hormones and genitalia, though many people are born with a genetic make-up that contradicts simple notions of sex and gender. The real issue is the interaction of biology and culture; as Simone de Beauvoir said in *The Second Sex*: 'One is not born, but rather becomes, a woman,' and precisely the same is true of becoming a man. After endless debates about whether gender roles are genetically or culturally determined, we are – surely – close to the end of that road. Most of it is cultural, but biological (especially hormonal) influences still play a huge role – especially when it comes to romance and reproduction.

Yet even the question of sexual attraction forms part of today's more fluid attitudes to sex and gender. A friend who'd had a series of heterosexual relationships through her twenties surprised herself by falling madly in love with a woman. She describes it as having fallen in love with a *person* who happened to be a woman. She feels confident that this will be a lifelong commitment for them both but says that, if it were to end, she supposes she would be as open to another relationship with a man as with a woman – it would all depend on the person, she now realises.

The old 'nature versus nurture' debate always ends up at the same point, whatever the context: we are born with certain genetic dispositions and our cultural conditioning shapes those dispositions in different ways. Sometimes, cultural influences overwhelm what we fondly imagine to be our biological destiny; sometimes genetic predispositions overwhelm other people's attempts to culturally condition us. A girl might be raised to fit the very feminine mould of her mother, turns into a tomboy, refuses to wear a dress, make-up or stockings, is only happy when she can appear indistinguishable from a man, and gravitates towards the girls – and the boys – who love her just like that. Or a little boy is given nothing but toy trucks and trains to play with, demands a doll of his own and wants to dress up in his mother's clothes, especially her silk underwear, and finally emerges as a determinedly heterosexual teenager with a keen interest in what his girlfriends are wearing, especially their silk underwear. Others, both male and female, might simply realise that they yearn to be the opposite of what they appear to be. Indeed, for many LGBTIQs, it goes beyond yearning to a certainty that nature has made a mistake in assigning them a gender that simply doesn't feel right to them.

In other words, we're all over the shop when it comes to questions of 'sex' and 'gender' – even the attempts to distinguish between those terms by saying one is about your genital organs and the other is about your own private sense of your own unique point on the gender continuum often collapse in confusion. Not everyone's genitals are unambiguous, yet some people have trouble even imagining how the concept of gender identity could be uncoupled from a sexual identity determined by genitalia. Others are so strongly compelled to adopt a homosexual identity, they can't grasp why other people can't see them the way they see themselves.

As in so many other areas of life, compassion changes everything. To our improved understanding of the fluidity and complexity of gender, we need only add the discipline of compassion to become the kind of society where we would no longer raise an eyebrow at anyone who happened to find themselves at a different point on the gender spectrum from our own.

Marriage equality

As recently as 2004, the then prime minister, John Howard, persuaded his parliamentary colleagues to amend the Marriage Act to include a definition of marriage as being exclusively between a man and a woman, and to explicitly prevent Australia from recognising same-sex marriages from other countries. Howard was clearly anticipating the time when there would be a serious push for marriage equality in Australia, and was doing his best to make it as difficult as possible for that to occur.

When the push finally came, in 2017, after the Abbott and Turnbull governments' refusal to settle the matter by a vote in federal parliament, the resulting public campaign for 'yes' and 'no' votes in the non-compulsory, non-binding postal survey showed just how far some of us still have to go in the journey towards true gender equality, in the broadest sense of 'gender'. All kind of red herrings were introduced into the debate, including the strangest of all – that marriage equality would somehow restrict freedom of religion. No one ever managed to show how this might happen and, in any case, since fewer than 30 percent of Australian marriages are conducted in churches, the majority of heterosexual couples have definitely declared that marriage, for them, has nothing to do with religion.

Another strange argument put forward in opposition to same-sex marriage was that marriage *exists* for procreation and the care of children. While marriage has, historically, indeed been about the protection of children, our current low birthrate means that many couples who have no intention of becoming parents are still keen to marry and, given the high rate of divorce and remarriage among older people, many couples are marrying when the woman is well and truly post-menopausal and nothing could be further from the couple's mind than procreation.

Although the postal survey's 62 percent majority in favour of marriage equality represented a clear victory for fairness and equality, the whole process highlighted the radical changes now taking place in attitudes to marriage. The LGBTIQ community has been keen to embrace marriage as an institution at a time when heterosexual couples have increasingly been either giving it a wide berth or trying and then rejecting it.

With somewhere between 35 and 40 percent of contemporary marriages predicted to end in divorce, it is hardly surprising that a large number of cohabiting couples have become wary of formal marriage. But that level of predicted divorce also tells us something about changing perceptions of marriage in our society: increasingly, it is being thought of more as 'legalising a relationship' rather than, as previous generations might have thought of it, entering into the institution of marriage.

Institutions are inherently conservative: they are about stability, continuity and preservation. The increasing emphasis on marriage-as-relationship rather than marriage-as-institution has meant that cohabiting couples are no longer under cultural pressure to marry, even when children are involved, and, if they do marry, are more relaxed about the idea of divorce than their grandparents might have been. 'If the relationship isn't working, why hang around?' is an increasingly typical statement of a young person, married or unmarried; to which their grandparents might once have responded: 'What's all this talk about a *relationship*? You're married, aren't you? Just get on with it.'

And same-sex marriage? At a time when fewer heterosexual couples are choosing marriage, and existing marriages are less stable than ever, it would have seemed particularly churlish to deny access to the legal status of marriage to any adults – anywhere on the gender spectrum – who wished to have their relationship formalised in that way.

A new world is coming, where the heat will go out of the battle of the sexes because in every situation where gender is irrelevant – especially the workplace – we will have learnt to focus exclusively on the person, not their gender. True workplace equality, like true marriage equality, demands that we become gender blind.

We still have a long way to go

Even in 2018, we're far from being gender blind when it comes to the workplace in particular. It's still too easy, too tempting, for people to slip into the comfortable prejudices they grew up with, and to fall short of the point already achieved by thought-leaders in this area, where the differences between *people* are all that counts.

So we continue to grind out the stereotypes. Here is an only slightly exaggerated selection of the stock-standard ways of distinguishing between men and women that still linger in the minds of many people:

- *Women and men are so obviously different, in so many ways, it's no wonder they see the world in such different terms, and have so much trouble getting along with each other. In fact, it's a miracle they manage to cooperate as well as they do. That book* Men are from Mars, Women are from Venus *was spot on.*

- *It's all down to their hormones: women have a menstrual cycle and men don't. I know some women think PMT is a myth, but I've seen it up close, at home and at work, and it's not pretty.*

- *Women are made to carry children and breastfeed, and men aren't — there's the basic reason for the difference.*

- *Menopause can be a problem — not just for the women going through it, but for the men who have to live or work with them. There's no point pretending it isn't a real point of difference between the sexes.*

- *Testosterone is the villain of the piece. Men are so driven by their sexual urges, they often act as if they can't help it.* (On this point, the evidence favours the conclusion that, at certain stages of the lifecycle and in certain situations, *people* are so driven by their sexual urges, they often act as if they can't help it.)

When confronted by the argument that most of the gender differences we talk about may be culturally rather than biologically determined, those who cling to gender stereotypes will say: 'So what? What difference does it make where they came from? That doesn't make them any less real.'

All this is typically couched in the terms of sweet reasonableness: 'Men and women are simply good at different things — they can be as equal as you like, but they can't be the same.' When asked to give some examples of the 'different things', men will often describe women as 'more emotional and less rational than men' and may cite driving a car (especially reverse parking) or reading a map as evidence of this. (There's just a smidgeon of evidence supporting the idea that men are better at judging distances than women are — and there's no mystery about why that should be so, in evolutionary terms.)

By contrast, the examples women give are more likely to involve how hopeless men are at asking for help when they need it, at discussing their emotional state, at listening attentively, or at spontaneously noticing that some domestic task needs to be done and doing it without expecting lavish praise.

From a medical point of view, of course, there are good grounds for treating men and women differently. There's also growing acknowledgement that most medical research has been carried out on men, and many doctors have traditionally regarded women as simply being a smaller version of men. As Deb Colville of Monash University wrote in *The Conversation*: 'Until the turn of this century, there was little sense in Western medicine that gender mattered. Outside the niche of female reproductive medicine, the male body was the universal model for anatomy studies ... Clinical trials mainly involved males.' In fact, there are significant gender differences in the nature and treatment of cardiovascular disease, for example, where men typically suffer the classic 'heart attack' and women are more likely to experience the less dramatic but, in the end, equally lethal 'heart failure'. As one doctor put it to me: 'Women don't really live longer than men; they just take longer to die.' The fact that blindness and dementia are both more common in women than men also suggests some as-yet-unexplained sex differences.

Biomedical questions aside, many people still insist on drawing sharp gender distinctions based on cultural assumptions. Ultraconservative Christians, for example, clinging to tradition and ignoring cultural evolution, will assert that men are the 'natural heads' of families and of churches, that wives should obey their husbands, and that only men can be ordained as priests. Indeed, conservative Christianity has a lot to answer for when it comes to perpetuating the culture of male supremacism.

The proposition from some men that 'I've got nothing at all against women – in fact I love women – it's just that . . .' is matched by the proposition from some women that 'the world would be a better place in every way if women were in charge'.

Well, *would* it be a better place?

Naturally, there's zero evidence either way. There was a time when, if you lived in Sydney, you had a female lord mayor, a female premier, a female governor, a female prime minister and a female governor-general. Was life noticeably better, or worse, for all concerned? Was life noticeably *different*, in or out of the corridors of power? And if so, was that about gender, or competence, or personality or . . .?

Was Margaret Thatcher or Theresa May a *different kind* of UK prime minister from John Major or David Cameron? Was Angela Merkel a *different kind* of German chancellor from Helmut Kohl? Was Quentin Bryce a *different kind* of Australian governor-general from William Deane? Was Gail Kelly a *different kind of* Westpac CEO from David Morgan? If, in any of those cases, a woman *was* judged to be a different kind of leader from her predecessors or successors, would anyone – especially the woman concerned – claim gender was the crucial determining factor? What about upbringing, temperament, intelligence, personal values, attitudes, prejudices, ambition or political convictions?

In mid 2017, an unseemly spat was reported between the lord mayor of Sydney, Clover Moore, and her deputy, Kerryn Phelps, over an alleged misunderstanding about the future role of the deputy, and whether or not an undertaking had been given that Phelps's position as deputy was assured. From media accounts of the conflict, it didn't seem different, in any way, from similar struggles between male politicians at all levels of government and throughout history. No worse. No better. Just very human.

When I give a lecture to a mixed audience and call for questions, the first few questions are almost always asked by men. Still. A mother recently complained to me that a new teacher at her daughter's primary school was paying more attention to the boys than the girls, tending to ignore the girls' questions while responding to the boys'. It was so overt, and so contrary to the ethos of the school, the kids themselves had noticed it. Another woman has told me that at meetings of the executive committee of her apartment-block owners' corporation, the female members of the committee sometimes bring their male partners; the other men on the committee then tend to discuss the agenda with those non-member male partners, ignoring the women who are actually members of the committee. And many women still habitually report that in meetings at work, or on committees of organisations, the men's voices tend to dominate, the women's views tend to be brushed aside and – most egregious of all – a man who repeats something previously said by a woman is more likely to be taken seriously than she was.

Conditioning is powerful, and the best-intentioned women and men are sometimes unable to shed the influence of all those years of watching how males and females interact – at home, at school, at work and socially. But there's a very ugly word that describes all this stuff: *sexism*.

'I sat next to a particularly pompous middle-aged man at dinner the other night,' a woman told me recently, 'and he spoke nonstop for almost half an hour, entirely about himself and what he had done and what he was going to do.' When he finally paused for breath, the woman said to him: 'That's interesting. Now, would you like to know anything about me?' He showed no inclination to pursue the conversation.

One of the ugliest manifestations of sexism has been the longstanding assumption that men in positions of power and influence are entitled to sexually exploit, abuse or assault women who come within their orbit. As we move towards genuine gender equality, especially in the workplace, such exploitation is coming to be seen for what it is: not only an abuse of power, but a perpetuation of gender stereotypes that are seriously outmoded and utterly unacceptable. The 2017 accusations against Hollywood producer Harvey Weinstein emboldened many women around the world – including in Australia – to speak out against such gender-based exploitation. Indeed, the growing willingness of women to 'name and shame' the men who have offended or assaulted them is yet another clear sign that the move towards true gender equality is gathering an unstoppable momentum.

Some women wanting to assert their independence and equality have preferred to retreat from the gender fray and take refuge in single-sex enclaves. Women & Leadership, Women in Theatre and Screen, the Women's Electoral Lobby, the Australian Women Against Violence Alliance . . . these are places where women can gather together to show the kind of respect towards each other that they have found wanting in a mixed-gender setting. There's an Australian Federation of Medical Women, too, with international affiliations, established not only so women can encourage and support each other in a traditionally male-dominated profession (though that is swiftly changing), but also to mentor young female doctors who, even in the 21st century, are likely to be bullied and harassed by senior male members of the profession. Resisting the trend towards equality, some of the specialist medical colleges are still accused of being run not only like a 'closed shop' but also like an 'old boys' club', with young females finding it just as hard to break down the doors as previous generations of women have done.

Socially, most women will sometimes want to spend time with other women, and most men will sometimes want to spend time with other men. 'Best friends' are usually, but not always, of the same gender. Some women and some men will always feel more comfortable in a single-gender association, society, club or activity. But the emergence of so many women-only organisations – and the persistence of men-only organisations – is testimony to the fact that we have not yet reached the stage of seeing men and women as equal partners in addressing society's ills, or meeting society's challenges. It was perhaps inevitable that the women's liberation movement – as a *women's* movement – would not devote as much of its revolutionary energy to showing us *all* how to cooperate as it would to encouraging women to go it alone.

That movement faced a huge task in getting gender onto society's agenda, and it has certainly succeeded in that – though, as part of that process, it had to create some excruciating distortions of language to force men to think differently. ('Chairperson' is finally, mercifully, giving way to 'chair' or 'president'; 'waitperson' seems unnecessarily cumbersome when 'waiter' will do perfectly well for males and females, just like 'writer'; 'foreperson' was apparently conceived in ignorance of the fact that the 'man' in 'foreman' derived from the Latin *manu*, referring to the hand, not the male gender, and has the same meaning as 'leading hand'. Similarly, 'manning' the phones – or the lifeboats – has nothing to do with gender, but only with hands.)

The next task is to bring that revolution to an end with one final decisive blow – quotas – and then get gender off the agenda again. But before we come to the quota question, here's another way of thinking about gender . . .

The gender of souls

In the course of my research for this book, I came across a paper called 'Advancing toward the equality of women and men', published by the Institute for Studies in Global Prosperity – a non-profit organisation founded in 1999, in association with the Baha'i International Community. Here's an extract:

> When viewed in its broader context, the discrimination against women in present day society is one of many symptoms of an ailing social order. We live in a world with rampant conflict and injustice. Individuals and groups compete with one another in pursuit of narrow self-interests. Insecurity and violence are commonplace . . . Our aim cannot be only to open room for women to participate in the affairs of society within the present social order. Rather, women and men must work shoulder to shoulder as they apply spiritual principles to the construction of a new social order characterised by justice, peace and collective prosperity.

And what might those 'spiritual principles' be? This institute – like the Baha'i movement itself – has no interest in trying to impose any particular religious doctrines or beliefs on anyone. They are using the term 'spiritual principles' to refer to the ideals, the virtues and the values we all aspire to when we are at our noblest: justice, fairness, equality, peace and harmony. From the Baha'i perspective, these are all 'spiritual' concepts, because they relate to the essence of human goodness and the spirit of goodness permeating a civil society.

The paper also urged us, in the spirit of justice, to move beyond cultural relativism in the treatment of women and girls: 'There are certain cultural beliefs or practices in every culture that are prejudicial towards, or are in some way harmful to, particular groups, especially women and girls who often occupy the most vulnerable positions in society.'

Because Baha'is are not embarrassed to talk about 'spirituality' in the context of gender issues, they are equally comfortable talking about 'souls'. Whether you share their level of comfort or not, most of us use the word 'soul' or 'spirit' in an entirely non-religious way to convey the idea of the essence of a person. And who would ever try to defend the proposition that, in their essence, women and men are different?

To quote the institute's paper: 'The reality of the human being is his or her soul and the soul, we firmly believe, has no gender.' That's another way of saying that, deep down, we are all *human*, before we are women or men. The recognition of that essential humanity we all share is, surely, the starting point for the remaining struggle towards true equality. That struggle will be 'joyous' because it is not based on acrimony, revenge or a desire to compete, divide, conquer or win, but only to cooperate in the process of bringing out the best in everyone, encouraging everyone to contribute what they can, and refusing to concede that gender has anything to do with that process.

The last frontier: quotas

It may sound like a contradiction of much that has gone before, but there is no point in kidding ourselves: we need to take one final big step before the work of the gender revolution can come fully to fruition and we can get on with the job of establishing the new social order where gender equality is simply taken for granted.

There would not be a man – or a woman – in Australia today who does not understand the concept of gender equality and is not aware of the issues involved. So why has our progress towards equality stalled? Why have key indicators like corporate boards and parliamentary frontbenches gone backwards? Why are there only nine female CEOs among Australia's top 200 publicly listed companies?

The answer to those questions lies in the relationship between attitudes and behaviour. The popular view is that, in order to change behaviour, we must first change attitudes. Well, that job appears to have been done: what man in a position of power and influence would not *say* he gets it? What captain of industry, boardroom powerbroker, senior public servant, partner in a major law or accounting firm, or political operator would not declare strong support for the idea of gender equality at every level of society?

So why hasn't it happened, 50 years after the subject came up?

It's because the popular attitude/behaviour model is wrong. Attitudes rarely lead to behaviour; it's the environment we live in that influences our behaviour, and those patterns of behaviour, in turn, shape our attitudes. The attitude change that really counts, therefore, is the one that comes *after* a behaviour change. And when you have a target audience – in this case, men at the top – addicted to their positions of supremacy, no amount of gentle persuasion is going to budge them.

Think about some other target audiences whose behaviour society has felt it appropriate to change. We were never able to persuade people who are addicted to fast driving to slow down until we began installing speed cameras and other measures like speed humps and cruise control that modified the driving environment and thereby exerted direct pressure on drivers' behaviour. Anti-drink-driving propaganda never had much impact until we modified the driving environment by introducing random breath testing. We were never successful in persuading people addicted to nicotine to give up smoking simply by nagging them. No matter how carefully we explained the health hazards of smoking, they didn't give it up in significant numbers until we changed the world they live in by increasing the price of cigarettes and imposing bans on smoking in all the places where they'd like to smoke. When we did all that – when we modified the unacceptable behaviour by modifying the environment in which it occurs – then we saw the attitudes of drivers and smokers change. (After their behaviour changed, they became far more attentive to the messages that reinforced their new behaviour.) Bribery works, too. So does torture. Those are appalling examples of the principle, but the principle still holds.

If we are ever going to see the radical behaviour change that is the necessary precursor to true cultural change, we have to change the environment, starting at the top, where decisions that affect gender equality are made and where it's possible to enact legislation to force the change: the boards of public companies, the boards of government agencies and instrumentalities like the Reserve Bank and the ABC, the upper echelons of the public service, the governing bodies of universities, the frontbenches of governments and oppositions (requiring, in the short term, a gender quota-based system of political parties' pre-selection of their parliamentary candidates, as well).

Interference? You bet. The heavy hand of regulation in areas where people feel they should be free to make their own decisions? Yep. Not 50–50, though: that would be too rigid. Perhaps a minimum of 40 percent women, a minimum of 40 percent men, and 20 percent 'floating'. And not forever, either. Ten years is all it would take to alter the cultural landscape so radically that gender equality at the top would look and feel normal, and we'd all have had time to get used to it. All of us – men *and* women – need to become so accustomed to seeing women functioning in senior positions that we no longer regard it as exceptional.

In areas where it would be more difficult to legislate – the boards of unlisted companies, the equity partners in legal and accounting firms, the medical specialists' colleges – we would merely have to hope that the radical changes going on elsewhere would exert enough social pressure to shame them into following suit.

Would this mean that some women would be stigmatised, seen as tokenistic 'quota women'? Inevitably. But that would be no worse for them than the stigma now attaching to the males who keep surrounding themselves with other males, as if they're too frightened to push the gender boat out. And does anyone believe that, in 2018, there are insufficient well-qualified and experienced women to fill at least 40 percent of the top jobs?

Given the maturity of this debate and the gross failure of the men in charge to do anything about it, the time has come for the community to insist on change, and for governments to respond. We've run out of time for this to be voluntary. Equality can't wait any longer. Targets are a feeble joke that men can laugh at behind closed doors. Quotas are essential.

The only people who will squeal about this will be men – especially men in the private sector who have made a career out of sitting on boards, and male career politicians who have come to believe that a frontbench position is their birthright. In an opinion piece for the *Sydney Morning Herald*, Jessica Irvine quoted prominent businessman and chair of the ANZ bank board David Gonski, speaking on *The Policy Shop* podcast in 2017: 'I have a very strong view that I don't believe that legislation should be telling private companies who to put on their boards, nor indeed how many of a particular type of person, or indeed what gender, geography or indeed persuasion that person should be.' Well, it's public rather than private companies that are under scrutiny here, and neither geography nor 'persuasion' are the issue: gender is the sole issue.

As Irvine commented, 'change hurts', and Gonski confirmed it: 'I do know that a lot of my colleagues have complained that there is actually an active bias at the moment towards women. It is hurting them.'

Apparently the bias hasn't been active enough, given the glacial rate of progress. A short sharp shock is clearly needed.

The growing chorus of women and men in support of quotas will not be silenced, nor should it be. Once the change has been made in those three key areas – boardrooms, senior public service, parliament – we will see the influence of that example spread more widely. Only then will we be able to hear the new harmonies of a society that has embraced the idea that men and women are partners in the same project, not combatants in a war.

Quotas are not magic wands. They will accelerate the present culture shift and generate a more dynamic, more urgent approach to gender equality, but even that will not be enough. The real task of ensuring gender equality begins in the home and in the classroom, and we must redouble our efforts to encourage parents and teachers to be more alert to the impressions they create and the inherited biases they might be unconsciously transmitting.

No one wants to see girls and boys – women and men – treated as if they are identical in all aspects of their lives. No one in their right mind would want to discourage little girls from wearing pink if they happen to love pink – nor boys, for that matter. No one could seriously suggest that sex differences across the whole gender spectrum are anything but a source of interest and wonderment as we grow through adolescence and into adulthood. *Vive la différence!*

But in the classroom, in the workplace, in politics, in management and leadership, the time has come to don the gender blindfold.

7

Religion's noblest role: Promoting compassion

Let love be genuine; hate what is evil; hold fast to what is good . . . If your enemies are hungry, feed them; if they are thirsty, give them something to drink.

Letter of Paul to the Romans, 12:9–20

A convergence no less spectacular than the gender revolution is occurring on the subject of God. In fact, as we move through these next decades of the 21st century, I imagine it will become increasingly difficult to spot the difference between atheists and theists. It will also become increasingly difficult to write religion out of the script.

The biggest upheaval in our conception of God in the modern era began with Friedrich Nietzsche's claim in 1882 that 'God is dead' – a declaration that has reverberated, and been widely misinterpreted, around the Western world. Much of what the rather incoherent Nietzsche wrote was in the form of cryptic notes published after his death, and philosophers have always struggled to make sense of his thinking. So what might he have meant by his most famous statement?

It's clear he did not mean that there was once an external, supreme being called 'God' – creator of the universe and ruler of the world – who was now dead. All he seemed to be saying was that that idea of a supranatural God, 'out there' somewhere, had lost its hold on the imagination of post-Enlightenment Europe. Which was true. More specifically, he was saying that the traditional idea of God as the author of human morality, via absolute imperatives, was dead. That was true, too, and has become even more true as we have come to realise that morality is a social construct, arising from our ever-evolving struggle to work out how best to live together in peaceful, harmonious communities.

In the wake of the Enlightenment, the idea of God in Western thought has undergone radical changes. There are still many people who fervently believe in an 'out there', all-knowing, all-powerful, supranatural entity or agency of some kind – judgemental, inconceivably mysterious, yet prepared to take an interest in the lives of individual human beings. But the big movement, like a silent tide, has been away from an 'out there' interpretation of God to an 'in here' view of God as a loving spirit that is within us and among us.

While theological debates rage about all this, the gradual move towards a more personal, interior view of God has had a curious effect: it has made it harder for atheists to declare that they don't believe in God if it's *that* kind of God people are talking about. The only remaining basis for argument is whether the spirit of love should be called 'God' at all, or simply 'the spirit of love'.

Let's put those arguments into perspective. What person of goodwill is *not* in favour of the idea that love – compassion, kindness, charity – is the most powerful force in the world? Who does *not* agree that the world would be a better place if we surrendered at least some of our petty vanities in favour of the common good? Who does *not* acknowledge that forgiveness ennobles both the forgiver and the forgiven? Who does *not* believe that a life of service to others is the most deeply satisfying kind of life, or that in any civil society we must respond to the needs of the poor, the marginalised, the disadvantaged?

The people who do believe those things are the source of a deep well of goodness in our society. What else they might happen to believe – about the nature of God, or the value of religion, or the nuances of difference between various religious doctrines, or the existence or non-existence of an afterlife – is of great private, personal significance for the individual, but is of no concern to the wider society and should not detract in any way from the vastness of our common ground on the subject of love.

The US psychologist Abraham Maslow (famous for his theory of a hierarchy of human needs) once asked: 'If God gets to be redefined as "Being itself" . . . or in some other non-personal way, what will atheists be fighting against?' It's a good question, especially if God is to be defined not as the author of some grand unifying principle or 'the mind of the cosmos', but as a loving spirit. Of course, atheists and theists will continue to disagree about whether there's any place for the idea that God *is* that spirit, and they may be in passionate dispute about the value of religion in fostering the spirit of loving-kindness in our society, but when it comes to the question of whether that spirit itself can be a powerful force in human affairs, there is very little left to argue about.

Religion's bad rap

Although 68 percent of Australians claim belief in God and more than 60 percent still choose to identify with some form of religion (including 52 percent who identify with Christianity), institutional religion has probably never been held in lower esteem in Australia than it is now.

That's hardly surprising, given the 2017 findings of Australia's Royal Commission into Institutional Responses to Child Sexual

Abuse, and given many people's negative experiences of the institutional church – though those experiences are more likely to revolve around boredom and irrelevance than abuse. For whatever reason, people now feel freer than ever to criticise religion.

A friend recently wrote to me, conceding a point I had made about the difference between institutional religion and the personal faith of an individual, but insisting that the net effect of any form of religion is negative: 'I will never agree religions do not do harm. They obstruct, lie for their own purposes and keep millions uneducated, uninformed and unenlightened. I prefer to believe in one another and in making a better world (though that's a challenge), not in made-up deities.'

Another has spoken of the intensely judgemental attitude of the minister at a church he was attending: 'There was no sign of compassion. He had this superior view that he had all the answers and if you didn't believe what he believed, then you were destined for the flames of hell. The amazing thing was that people seemed to go along with it. He had quite a big congregation. And although he was a raging male chauvinist, the majority of them were women.'

Although such remarks emphasise how religion continues to be a fault line – and sometimes an unbridgeable chasm – between believers and non-believers or ex-believers, there are signs that the rise of the 'spirituality' movement (often loosely associated with Eastern mysticism) might be rehabilitating the idea of faith. The growing number of people who use yoga, meditation or mindfulness training as a form of spiritual exercise may describe themselves as 'spiritual but not religious' (SBNR), even though both those practices are, in fact, religious exercises in the Hindu and Buddhist traditions. What SBNRs mean to convey is that their lack of interest in religion, or perhaps even their explicit rejection of institutional religion, should not be interpreted as a lack of interest in the mysteries of existence, nor as an embrace of atheism.

It has become fashionable to talk about Australia as a nation that has turned its back on religion – or, at least, on Christianity. The emergence of the so-called New Atheists, encouraged by the writings of Richard Dawkins in particular, has created the impression that atheism is on the march and religion is in retreat, but the truth is more complicated than that.

It's certainly the case that Christians are not attending traditional churches in the numbers they used to, though an unknown but apparently growing number now attend informal 'house churches' in private homes. The number of people who go to a conventional church monthly or more often is down to about 15 percent of the population, though the figure rises above 25 percent at Christmas or Easter. Against the trend, there are pockets of strong growth in Pentecostalist churches like Hillsong, and in some Anglican and Roman Catholic cathedrals.

The Australian religious landscape has become more diverse, as an inevitable consequence of Australia's culture having itself become more diverse. As support for Christianity wanes, support for other religions gradually increases, so the evidence suggests Australia is far from being finished with religion. The question is whether Australia is ready for a new approach to religion – and a new level of tolerance of religious difference – that reflects this changing landscape.

What the 2016 census said about religion

When the 2016 census results were released, anti-religionists worked themselves into a lather of excitement about the apparent increase in the number of Australians ticking the 'No religion' box. In the five years since 2011, that figure rose from 21.8 to 29.6 percent.

Or did it?

After a great deal of lobbying from interested parties, the Australian Bureau of Statistics moved 'No religion' from the bottom of the list of religions, where it had previously been located, to the top of the list for the 2016 census. This was done, it was said, to correct the bias associated with 'No religion' being last on the list. (Incidentally, about 10 percent of the population chose not to answer this question at all.)

As of now, therefore, we simply don't know the true figure. Did it increase because the number of people not wishing to identify with a religion had actually increased, or did it increase because, as predicted, items at the top of the list attract more support than those at the bottom? If the number of people choosing 'No religion' had been artificially deflated by being last on the list, then, logically, it might equally have been artificially inflated by being placed first. Given recent trends here and elsewhere, the strongest probability is that there was an actual increase, but perhaps not as great as the 7.8 percent reported. To establish the true figure, we would need to experiment further with the positioning of 'No religion' on the list, to see if the increase holds. (If there was some artificiality built into the 2016 figure, it would have been boosted to an unknown extent by the pre-census propaganda urging people to tick 'No religion' unless they were active, practising members of a faith community. This must have been the first occasion in the history of the census when such overt persuasion was focused on trying to influence people's behaviour on census night.)

Whatever the true figure, the increase in 'No religion' was consistent with a long-term trend in that direction, and it emboldened some anti-religionists to call for greater secularisation of Australia, perhaps confusing Australia's commitment to freedom *of* religion with the anti-religionists' goal of freedom *from* religion.

In the weeks following the release of the census data, the claim was made that 'No religion' is now the biggest single category of religious identification. In fact, the 60 percent (rising to 66 percent in New South Wales) who identify with one of the religions being practised in Australia – Christianity, Islam, Buddhism, Hinduism,

Judaism etc. – is exactly double the number who claim no religion. While it's true that more people ticked 'No religion' than any one of the individual Christian denominations, the cumulative 'Christian' figure was 52 percent, representing over 12 million Australians. That figure represents a sharp drop from the 62 percent in the previous census, but shows a majority of Australians still choosing to identify as Christian – even if only with Christian values rather than Christian beliefs.

The claim that 'No religion' is now the biggest single item on the list of religions masks the fact that 'No religion' is itself a complex category, in the same way as 'Christian' or 'Muslim' or 'Buddhist' are complex categories. Just as 'Christian' embraces many denominations – Catholic, Anglican, Uniting, Baptist, Pentecostalist etc. – and Islam, Buddhism, Hinduism and Judaism all consist of several (sometimes warring) factions, so, if you were to break 'No religion' down, you would find a similarly diverse range of subcategories.

That range would include the large and growing band of people, especially young people, who identify as SBNR; the militant anti-religionists who would like to adopt *'No religion!'* as a slogan; the roughly 8 percent of Australians who do not identify with any religion but still claim to believe in God 'or some higher power'; those who are completely uninterested in the topic; the agnostics who are not prepared to commit themselves to either theism or atheism, but who would not rule out some form of religious faith or practice in their future, even if it has no role in their present life. And, if the pre-census propaganda bore any fruit, the 'No religion' figure would also presumably include people who still think of themselves as basically Christian in their values and orientation, while not wishing to be associated with any religious institution.

So it would be wrong to equate 'no religion' with 'anti-religion' (let alone with atheism), particularly as there's a discernible streak of faith-envy in Australia among those who once had religious faith but no longer do, or whose parents still do but they don't, or who occasionally meet someone whose religious faith seems to animate them in an attractive way.

Further decline in Christian faith and practice seems likely, but Islam is certainly not the 'threat' so often imagined; at present only 2.6 percent of the Australian population is Muslim, and our fastest-growing religion is actually Hinduism – currently around 2 percent and growing rapidly, largely in response to immigration from the Indian subcontinent. In New Zealand, Hinduism is already the second-biggest religion after Christianity, and that is likely to be replicated here.

In spite of the large number of Australians wishing to identify with Christianity, the fact is that most Australians simply never enter a church, not even for weddings: as previously mentioned in relation to marriage equality, about 70 percent of weddings are now conducted on non-church premises. Yet, when surveyed, 90 percent of *non-churchgoers* say they like having a church in their local neighbourhood, presumably because they think of churchgoers as people who are likely to be upright citizens, good neighbours, given to charitable works and committed to showing kindness to others.

And while Australians are staying away from church in droves, they are sending more and more of their children to church-run schools: about 40 percent of secondary school pupils now attend non-public schools, and the vast majority of those are faith-based. The reasons for that are complex; there is no suggestion that every parent who chooses a church school for their child is hoping the child will 'get religion'. When parents discuss this, they often refer to the values of the school, the emphasis on discipline and, in some cases, their belief that private education in Australia is generally of a better quality than public school education, regardless of any religious association.

Why religion survives

To predict the death of religion – in Australia or anywhere else – would be to miss not only the lessons of history, but also the present global situation. About three-quarters of the world's population identify with one of the four great world religions: Christianity, Islam, Hinduism and Buddhism. The respected Pew Research Center estimates that that figure will rise to 80 percent by the middle of this century, by which time Islam will have passed Christianity as the biggest of the four, there will be more churchgoers in China than in the US, and China will have become the world's biggest Christian country *and* the world's biggest Muslim country. Confirming the ineffectiveness of prohibition, religion's most dramatic growth has been in the countries where it was once banned – most notably Russia and China.

Religion survives, even in places like Scandinavia, which has the lowest rate of church attendance in the world, because of the answers to existential questions it offers the faithful; because of the inspiration and comfort people draw from its grand narratives (increasingly, in the West, such inspiration relies on the metaphorical truth *in* the stories rather than belief in the literal truth *of* the stories); and because of the powerful sense of belonging people derive from their membership of a faith community. Indeed, that sense of connection to a community of like-minded people is sometimes stronger than the commitment to the institution's formal articles of faith. It survives in places like Nigeria, which has the highest rate of church attendance in the world, because of the consolations and hope it offers to people struggling to survive in the midst of social and economic chaos.

Religion survives everywhere, in one form or another, because of the benefits – spiritual, emotional, physical – that flow from the combination of religious faith and practice. At its best, and in spite of all the horror stories of institutional corruption, faith-based violence and personal disillusionment, religion encourages people to live noble, rather than merely moral, lives. Perhaps it's no wonder that 60 percent of Australians still choose to identify with it, in one form or another.

A good question to ask is why, when the practice of Christianity is in such sharp decline, does a persistent 15 percent of the population still attend church regularly? What are they getting from it that non-churchgoers are missing out on – apart from the health benefits of religious faith and practice already mentioned in chapter 2, including lower rates of anxiety and depression and quicker bounce-back from depressive episodes?

Regular churchgoers speak of the value of a retreat from the routines and pressures of daily life; a time to contemplate the mysteries of existence; an opportunity to join in singing well-loved hymns; exposure to a spine-stiffening sermon (or 'homily') that encourages the faithful in their commitment to a life charac-terised by kindness, charity and compassion. They will also point out that there is nothing else in their life that offers this blend of contemplation, inspiration and encouragement. As one regular churchgoer told me: 'You come out feeling uplifted. And you feel more determined to lead a good life. By the time you've heard one of our minister's sermons, you could never oppose marriage equality, or support what we're doing to people in those detention centres. Christianity is all about compassion, in the end.'

If that were the universal experience of churchgoing, there would be good grounds for encouraging more of it! But it's not always like that. There are some churches (just as there are some mosques, temples and synagogues) where the emphasis is on a particular set of beliefs characterised as the One True Way. There are faith communities that believe their main role in life is to persuade others to convert to their point of view and to subscribe to their set of beliefs. There are fundamentalists in every religion who take a highly prescriptive, legalistic approach to their faith and who are keen to duel with those who see things differently – competing 'scripture verses at ten paces'. Hardline, dogmatic Christians who want to attack what they see as offensive passages from the Koran, for example, inevitably find themselves having to defend equally offensive passages from the Bible, such as Jesus's reported assertion that he 'came not to bring peace but a sword' or that his intention was 'to set a man against his father and a daughter against her mother' – let alone trying to defend some of the bizarre prescriptions in the Old Testament book of Leviticus that seem to have no relevance to contemporary culture, such as the harsh prohibitions against people with physical disabilities prescribed in the book of Leviticus.

Convergence rather than conversion

In any civil society, one of the most searching tests of our commitment to the ideals of tolerance, kindness and mutual respect is to see how we treat those whose beliefs happen to be different from ours. The starting point is simply to acknowledge that people are free to believe whatever they choose to believe and to act on those beliefs, subject only to the constraints of the law and the limits to what is morally and socially acceptable within the community where they live. We also need to acknowledge that everyone's beliefs seem strange to those who don't share them – half the world doesn't understand what the other half is on about, whether it's religion, politics, music or the love of Latin.

Leaving aside the specifics of belief – and even leaving aside their different conceptions of God – the striking thing about religions is that they all, at their core, recommend a life of kindness, compassion, peace, harmony, respect and service. They all urge us not to pursue personal happiness as a life goal, but to strive instead for the more deeply satisfying state of holiness (a religious word for 'wholeness') that brings a rich sense of meaning and purpose to life by shifting the focus away from the self to the needs of others.

Many non-religious people – including some ancient and modern philosophers – would urge us to live by those very same principles, but the *societal* value of religion (quite apart from its private value to the believer) is that it creates an institutional framework and a set of rituals and practices designed to reinforce those principles and foster the values that underpin them.

The religious emphasis on love (charity, compassion) as a way of life doesn't only provide some encouragement to those who want to foster interfaith dialogue; it also points to another vast area of common ground between religious faith and the beliefs and practices of the growing number of SBNRs. In conversations with SBNRs, a central theme typically emerges: their commitment to the idea that we are 'all one'; that we are all connected not only to each other through our common humanity, but also to the Earth and the wider cosmos that sustain us. And that insight invariably leads to another: since we are all one, it makes no senses to treat each other with anything other than kindness and respect. Many people who wouldn't identify as SBNR – let alone as religious – would say roughly the same things about oneness and connectedness being the deepest truth about us.

Here, then, is the great intersection between the religious and non-religious streams of thought in our society. Call it a common commitment to the Golden Rule ('treat others as you would like to be treated') as the heart of our moral code. Call it, if you prefer, a shared conviction that we can only survive as a species if we learn the lesson of compassion. Without that, communities fall apart, and without strong communities, societies fall apart.

If we are evolving as a species, that doesn't mean we've 'grown out of' religion. It doesn't mean that we are so clever that we can now get machines to do whatever we want them to do (and remember the warning in chapter 1: if we push artificial intelligence to its logical conclusion, those machines may soon start deciding for themselves what they want to do, including what they want to do with us). It doesn't mean that we have evolved into more 'rational' beings; we are, and have always been, a complex mix of the rational and emotional, in which the emotional usually prevails.

What it does mean is that there's a lot of history to learn from, so it might be time to ponder anew the alternative approaches to the presence of religion in our midst. If we allow religion to provoke feelings of antagonism, rivalry, prejudice and hatred towards those whose beliefs are different from ours, history tells us the probable consequences will be tension, anxiety, conflict, violence and war. If, on the other hand, we adopt an attitude of tolerance, kindness, compassion and respect towards those whose beliefs we can't share, the probable consequences will be peace and harmony.

The clock on species survival is ticking. It's time, surely, to look beyond each other's particular belief systems and to search for the signs of our common humanity. It's also time to back off the struggles over the value of religion per se, and to acknowledge the equal value to our society of those whose religion encourages a commitment to compassion, and those who get to that same destination via a different pathway.

8

Politics: Is this the best we can do?

The things that unite us are greater than the things that divide us.

Claim made by almost every political leader on
election night, after having exploited 'the things
that divide us' throughout the campaign

In the mid 1960s, British Labour prime minister Harold Wilson
made a remark that has become a political cliché: 'A week is a long
time in politics.' The week I began work on this book coincided
with the resumption of federal parliament after its long summer
break. Here's what happened in that one week: Senator Cory
Bernardi announced he was splitting from the Liberal Party to
form a new conservative party; Malcolm Turnbull, apparently
as part of a premeditated strategy for shoring up backbench
support ('rallying the troops'), unleashed such a vicious personal
attack on Bill Shorten that he positioned himself irrevocably as
'just another politician' in the minds of many voters who had
previously thought he was above that kind of grubby behaviour;
the treasurer, Scott Morrison, brought a lump of coal into the

House of Representatives, in flagrant contravention of the standing orders, and used it to ridicule the Opposition's commitment to clean energy; Pauline Hanson's One Nation party polled 23 percent in a survey of Queenslanders' voting intentions; the Q Society, mentioned in my earlier reflection on free speech, held its infamous Sydney meeting.

Quite a week, really. And each of those events related, in some way, to our growing uneasiness about the state of the body politic.

Growing uneasiness? The Australian National University's long-running Australian Election Study, led by Professor Ian McAllister, reported record low levels of interest in the 2016 federal election and record low levels of satisfaction with democracy and trust in government. Professor McAllister described the findings as nothing less than 'a wake-up call to Australia's political leadership'.

Disillusionment with politics is widespread. About 75 percent of Australian voters feel that way, and it's become an increasingly popular perception of Australian politics that 'the system is broken'; in fact, a 2017 poll conducted for the newDemocracy Foundation found that 54 percent of Australians agreed with that proposition, while only 39 percent agreed that our current system of parliamentary democracy is 'the best there is'. When asked to pick the three least-trusted categories of people in society, a whopping 69 percent put politicians on their list (compared with 36 percent who included journalists, 34 percent lawyers and 32 percent bankers, the next three least-trusted categories).

At about the same time as that research was published, an international survey conducted by Ipsos cast some light on why perceptions of politicians are so negative: 70 percent of Australians believe the nation 'needs a strong leader to take the country back from the rich and powerful', 68 percent believe 'the economy is rigged to the advantage of the rich and powerful', and 61 percent believe 'traditional parties and politicians don't care about people like me'.

If any of that seems new or surprising, it shouldn't. Glancing back through some of my old research reports, I came upon this: 'Many members of the Australian middle class felt they had been overlooked by both the major parties.' In the same report, politicians were being roundly criticised for being power-hungry, for their childish behaviour in parliament, and for the obvious relish they took in making personal attacks on each other. The major parties were seen as converging towards the middle ground, making the traditional distinctions between them increasingly meaningless and voters' choices therefore less clear-cut than they once were. Personalities seemed to have become so significant in federal politics that '*who* you vote for was beginning to seem more important than *what* you vote for'. That was in 1982.

Not much has changed in those 35 years, it seems, except that there is now a more urgent sense that something needs to be done about the state of federal politics and that perhaps the system itself is at fault. One symptom of that may be what looks like an unsustainable churn rate of prime ministers: in the eleven years from the Kevin 07 election to the publication of this book, no prime minister had survived his or her government's full term. Not one. It's reached the point where paramedics, I'm told, can no longer use the once-standard question 'Who is the prime minister?' as a reliable test of cognitive function of the bewildered or concussed. (Still, we need to remind ourselves that voters don't choose prime ministers; governments do, and a government can change its leader as often as it likes. When Kevin Rudd and Tony Abbott each complained, as they were pushed off their pedestal, that *the people* had elected them prime minister, they were simply wrong, even though it must feel like that to the leader of a party in government.)

Reinhold Niebuhr, the US theologian quoted in chapter 2, wrote: 'Man's capacity for justice makes democracy possible, but man's inclination to injustice makes democracy necessary.' That was in 1944, when the world was at war. Today, Niebuhr's assertion might seem a little too lofty for comfort, especially as many Australians – and Americans – would now say that democracy is no protection against injustice, especially if we regard inequality as a form of injustice. Our own brand of democracy has reached a point in its evolution where we *expect* ruthless, self-protective pragmatism from our politicians, rather than idealism; where noble sentiments are likely to be dismissed as 'the vision thing'; where winning is everything, civility is in short supply, and the lack of respect between political opponents – sometimes amounting almost to loathing – only serves to reinforce voters' cynicism about all of them (a cynicism deepened when voters occasionally learn that some of these combatants are actually quite friendly with each other offstage).

Even to mention the word 'compassion' in the context of politics might seem bizarre, yet it is the lack of compassion towards their opponents and the lack of compassion as a driving force in social policy that lies at the heart of the opprobrium now attaching to politics.

It's an odd thing that 'ideology' has acquired such negative connotations in the present political climate, considering that it's a word traditionally associated with the exploration of ideas, and even with the concept of – dare I say it? – idealism. Today, it's more likely to be used as a term of abuse. In an interview with the *Australian Financial Review*'s Laura Tingle at the end of 2016, Prime Minister Malcolm Turnbull dismissed ideology as 'a fact-free zone'. Well, of course it is: the exploration of ideas necessarily takes us beyond bald facts into the realm of concepts and possibilities, and idealism is about nothing if it isn't about noble aspirations – the very things the voters were hoping for from Turnbull – rather than mere pragmatism or bean-counting.

The retreat from idealism – ideology – might be one reason why governments of all persuasions have been able to blind themselves to the moral dimensions of our asylum-seeker policy, or our disgraceful failings in the treatment of Indigenous Australians, or the growing problem of income inequality. Moral disengagement makes even our participation in an 'unjust' war seem less odious.

It might also help to explain why voters have become so disillusioned by politics and why, when they think about politics and politicians – which they mostly try to avoid doing – they tend to focus on their grievances. While many people do acknowledge that politicians are hardworking and that some of them enter parliament with high ideals and sincere aspirations to contribute to the betterment of society, the more general perception is, unfortunately, less charitable than that: political ambitions are often assumed to be more about power than service; more about ambition for personal advancement than civic duty. (The former NSW minister Rodney Cavalier once remarked that parliament is an inherently unhappy place, because the members of the Opposition all want to be in government, the backbenchers all want to be on the frontbench, and the frontbenchers all want to be leader.)

Tony Fitzgerald, the retired judge who led a famous inquiry into political corruption in Queensland, is scathing in his assessment of contemporary federal politics. Writing in the *Canberra Times*, he described politics today as 'a clash of interests, not ideas. The major parties, which receive large sums of public money to finance their campaigns, are controlled by professional "whatever it takes" politicians driven by self-interest and ideology and addicted to vested-interest funding.' He observed 'widespread public contempt for politicians who themselves repeatedly assert that (other) politicians act improperly and accuse each other of misconduct and egregious character defects'.

Fitzgerald's criticisms are widely echoed. However unjustified some of the criticisms might be in individual cases, they tend to point in the same general direction. Here are fifteen of voters' most common complaints:

- Governments and oppositions seem unable to work together in a mutually respectful, productive, collaborative manner, or to accept that good ideas could come from either side of politics.

- They spend as much time attacking and belittling their opponents' policies as advocating and explaining their own.

- Too many politicians seem more interested in furthering their own careers than in serving the country.

- Politicians have an inflated sense of their own importance; they think of themselves as a superior 'political class' – VIPs – a view reinforced by the self-indulgent opulence and insularity of Parliament House itself.

- Politics only ever seems to be about economics – even so-called education reforms only seem to be about funding.

- They only show real interest in 'us' at election time.

- Political campaigning is all about the endless recitation of slogans, as if politics were no more significant or substantial than the marketing of consumer products.

- The leaders' TV debates at election time are usually stilted and unproductive, and often embarrassing; extended one-to-one media interviews are better.

- Political donations, wherever they come from, are a scandal, because self-interest is generally assumed to be the motivation for making them (especially when corporations make donations to both sides).

- Too many politicians have only ever worked in politics, so they lack an understanding of 'normal life', and the longer they stay in politics, the greater the disconnect between them and us.

- Party factions exert too much influence on the selection of candidates for election, and on the choice of leaders and frontbenchers.

- They seem to be poll-driven, with one eye constantly on the regular results of Newspoll, Galaxy and Ipsos voting-intention surveys, and poor polling is sometimes the catalyst for replacing a prime minister. The *Sydney Morning Herald*'s Peter Hartcher describes the current situation as 'a parlour game of polls and perceptions'. (A paradox: these allegedly poll-driven politicians choose to ignore public opinion research on some issues – negative gearing of investment properties and the treatment of asylum seekers being two such cases at the time of writing.)

- They too often resort to fear tactics as a way of staying in power – once it was 'the yellow peril', then communism, now terrorism.

- They run presidential-style election campaigns that perpetuate the myth that the voters choose the prime minister.

- The 'best people' (however that might be defined) don't go into politics. (This is patently untrue, since some very fine people have sat in the federal parliament, but the perception is strong, and it seems to be associated with the view that the two-party system crushes idealism, limits the influence of individuals and, in some cases, causes 'good' people to leave politics in despair.)

Perhaps you have more items to add to your own list – and more positive things to say, as well. But the essence of those criticisms is captured in the following three propositions about the system itself . . .

'Adversarial politics has had its day'

The adversarial parliamentary system is widely judged to be less relevant than it was when political philosophies were more clearly articulated and left and right more easily identified. The age of convergence applies as much to politics as to gender or religion.

Many Australians would still say that Labor is more likely to be focused on 'the workers', on the disadvantaged and marginalised, and on the redistribution of wealth, whereas the Coalition is the friend of big business and is more focused on protecting the wealth of the already-wealthy than addressing the needs of the poor. But there is less confidence in such characterisations than there used to be, since both sides of politics tend to speak the same language (the language of economic rationalism) and to aspire to occupy the same middle ground, 'centre left' and 'centre right' being about as daring a label as anyone is prepared to wear.

Even in terms of party behaviour, convergence is happening: the 1982 report I quoted earlier referred to the sense that the Labor Party was rather more 'murky' and 'mysterious' than the Coalition, and more beholden to its factions. Today, both major parties are considered to be highly factionalised and, particularly when it comes to abuse of parliamentary allowances, receipt of 'suspect' funding and vulnerability to outside influence from powerful lobby groups, there is no perceived difference between them. Nor is it easy to predict which party will embrace which policy – adversarialism trumps idealism.

The adversarial model, based on the British legal system, is seen as relying on stark philosophical differences that are no longer as valid as they once were. But it is also widely criticised on the grounds that adversarialism itself foments hostility and competition, rather than cooperation, and is notoriously unproductive and wasteful of intellectual and emotional resources. 'Look at the time and energy they squander getting stuck into each other' is a typical response to Question Time in the House of Representatives. Indeed, Question Time is often regarded as a showcase for the futility of adversarialism, and for the worst and most childish excesses of parliamentary behaviour. For as long as I have been researching Australians' attitudes, parents have been saying: 'I wouldn't let my kids behave the way they do in parliament.'

The adversarial system rests on a political fault line that, these days, produces few authentic tremors, though there are plenty of confected tremors designed to maintain the illusion that the two major parties are engaged in a titanic struggle of ideas. The two-party system – give or take a few independents and some minority parties in the Senate – staggers on, way past its use-by date, because that largely fictional fault line serves the interests of the major parties themselves. When, on election night, the victor utters those immortal words, 'The things that unite us are greater than the things that divide us,' everyone knows that the whole election strategy relied on exploiting the things that divide us.

Worse, the two-party system creates fault lines in the community at large. People still tend to identify as Labor or Coalition voters (though fewer of them are as rusted on as voters were in the past, and the numbers prepared to join a party are rapidly dwindling), and that identification tends to be divisive in a way that exaggerates our differences of opinion. In a truly civil society, we would debate issues with each other, often with passionate conviction, but those issues would rarely be about whether we should be a free-market or socialist society, since we have long since evolved into a blend of both, and we like it that way. The further we retreat from two-party partisanship, the easier it will become to respect each other's views, and take them into account.

Meanwhile, voters tend to express their displeasure with the adversarial House of Representatives by regularly installing a hostile (or, at least, unpredictable) Senate that they expect to act as a restraining influence on the government of the day: one-third of voters in the 2016 Senate election voted for minor parties. 'Unrepresentative swill' the Senate may be (in the famous words of Paul Keating), but its ability to curb the otherwise untrammelled legislative ambitions of any government is still seen as a welcome safeguard built into the system.

'Treat parties and leaders like brands and we will, too'

The injection of consumer mass-marketing strategies into political campaigning has lowered voters' esteem for the institution of parliament and those who work in it.

In the commercial setting, advertising and other marketing techniques are widely admired for adding a certain zest to the marketplace; they are a welcome source of colour and movement that we know to be relatively trivial in the scheme of things, but still fun. No one is in any doubt about the purpose of these techniques: they are transparent – and perfectly legitimate – attempts to encourage consumers to buy brand X or brand Y in product categories where, generally speaking, those consumers know that most competing brands are almost indistinguishable from each other. If the supermarket is out of brand X, brand Y will usually do just as well.

Voters used to think politics was different from all that; more serious, more significant, possibly even more noble. But the gradual shift in the direction of 'selling' leaders and parties like brands, and wrapping policies in endlessly repeated slogans, has had a dramatic effect on voters' perceptions of the whole enterprise. The relentless emphasis on targeting the 'swing vote' strengthens the impression that this is about marketing brands, not ideas. Meanwhile, ironically, the ranks of undecided voters continue to swell, as unswerving commitment to one side or the other seems increasingly inappropriate.

Slogans are a big part of the problem. *Stop the boats*, *Jobs and growth* (ever noticed the remarkable phonetic similarity between that notorious pair of three-worders?), *Continuity and change* (that one vanished pretty quickly after it emerged that it had been used in a satirical US TV show), *Putting people first* (you mean you might have contemplated putting them second?). It's not only the words themselves that are the problem; it's the mentality that says political leaders and parties should be marketed just like commercial products – though successful commercial marketeers have long known that: (a) endless repetition of the same message rapidly leads to boredom, irritation and switch-off (repetition *with variation* is the secret to keeping consumers' attention, and even then only if the message is about *them*); and (b) all your energy should be devoted to selling the benefits of your own product, not denigrating your competitor's.

The reliance on slogans has been steadily gaining momentum since 1972, when Labor's 'It's time' campaign was credited with having defeated the Coalition government led by William McMahon. It didn't. A political truism worth repeating is that oppositions hardly ever win elections; governments lose them. The rudderless and widely ridiculed McMahon government lost office all by itself in 1972. 'It's time' certainly summed up the mood of the electorate, but it didn't create that mood.

Slogan-based campaigning reached its nadir with 'Kevin 07', a slogan completely devoid of content. That slogan didn't win an election for Labor either; the 2007 election was comprehensively lost by the tired and dispirited Coalition government led by John Howard, a leader who made the common mistake of clinging too long to office.

It's pretty easy to imagine how voters' perceptions of politics and politicians are affected when they see political parties being marketed like Coke or Pepsi: the whole process is trivialised in their minds. Parties come to be seen as the equivalent of brand A or brand B, including the perception that there's not much difference between them. Leaders come to be seen as walking billboards bearing slogans devised by marketing consultants rather than ideas and visions created by political philosophers, economists, demographers, geographers, urban planners or social scientists, and relying far too heavily on those notoriously unscientific 'focus groups'.

If you seriously think the most creative and best-funded ad campaign should win you an election, then surely you have lost sight of the very essence of democracy. If you think a slogan can capture the minds of voters, then you have abdicated any right to be taken seriously. And if 'stop the boats' actually did win you an election, that would be all the proof anyone needed that politics had lost its way. The three-word slogan strategy didn't win the 2013 election for the Coalition, because, yet again, the Opposition didn't win: the Rudd Labor government lost all by itself, sinking under the weight of its leader's hubris.

We need only look to the 2016 US presidential campaign to see the natural endpoint of the process of turning politics into commercial marketing. In the land of the brand, Donald Trump is nothing if not a brand.

'Career politicians can't be true representatives of the people'

This is perhaps the most lethal, and yet the most problematic, of the charges levelled against the parliamentary system, particularly at the federal level. On the one hand, people acknowledge that, as in any other field, experience should mature politicians and improve their performance. On the other hand, some of the longest-serving politicians ('old warhorses') are often perceived as the worst offenders when it comes to mindless adversarialism, obstinacy, petulance and an unwillingness to take alternative views into account.

The nub of this criticism is that because of the very nature of a federal politician's life – well paid (with spectacular additional benefits, including generous pensions), constantly feted as VIPs because they are members of parliament (almost as if they are the masters rather than the servants of the people), with long periods of time spent away from home and family, and from the voters who elected them – their lives are a far cry from the lives of those they are meant to represent.

The very idea of people seeking to make politics a career, rather than a period of one's life devoted to this form of public service, strikes some people as inappropriate, even though it is an established fact of life in most democratic systems like ours. Many voters acknowledge that politicians work long hours and have a hard life, especially if they are constantly in the media spotlight, but there is a deeply ingrained view that their life in the hothouse of parliament is so insulated from the rest of us, it must be easy for them to lose touch with what life is like in 'the real world'.

One obvious solution we'll never adopt

Given all that discontent, and the growing doubts about the integrity of the present system, it's not surprising that increasing attention is being given to alternatives. So here's my two cents' worth.

Consider this possibility: instead of holding elections to choose members of our parliament, they could simply be chosen at random from the electoral roll, just as jurors are chosen. This is the closest thing to true democracy you can imagine, where every citizen has a statistically equal chance of being asked to serve in the parliament.

They would not be expected to devote their whole lives to the job; they might be appointed for a one- or two-year term, involving, say, five days per month spent in Canberra, being thoroughly briefed by senior public servants and other experts on the subject of proposed legislation, and then voting. It would be like the so-called 'deliberative democracy' process – sometimes called citizens' juries – already adopted by some local govern-ment councils across Australia, from Geraldton to Melbourne, to supplement the work of the council by reviewing, for example, the framing of an annual budget. The citizens' panel appointed by the South Australian government to consider proposals for the dumping of nuclear waste in that state was an expression of the same idea.

Randomly selected MPs might choose to hold meetings and conduct research in their own electorates to canvas the views of their community, though, having been selected at random, the assumption would be that they themselves would be a broadly representative group of Australians, capable of making responsible decisions without the heat and pressure of party-political rivalries.

Yes, there would have to be some form of vetting to make sure those chosen were competent to carry out the duties of a member of this kind of parliament. Yes, electorates might need to be smaller and more numerous than they are now, so we have a larger and more broadly representative pool of MPs – a minimum of 500 would be good – or perhaps we could simply select two or three people from each electorate to go to parliament. Yes, there would have to be a completely different way of appointing ministers charged with monitoring the work of public service departments and initiating policies. Yes, any such reforms would give more authority and influence to the senior ranks of the public service, and why not? (Belgium serves as a rather instructive example of a country that was run for 598 days by its public service, without an elected government.)

Public servants, after all, are the real experts in public policy: when a new minister is appointed under the present system, the first thing she or he must do is undertake a crash course in the policies being implemented by the department, and the issues that arise in that area of public policy. New ministers are, almost inevitably, amateurs in the field covered by their portfolio. To complete the picture, I'd envisage the appointment of a professional Speaker of the parliament, drawn from the judiciary, with the whole parliamentary process managed by professional staff.

I'd also imagine an elected, non-political head of state supported by an advisory body of heavyweights – perhaps such people as the chief justices of the High Court, the Federal Court and the Supreme Courts of all the states and territories, the governor of the Reserve Bank, the chief of the defence forces, a senior academic moral philosopher, an Indigenous Australian chosen by an Aboriginal council of elders, and . . .? That body, in close consultation with the head of each public service department, would be charged with choosing ministers from the world of business and the professions – people who have demonstrable expertise in the field covered by each department's responsibility. (This is the US system of cabinet appointments, in essence, but it's used elsewhere, too. Emmanuel Macron, for instance, was an unelected minister of finance in the French government before he ran for the job of president.)

It's no surprise to learn that the subtitle of David Van Reybrouck's recently published book, *Against Elections,* is *The Case for Democracy*, since almost every aspect of our present electoral system takes us away from the core values of a true democracy.

I recognise the improbability of our entire system being reformed in the foreseeable future, but before we come back to earth with some more realistic possibilities, consider some of the benefits that would flow from replacing elections with a system based on a random selection of MPs:

- All complaints about inadequate representation of women and assorted minority groups in parliaments elected under the existing system would evaporate. Gender, ethnicity, socioeconomic status, age, occupation, education status, disability, religious beliefs or the lack of them . . . all potential bias would be eliminated by the strict statistical randomness of the selection.

- Doing away with the preselection of candidates by parties would mean the elimination of any opportunity for the egos of power-seekers to jostle with each other.

- While MPs would inevitably disagree with each other about all sorts of issues, and robust interrogation of those issues would be encouraged under the guidance of experts in the field, there would be no *institutionalised* adversarialism – this would be a truly democratic forum, with no 'sides', based on the idea that when a random selection of citizens is assembled and briefed on any issue, they will reach a satisfactory conclusion.

- There would be no election campaigns, no advertising slogans, no policy speeches and no political party propaganda. Therefore, there would be no need for political donations and no associated scope for corruption.

- Political parties could still exist as forums for community discussion and advocacy of political issues and the formulation of particular policy proposals, with as much right to be heard as any other interest group.

- There would be no career politicians, so MPs would be unconstrained by any thought of how a particular vote might affect their career.

- There would be no more opportunities for salivating journalists to engage in endless speculation about 'leadership tensions'.

- People selected as MPs would receive a modest honorarium, but no lavish salaries or other benefits – this would be regarded as part of a person's civic duty. Employers would be expected to support people selected as MPs (rather as, in the past, they had to support people called up for National Service training), and self-employed people could seek some support to compensate them for time given to the parliament.

There are people who think even that model is too timid a departure from the present system. They are the advocates of voters' full, online participation in every vote on every piece of legislation. Let others advocate that; for reasons that relate to the underlying themes of this book, I think the value of a live forum should not be underestimated – it is highly unlikely that any system of government incorporating online referenda could ever approach the value of the comprehensive personal briefings and dynamic interactions that occur in the 'deliberative democracy/citizen jury' environment.

But we know this is all quite unlikely to happen in our lifetime. Dennis Altman of LaTrobe University wrote in *Griffith Review* 57:

> While new forms of consultation and participation might supplement representative government, they are unlikely to replace it. When the federal government sought to resolve same-sex marriage through a referendum there was strong opposition from many of those most affected, who insisted on the primacy of Parliament . . . We need strong social movements to keep pressure on governments, but we also need good people in government to develop and enact progressive policies.

Altman's is probably the dominant view.

In any case, it's hard to imagine any parliament voting itself out of existence in favour of some purer form of democracy . . .

. . . so let's be more pragmatic

If you were prepared to regard a statistically random selection of MPs as the gold standard (even if it's fantasy gold) then it might be interesting to see how the present system could be modified to introduce some of the benefits that would flow from random selection without adopting random selection itself.

For example, we might consider limiting every parliamentarian's service to two terms. If you haven't made a substantial contribution in two terms – six years or perhaps eight – you're probably never going to. That would eliminate the possibility of politics becoming a career, with the associated ugliness of power-seeking, especially if we were prepared to introduce appointed rather than elected ministers from outside the parliament.

The idea of appointing non-elected ministers has been endorsed by such clear thinkers and devoted servants of the body politic as Greg Combet, former ACTU secretary and a minister in the Rudd and Gillard Labor governments, and former WA premier turned academic Geoff Gallop. Delivering the 2010 Annual Hawke Lecture, Professor Gallop said: 'Having ministers less trapped by the imperatives of electoral and parliamentary politics should allow for better management and more innovation.' He was raising the possibility of non-elected ministerial appointments being part of a broader restructure of the political system once we become a fully independent republic – which most Australians, even John Howard, think is inevitable. Indeed, the transition to a republic would be a wasted opportunity if it did not include some re-examination of the whole system.

Apart from the obvious benefit of having actual experts in ministerial posts, such an approach would ensure that ambition for ministerial office played no part in a parliamentarian's life, and would therefore go some way towards the highly desirable goal of switching MPs' focus from power to service. In dreaming of that separation of power and service, I'm entirely persuaded by Plato's famous remark that the desire for power should be the very thing that disqualifies a person from attaining it – yet another good reason for selecting members of parliament at random from the electoral roll!

Many people are pondering ways of overhauling the system, notably Richard Walsh, the former publishing executive and editor of *OZ* magazine in the 1960s. In his 2017 book

Reboot: A democracy makeover to empower Australia's voters, Walsh does not suggest scrapping elections in favour of random selection of MPs – indeed, he is a passionate supporter of Australia's combination of compulsory and preferential voting – but he, too, favours the appointment of experts from outside the parliament to serve as ministers. That view was shaped by his personal experience of several summits that have convinced him of the value of people listening to 'experts, not orators'. Walsh also favours a popularly elected president supported by an advisory council of 'national treasures', including showbiz luminaries (a bit different from the more sober bunch I have in mind).

The founder of the newDemocracy Foundation, Luca Belgiorno-Nettis (who is also head of Transfield Holdings), differs from Walsh on the subject of elections: he (like me) wants to do away with them. But he agrees with Walsh on many other points, including the abolition of the Senate. As a measure that would take us some way in that direction, Belgiorno-Nettis favours supplementing the existing Senate with a citizens' senate – an echo of the democracy of ancient Athens. Meanwhile, newDemocracy is involved in promoting the idea of deliberative democracy at the local level: the organisation was engaged by the Victorian government to design, select and run a 100-member citizen jury charged with making recommendations for overhauling the operations of the Geelong city council. While the growing use of citizen juries in local government is an encouraging sign of some shifts in our thinking, it does not of course suggest that radical parliamentary reform is just around the corner.

And yet, if the present chorus of discontent becomes even louder and more sustained, then at least some of the reforms now being proposed could become reality. As Richard Walsh says in *Reboot*: 'To have the courage of reform, perhaps we need to remind ourselves of two of the greatest achievements of our past: extending the vote to women and the introduction of Tasmania's

Hare-Clark system of voting. They were two very brave new ideas in their times; they were ultimately embraced and are now over one hundred years old.'

In his Hawke Lecture, Geoff Gallop also said: 'To argue that our nation is incapable of debating and acting on political reform at the same as it moves forward with economic and other reforms is to underestimate the capacities and misrepresent the interest of the electorate.'

Meanwhile . . .

When it comes to federal politics, reform of the institution is not the only or even the most urgent option. Right now, we should be demanding much more from the present system. We are the voters, after all; MPs are merely our representatives. Parliament is *our* institution, not theirs: we send them there to work on our behalf, not to jostle and bicker as they climb the greasy pole of power, nor to trash the institution by unseemly behaviour. MPs will conform to the standards we set for them if they know what those standards are, and if they know we *care*. If we give in to cynicism or despair, we will have forfeited our right to complain and, humans being human, those standards will inevitably slip.

Socrates said that personal fame counts for nothing if your life isn't itself a life of virtue, and the same goes for political power. We could certainly demand more virtue from our politicians, starting with a more respectful attitude towards each other as legitimately elected members of parliament, and an inflexible commitment to telling the truth.

In his *Canberra Times* article, Tony Fitzgerald offered a pretty good summary of what 'virtue' could mean in federal politics: not misleading or deceiving or withholding material information unless it is in the public interest to withhold it; not having regard to any matter except the public interest when making decisions; not spending public money for any purpose except the public benefit; not using public office or information gained in the course of public office for personal or political benefit. For Fitzgerald, the obvious starting point for encouraging higher standards of behaviour is the establishment of an effective national anti-corruption organisation and an independent parliamentary integrity commissioner with investigative powers.

We should demand better parliamentary behaviour, and keep on demanding it. We should insist on more big-hearted, open-minded courtesy in debates both inside and outside parliament. (ABC TV's *Q&A* program provides regular examples of the kind of thing we *don't* want.) We should complain to our local member every time we are appalled, offended, disappointed or disgusted by the behaviour of them or any of their colleagues.

Instead of ridiculing our parliamentarians or simply switching off, we could become far more engaged in the political process – attending public meetings, joining current affairs discussion groups, online forums and pressure groups like GetUp!, meeting with our local member whenever the opportunity is presented (most good local members regularly show up in shopping centres and other places to meet any constituents who would like to talk to them). Perhaps we might also heed the suggestion by Andrew Leigh, the federal member for Fenner in the Australian Capital Territory, that one day of each election year be declared 'Deliberation Day' – a public holiday set aside for local community meetings and other events designed to encourage vigorous debate on our nation's future. We need to seize every opportunity available to us to make our views known – especially our serious concerns and our suggestions for addressing them. Mere bleating is actually counterproductive because it widens the gap between us and those who are supposed to represent us.

How many of us took active measures to discourage the government of the day from committing our troops to the invasion of Iraq, even though, at the time, most Australians were opposed to our participation in that recklessly miscalculated and morally dubious adventure? How many of us maintain relentless pressure on our MPs over successive governments' abuse of the human rights of asylum seekers? How many of us raise our voices – and keep raising them – when we feel demeaned by listening to politicians' flagrant distortions of the truth, or their evasion of perfectly reasonable questions from journalists? We roll our eyes and mutter about such things, but perhaps we need to send more messages to Canberra rather than to each other.

'Every nation gets the government it deserves.' That proposition, first articulated by the French lawyer and philosopher Joseph de Maistre (1753–1821), has been endlessly quoted in all sorts of contexts ever since, because of the deep truth it contains. If we lose interest in politics, cease paying close attention to it, or simply wash our hands of the whole enterprise, then whatever government we get will indeed be the government we deserve.

One of things most commonly said about the state of contemporary federal politics is this: 'I've never known it to be this bad.' (I've heard precisely those words uttered countless times over the past twenty years, by the way. In 1999 I wrote in a research report: 'Esteem for politicians has sunk to a new low . . . There continues to be a widespread perception that Federal politics lacks inspiration, vision and leadership.') Sometimes I wonder whether 'I've never known it to be this bad' is simply another way of saying, 'I've never known people to be so disengaged from politics.' You might want to argue that people are as disengaged as they are right now *because* of the parlous state of politics – in particular, because of the depth of their disappointment in the current crop of leaders. There's truth in that, but the larger truth is that to disengage is to abdicate your role as a citizen.

If you're not in favour of structural reform – or even if you are – the immediate strategy for lifting the political game and – don't laugh – for making us proud of our representatives is to let them know we care; to let them know we want their integrity and their ideals to be on display; to let them know we'd prefer they listened to us, and to their consciences, rather than to their party whips or backroom strategists.

Yes, we can wait until an election to express our displeasure with whomever is in government. But if we expect no better from their replacement, those low expectations are likely to be met and our cynicism to deepen. To fall silent between elections is to acquiesce.

One day, we might decide to appoint our ministers from outside parliament, or even to select our representatives by random ballot. Today and tomorrow, we have to extract the very best we can from what we have.

To start the ball rolling, why don't we stop calling MPs 'politicians', and insist on calling them 'parliamentarians'? That might go some small way towards reminding them of their true role, and might even encourage them to show more courtesy and respect towards each other, towards the institution, and therefore, by implication, towards us.

9

'Choice': The big threat to public education

It is in fact nothing short of a miracle that the modern methods of instruction have not yet entirely strangled the holy curiosity of enquiry; for this delicate little plant, aside from stimulation, stands mainly in need of freedom.

Albert Einstein, *Autobiographical Notes*

Although we have traditionally been inclined to brag about Australia's education system, the melancholy truth is that it used to be more brag-worthy than it is now, with declining performance of school pupils – especially in maths and science – a serious concern. In June 2017, UNICEF ranked Australia's education system 39th out of 41 high- and middle-income countries, and our participation rates and public funding for early childhood education were judged to be abysmally low.

So what went wrong? The chief problem is that we became complacent about the plight of children affected by poverty and disadvantage and, in the process, degraded our entire public education system. Compassion changes everything, and so does the lack of it.

Warning: If you are convinced that government (i.e. public) money should be given to non-government (i.e. private) schools and that those schools should not be made accountable for what they do with the money, you might like to skip this chapter. I'm about to make the suggestion – self-evidently sensible to many people, shocking and even absurd to others – that the funding model for schools in Australia is deeply flawed, seriously disadvantages the public education system, and is directly contributing to an overall decline in our educational standards.

As part of the argument, I'll be suggesting that: (a) in the immediate short term, any schools that receive public funding under the present cockeyed arrangements should be made transparently accountable for what they do with it, and (b) in the longer term, we should gradually phase out all grants of public money to schools established as an alternative to the public system. I should emphasise that I'm not remotely opposed to such schools; on the contrary, I support their existence to the hilt. I'm just against the idea that they should receive any funding at all from the very limited public purse.

If this alarms you, makes you uncomfortable, or leads you to call my sanity into question, please skip to chapter 10.

Still with me?

Perhaps I should begin by summarising my own experience of schools, so you can judge for yourself where my prejudices might lie.

My schooling began in 1943, at St David's – a private kindergarten in Melbourne's East Malvern. I entered first class at Murrumbeena State School, learned to write on a slate, and loved everything about it.

Then to Sydney in 1945, and to second, third and fourth class at Roseville Public School. My fourth class was actually a composite third/fourth class, comprising over 40 boys; the previous year there had been almost 50 boys in my third class. Too many, you might think, but as economist Ross Gittins reminded us in his 2017 Jean Blackburn Oration, all the subsequent effort that has gone into reducing class sizes has done little to improve outcomes.

At the end of fourth class, my parents received a mysterious letter from the Department of Education, advising them that I had been offered a place in an 'opportunity' class at Artarmon Public School. They had no idea what that meant, and neither did I – I only knew I didn't want to leave my friends at Roseville Public. But the decision was made and, at the beginning of 1948, I rolled up at Artarmon to be introduced to the formidable Miss King, who would be my teacher for fifth and sixth class – by far the best teacher I ever experienced in my eleven years of formal schooling, and those two years by far the most enjoyable and productive of all my time at school. The class was co-ed (though the playground was strictly segregated) and there was never a hint, from Miss King or anyone else, that boys and girls should be treated differently.

A second mysterious letter sealed my secondary school fate. Hoping to attend North Sydney Boys High with my Artarmon and Roseville school friends, I was shocked when my parents told me I had been awarded a free place at Sydney Grammar School (one of the many tests we did at Artarmon had been some kind of generic, all-schools scholarship exam). Miss King, a passionate advocate for public education, was appalled, and could offer only grudging congratulations. My classmates were quick to apply the label 'private school snob', common in the 1940s and 50s.

In 1950, Sydney Grammar was still recovering from the war years. Several staff members had gone away to serve in the armed forces and those who had remained were typically old, tired and less well qualified than those subsequently appointed to invigorate the place under a new headmaster who arrived from England in 1951. He was known as 'the rod' because corporal punishment was a big feature of Grammar culture then. So was sport. The arts were not.

All the teachers were male, and not all were incompetent. Some were outstanding, like the senior science master who ran a brilliant program in a demountable laboratory building. Like other GPS schools, Sydney Grammar had expansive playing fields and a rowing shed equipped with state-of-the-art racing shells. The school was regularly sending boys on to university, producing its fair share of Rhodes Scholars and stars in medicine and law.

And it received not a penny of government funding. No private school did. No Catholic school did. These were understood to be determinedly independent schools, firmly located outside the public school system. Parents chose to pay what was necessary to send their children to such schools because, for whatever reason, they wished their children *not* to be educated by the state. What might those reasons have been? The presumed 'values' of the school, perhaps; specific religious affiliation; a family tradition of going to a particular private school (especially a private boarding school for children from rural families); access to 'old school tie' networks; something vaguely identified as 'polish'; and, let's be frank, in some cases it was because a child would have struggled to gain entrance to one of the better high schools.

Although there was some agitation from the Catholic Church seeking 'state aid' for its schools, the idea that public funds would ever be used to support non-public schools would have appeared ludicrous to most people in the 1950s. The whole point of these independent schools was that they *were* independent. They had their own culture, their own style, their own uniforms, their own employment policies, their own boards of governors, their own way of doing things . . . and their own financial arrangements, funded by the fees paid by parents who had chosen to reject state-funded education for their children, plus bequests from wealthy former pupils, money raised by capital appeals, and whatever grants might be made by the churches who owned almost all private schools. Sydney Grammar was one of very few exceptions, though its government charter specifies that it exists, among other things, to 'promote religion'. Other non-denominational exceptions included Brisbane Grammar, Toowoomba Grammar and Ipswich Grammar in Queensland.

The broad community attitude to private schools, at that time, was analogous to the attitude to private car ownership. The government provided public transport that most people used. If you wanted your own private transport, you paid for it yourself. Obviously. The government didn't say: 'Oh, you don't like our buses? Here's some cash for you to put towards buying your own car, or perhaps you and a few friends might like to chip in to buy and run your own bus.'

Today, in the case of private schools, that's more or less exactly what governments are saying. 'Oh, you don't like our public schools? Never mind, we're making it easier for you to send your child to a non-public school by pouring billions of dollars into those schools every year.'

An imperfect analogy. But the basic idea is the same: public money should build public schools and provide public education. People who wish to opt out should be absolutely free to do so, provided they can afford to pay for the alternative. What business does the state have subsidising a parent's decision to choose the private alternative for their child? (The most extreme case of this is perhaps the schools run by the Exclusive Brethren sect, who not only wish to educate their children outside the state system, but to prepare them for a life of disengagement from society – in which, for example, they will not participate in the democratic process. They are, of course, free to do what they wish within their own sect, but should the rest of us be subsidising their separateness?)

It's a strange thing, by international standards, for governments to offer such generous subsidies to non-public schools that they amount to an incentive for parents to choose private education. Which is what has been happening at an accelerating rate: already, more than 35 percent of all schoolchildren in Australia are in non-public schools, and if you look only at secondary schools, the national average is closer to 40 percent.

There's a certain inevitability about what will happen next: when governments take money out of their limited education budget to give to groups and institutions who want to run their own schools, less money will be available for the public system, and its overall quality will suffer. And if the government puts enough money into subsidising non-public schools, isn't it equally inevitable that, over time, public schools will suffer from the fragmentation not only of the education budget but of the school population, too, through the loss of all the pupils (especially those from better-educated and more affluent families) who would have kept the public system robust by staying in it?

It's not an attractive idea, but isn't it likely that by heavily subsidising the growth and development of the non-public sector, governments would also contribute to a widening of the gap between privilege and disadvantage in society at large? Leading educationalist Barry McGaw believes so; he has long warned of the danger that the public secondary school system might become a residual service for those unable to afford the alternative. And in a report commissioned by the Public Education Alliance in 2007, Lyndsay Connors, the former chair of the NSW Public Education Council, warned that the national system of funding schools was helping to entrench social disadvantage.

It's only grown worse since then. Here's the assessment of Ken Boston, the former director-general of the NSW Department of Education and Training and one of Australia's most experienced and widely respected education administrators, who was a member of the 2010–12 federal government inquiry into school funding: 'Equity and school outcomes have both deteriorated sharply since we wrote the Gonski report . . . The present quasi-market system of schooling, the contours of which were shaped by the Hawke and Howard governments, has comprehensively failed. We are on a path to nowhere.'

Comprehensively failed? A path to nowhere? It's surely time to ask: how did we get ourselves into such a mess that one of our most respected educationalists could say such things? In fact, Boston's bleak assessment matches the prediction made by Scott Prasser, writing in *The Conversation* at the time of the Gonski report's release: 'The main proposals and the government's response to them hold little promise for school funding to become more effective and equitable in the near future.'

It's not just a funding issue. Real educational reform is about far more than who gets the money. It's mainly about what we think public education is *for*, and how we might best achieve the objectives we set for it.

In a 2017 paper written for the Whitlam Institute located within Western Sydney University, Associate Professor Justine Grønbæk Pors of the Copenhagen Business School asks: 'What does education need to be if we still want democratic societies . . . and children who are citizens, not just performing well in labour markets?'

Drawing on the Danish experience, Pors exposes the negative effects that arise from a focus on marks-based classroom performance at the expense of education in the broader sense. In Demark as in Australia, standardised testing and educational rankings have had demonstrably adverse effects on school pupils. Australia's adoption of the National Assessment Program – Literacy and Numeracy (NAPLAN), for example, has moved us no closer to improved outcomes while contributing to increased anxiety and stress among the children subjected to the testing – effects which inevitably diminish those children's capacity for learning.

At the same time, school principals feel pressure to shift their focus from education to management in order to cope with the increasing demands of standardised testing, school rankings and the onerous regimen of reporting on school performance. Which is not, of course, to say that schools should not be accountable for their performance, but only to suggest there must be a way of doing it that gives teachers the freedom to teach in ways that respond directly to the needs of their pupils, and gives those pupils, in turn, the freedom to learn.

In *Freedom to Learn*, the eminent US psychologist and educationalist Carl Rogers wrote this: 'When we put together in one scheme such elements as a prescribed curriculum, similar assignments for all students, lecturing as almost the only mode of instruction, standard tests by which all students are externally evaluated, and instructor-chosen grades as the measure of learning, then we can almost guarantee that meaningful learning will be at an absolute minimum.'

Research commissioned by the Whitlam Institute and carried out by Newspoll in 2013 reported disturbingly high levels of stress among children in years three to ten in response to their experience of NAPLAN testing – a classic example of the 'standard tests by which all students are externally evaluated' that induced such despair in Carl Rogers. In an introduction to the report, the then-director of the Whitlam Institute, Eric Sidoti, noted that feverish media coverage had accompanied the 2013 testing, including commercial advertising: Nature's Way Kids Smart Omega-3 Fish Oil, for example, 'sparked a backlash when they marketed their children's dietary supplements as "Key ingredients for NAPLAN results and a healthy future"'. And the educational soft toy company Kimochi promoted their products as NAPLAN stress-relievers, quoting 'many teachers' who claimed that 'some students show increasing levels of stress before the tests, including sleepless nights and crying, the feelings related to these tests can be difficult for both children and their parents to deal with.'

'Sleepless nights and crying' hardly sound like the sort of responses you'd expect from a child who is relishing the experience of learning.

The Newspoll/Whitlam Institute research reported that 40 percent of parents of children undertaking the NAPLAN testing claimed their children exhibited some form of stress or anxiety. The anxiety was sometimes very explicitly tied to the anticipation of the test: fear of 'freezing up' occurred in 20 percent of cases; fear of parents' reaction to the results in 13 percent of cases. In other cases, more general symptoms were reported, including sleeplessness, feeling sick and crying.

As long as NAPLAN results and the associated school rankings continue to dominate political and policy discussion of education, we will continue to drift away from any consideration of the real purpose of education. Which is what? To teach children the knowledge and skills they need, including numeracy and literacy, to live the fullest, most satisfying life they are capable of living – intellectually, creatively, morally, emotionally, vocationally, socially? To expose them to the richness of our culture, especially our musical and literary canon? To introduce them to the realm of science and technology and to show them how science can improve the health and wellbeing of society? To transmit the values embedded in our cultural traditions, including our religious traditions? To 'socialise' them in ways that will allow them to operate comfortably as citizens of this society? All of the above, and more.

It would be a very narrow interpretation of the purpose of education to say that it should be about giving children as much information as possible. (Albert Einstein again: 'If you want your children to be intelligent, read them fairy tales. If you want them to be more intelligent, read them more fairy tales.') It would be equally narrow to suggest that it is only about transmitting the skills required to earn a living. Every child, surely, is entitled to an education that stimulates their imagination, fires their creativity and equips them to function – to the extent of their capacity – as fully-fledged members of this society, with a commitment to building up the common good through their multiple roles as citizens, neighbours, workers, friends and family members.

And yes, we need to talk about how to find the money to achieve all this. Most particularly, we need to talk about how to fund the best possible education for every child in our society, regardless of their parents' ability to pay. But the question of education's purpose should always precede the question of funding.

How did we get ourselves into this mess?

This is not a history book, so I won't be trawling through the events that led Australia to go from a well-funded, world-class public education system to the current hybrid model that sees around $12 billion of public money pouring into the coffers of non-public schools every year, and overall education standards in steady decline. The history has been well documented elsewhere but, in essence, the process began in 1962, when the Catholic Church spooked Prime Minister Robert Menzies by closing six Catholic schools in the regional town of Goulburn, in protest against the failure of the NSW government to provide additional toilets at one of those schools. Nowhere in all the coffers of the Church, apparently, could the cash be found to pay for an extension to a school toilet block. As a result of the school closures, roughly 2000 Catholic pupils rolled up at Goulburn's local public schools where, naturally, there were insufficient places available.

The so-called 'Goulburn school strike' was unsuccessful in the short term, and the Catholic kids went back to their Catholic schools after a couple of weeks of chaos. Longer term, the ruse paid off handsomely, and is still doing so. In the campaign leading up to the following federal election, which he won, Menzies offered new science blocks to all non-government schools, and the cry of 'no state aid for non-state schools' gradually faded to a whisper: the concept of public funding of non-public schools had been institutionalised. Thirty years later, under John Howard's prime ministership, the steady increase in federal money available for non-public schools was dramatically accelerated and the current hybrid system – hailed by many of its supporters as a victory for 'choice and competition' – came to be regarded as the norm for Australia. Towards the end of the Howard government's eleven-year term of office, economist Ross Gittins wrote in his *Sydney Morning Herald* column of 23 May 2007 that 'in the case of schools, Howard's greatest achievement has been to bias federal grants heavily in favour of private schools – particularly the least needy'.

Confirming Gittins's view at that time, the *Sydney Morning Herald* was reporting that a leading private boys' school with an operating surplus of $4.1 million for the year had received $3.3 million in government funding, and a private girls' school that had received $2.5 million in government funding had reported a net surplus of $2 million for the year.

The escalation of recurrent funding to non-public schools has continued. Some of the wealthiest private schools in the country continue to receive generous handouts from the public purse, and the total annual allocation to non-public schools now stands at around $12 billion. Since that $12 billion more than covers the total bill for salaries of teachers in the entire non-public sector, it's worth noting the 2017 observation made in their paper 'The vanishing private school' by former public school principals and fellows of the Centre for Policy Development, Chris Bonnor and Bernie Shepherd: 'Over the years, our federal and state governments, apparently without comparing notes, have raised private school funding to the point where those schools can no longer be considered private . . . If a private school is defined by who pays then they are rapidly becoming public.'

'Choice and competition'

A moment of truth came for me when I was being shown around a new state-of-the-art building at a private girls' school. 'Look at the aesthetics of the door furniture,' my guide urged me, pointing to an admittedly very stylish door handle that I might easily have overlooked in favour of larger signs of opulence. 'We don't want the girls to feel as if their school is shabby by comparison to their homes.' There seemed no danger of that. In fact, I wondered if a bit of shabbiness might have been just the reality check the girls needed, but restrained myself from saying so.

My exposure to those door handles set me thinking about this concept of 'choice and competition' in the school system. Like most comparable societies, Australia insists on compulsory schooling for its young, and on a broadly uniform curriculum; indeed, there's a trend towards a national curriculum in key subjects, replacing state-based curricula, precisely because of our desire to see all Australian school pupils exposed to broadly the same material. If we want a standardised curriculum, that means we don't want schools to be offering *curriculum* choice, so what kind of choice *do* we expect them to be offering? I guess the answer is 'door handles' – at least as a metaphor for all the extras money can buy: superior playing fields, strong music programs, well-stocked libraries, state-of the-art laboratories, wall-to-wall computers, stylish uniforms and, perhaps, better-paid, better-qualified teachers . . . and the indefinable 'something' that parents who send their children to non-public schools believe money can buy. If the essence of choice comes down to such things, then this surely strengthens the argument in favour of parents being asked to foot the bill for what they want.

In her 2017 paper 'Are we sifting and sorting our children . . . and then scattering them among too many schools?', Lyndsay Connors argues that the provision of more choice in a school system implies that more places will be created than are needed. In other words, a system based on 'choice and competition' is going to be inherently wasteful, through oversupply. (Remember: this is not some toothpaste or fast-food market we're talking about; this is our system for delivering compulsory, high-quality education to every Australian child.)

Through her experience with the ACT Schools Authority and, later, with the Commonwealth Schools Commission, Connors has observed that excess places in the school system tend to work their way down to the most economically disadvantaged and socially troubled schools. In other words, the more choice you create, the more competitive the system becomes and the more lopsided the outcomes, as parents naturally strive to find places for their children in the 'better' schools, leaving the 'worse' schools – poorer, less well resourced, higher pupil turnover, more disadvantaged families – with plenty of vacancies.

Internationally, there's little comfort for those who push the 'choice and competition' line. When Sweden introduced a market-based strategy through a school voucher system that allowed public funding to be applied to any school you chose, the average performance of its school pupils in all grades fell thereafter. Another result was increased stratification and segregation of students by socioeconomic status and ethnicity. (Sound familiar?) In Chile, the move to a 'choice and competition' model of school funding has been so spectacularly unsuccessful, moves are now afoot to restore the original system, where, as in most countries, *no* public money goes to non-public schools.

In 2016, the Australian Council for Educational Research (ACER) published an issue of *Policy Insights* in which its CEO, Geoff Masters, examined evidence from several countries that have been pursuing 'choice and competition' strategies. He observed that those tend to be the countries that have experienced the greatest declines in student performance over the past decade. 'Major English-speaking countries saw significant declines in reading levels, and similar declines in mathematics.' Although Masters was careful not to draw any direct cause-and-effect conclusions from this analysis, it's hard to miss a strong whiff of causality.

Why? I believe the Connors hypothesis fits the facts rather well: the drive for more choice creates excess supply; more supply encourages parents to move their children 'upwards'; already disadvantaged schools become more disadvantaged, increasing inequity and dragging down the overall performance of the system.

Some alarming new evidence about the growing inequity in our school system emerged from the OECD's 2017 Programme for International Student Assessment (PISA), based on millions of fifteen-year-olds in over 70 countries. Australia is now among the countries with the largest gaps between its advantaged and disadvantaged students in relation to access to qualified teachers and material resources. Perhaps Ken Boston got it wrong: perhaps we're not going 'nowhere'; perhaps we're actually heading in the wrong direction.

The Howard government had always defended its breakthrough increase in funding for non-public schools on the grounds that it was promoting freedom of choice, but the price of that freedom was a market distorted by the generous protection of non-public schools. In the process, there has been an inevitable erosion of the public education system's once-proud status as a symbol of our commitment to egalitarianism. Whatever other consequences you might imagine flow from such a sustained boost to the non-public schools sector, one thing is clear: we have moved from an essentially one-class education system, with a relatively small minority of families choosing to opt out of it, to a two-class system where public schools have already come to be seen by many parents as places where you send you kids if you can't afford anything better.

Once parents become conditioned to the public/non-public hybrid model of government funding, those who want to keep their children out of the state system would feel, quite understandably, that they were being hard done by if they were asked to pay the true market price for the education they want to buy for their children. There is a particular irony in this, since many of the most passionate advocates of public funding for non-public schools are also advocates of the free market. As far as non-public schools are concerned, 'freedom to send my child to the school of my choice' has become 'freedom to send my child to a non-public school, as long as it's heavily subsidised by the state'. Different thing entirely.

By 2010, the schools funding system had become so messy, and so impenetrable to all but those most directly involved in administering it, that the Labor government, with Julia Gillard as its minister for education, set up a committee chaired by businessman David Gonski to unravel the chaos and recommend a new funding model. More than enough has been written elsewhere about the recommendations of that committee. In essence, it confirmed that overall educational standards were in decline, that the gap between the wealthiest and poorest schools was widening, and that the funding process should be radically reformed in favour of the schools in greatest need.

As a result, education spending did indeed go up, yet overall education standards have continued to decline and, in 2017, Ken Boston went on record to identify the fundamental flaw in this entire process: the fact that, in setting up the review committee, the government had insisted that no school would lose a single dollar of funding as a result of the changes. It beggars belief how anyone could have been expected to design a realistic reform process when one of the most glaring faults in the existing model – the generous grants of public money to already-wealthy private schools – couldn't even be addressed. No wonder Boston has since described this as the albatross around the neck of the committee.

In fact, the *real* albatross was, and remains, the idea that has become conventional wisdom: that public money should be used to subsidise schools specifically established to *compete with* the public system.

Following a revised funding proposal in 2017, popularly known as 'Gonski 2.0', public education advocate and national convenor of Save Our Schools, Trevor Cobbold, challenged the claim by prime minister Turnbull that this new funding model was fair and 'needs-based'. Relying on data supplied by the Commonwealth Department of Education, Cobbold argued that, on the contrary, 'Gonski 2.0 is the best special deal private schools have ever had'. According to Cobbold's analysis of projected funding, the revised model 'entrenches inequity in school funding between public and private schools' and will perpetuate the chronic under-funding of the public system.

The key to reforming school education: teacher quality

Here's another quote from Ross Gittins's illuminating 2017 Jean Blackburn Oration: 'It's a great pity that the crazy way we fund our schools – two levels of government funding differently three different school sectors – keeps us so preoccupied that we rarely turn our mind to the more important question of *how* we can improve our schools' ever less-impressive measured performance.'

Well, it's not a secret, is it? The answer that towers above all others is: *teachers, teachers, teachers.* Teacher quality – underpinned by a world-class curriculum – matters more than any other single factor in the system, even though many other factors obviously matter as well, ranging from adequate toilet blocks and recreation facilities to every school having sufficient musical instruments for kids to play on, and teachers properly qualified to teach them how to do so.

Why do I mention music, specifically? Drawing on a wide range of studies for his 2014 book *Free Schools*, David Gillespie concluded that 'the most consistent [positive] effect on academic performance is from students who do music or play in the school band'. This would be no news to eminent Australian conductor and music educator Richard Gill, who has always maintained not only that listening to music develops areas of the brain that other activities don't, but that actually *making* music and especially composing music are breakthrough experiences in our cognitive and emotional development. Implication: schools that lack teachers capable of running a serious music program significantly disadvantage their pupils, so imagine the compound effect if such schools were *already* disadvantaged.

School-teaching has more impact on the kind of society we will become – more impact on the heart of the nation – than any other profession you can think of. Teachers, in today's world of busy, often overstretched parents, play an even more formative role than they did when I was at school – and it was already huge back then.

Education outcomes are primarily a reflection of teacher quality. We therefore need to train them better, monitor their performance more rigorously and support them throughout their careers. We need to provide teachers with programs of continuous professional development that bring them up to date with new thinking in their own discipline, keep them abreast of the latest findings from educational research, help them find better ways of engaging and motivating 'problem' students, and encourage their deeper understanding of the changing sociocultural context from which their students come. Such 'lifelong learning' programs could occur particularly in the periods between terms when pupils are on holiday and which have traditionally been time off for teachers, too. (Fully committed, professional teachers need only four weeks' annual leave, like the rest of us; forget 'short hours and long holidays' as a reason to become a teacher, if it ever was.)

A radical improvement in teacher quality must begin in the universities where teachers are trained, starting with a more rigorous and comprehensive selection processes. Some medical schools, for example, combine school exam results with an assessment of all aspects of an applicant's background and experience, often supplemented by personal interviews; why not adopt that model for selection of student teachers?

We should expect far more from our teachers, and we should nurture them constantly as they strive to meet those higher expectations. We need to revolutionise the way they operate – learning, again, from the example of the medical profession with its intensive ongoing training of newly graduated doctors and the requirement that all doctors undergo continuing education throughout their careers or lose their registration.

There needs to be far more emphasis on professionalism, more commitment to teamwork and mutual support, more access for teachers to mentors and counsellors. Perhaps fresh graduates need to be 'apprenticed' to senior, more experienced teachers, spending their early years working as trainee teachers under close supervision, and then returning for some postgraduate work – such as a graduate certificate or master's degree – after they have had some sustained exposure to the life of a school and the experience of being in a classroom.

The good news is that the process of significantly upgrading the teaching profession has already begun. National professional standards for teachers – public and private – have been devised, defining the steps required for teachers to move from Graduate status to 'Proficient', 'Highly Accomplished' and 'Lead' status. The states are now developing new strategies for the training, support and continuing professional development of teachers that, in many ways, echo the approach of the medical profession. For example, the NSW Educational Standards Authority (NESA), established in January 2017, has rigorous procedures for the accreditation, mentoring and monitoring of teachers, and will require teachers at every stage of their career to devote prescribed minimum amounts of time to participation in formal professional development activities – just as doctors and most other professionals must – if they are to retain their accreditation.

Needless to say, not all older and more experienced (or more jaundiced) teachers have welcomed these developments involving incursions into what was once regarded as 'spare time'. But the long-term positive effects on the profession will be profound. Given the disturbing rate of disenchantment and burnout among teachers in the public school system, we need better ways of ensuring that those who are struggling in the classroom are identified and supported – and re-energised where possible – before their pupils suffer.

We often nod approvingly in the direction of Finland when we worry about how we could do better with our school education. In Finland, students vie for places in teacher-education degree programs in roughly the same way Australian students vie for places in law and commerce. Teachers are paid handsomely and generally have postgraduate qualifications. It's a highly respected profession ... as it will become here, over time, if we decide to fund a revolution in the selection, training and continuing professional development of this most precious resource.

How badly do we want a better system?

The question is: do we really want a robust, properly resourced, world-leading public education system in Australia?

If the answer is 'yes', it would need a bipartisan commitment by our parliamentarians to bring about the changes necessary to achieve it. To start the process, it would take just a few courageous leaders to look at the evidence and say: 'This can't go on.' And, of course, it would take time – twenty years? – to implement the gradual phasing-out of public funding of non-public schools.

If we insisted that the organisations – and the parents – who want non-public education for their kids should pay for it themselves, public schools wouldn't be the only beneficiaries: universal, free preschool education for four-year-olds would become an affordable possibility, and TAFE colleges, currently squeezed for funds, could presumably share in the restoration of public money to public education. Otherwise, the technical and vocational education sector will continue to be disrupted and fragmented by the same mentality that drives the obsession with 'choice and competition' in the school system. Our willingness to put public money into non-public technical and vocational education has seen the NSW government contribute $1.8 million to McDonald's for staff training. Need I say more?

When we weaken our public education system by pouring public money into non-public schools, the result is not just a widening gap between rich schools and poor schools. The greater consequence is societal: whether intentionally or not, we are using our schools funding system as an instrument to promote public/private school-based class divisions on a scale never before seen in Australia. If a strong public education system is a potent symbol of a society's commitment to egalitarianism, what shall we say about a society that deliberately weakens its public education system by siphoning off billions of dollars every year to the non-public sector? The sad truth is that our school funding arrangements are creating a fault line that threatens to further undermine our social cohesion.

To fiddle at the edges with any funding model that perpetuates the present situation is to stand in the way of our progress towards becoming a great society, underpinned by great public education.

PART III

THE WAY WE COULD BE

10

The real state of the nation

Patriotism is a lively sense of collective responsibility. Nationalism is a silly cock crowing on its own dunghill . . .

Richard Aldington, *The Colonel's Daughter*

When it comes to people believing they live in the best country in the world, Australians are no exception to the general rule. 'Just take a trip overseas,' we say to each other with a knowing look, 'and see how you feel about this place when you come home.'

That's precisely what most people, in most countries, say when they get home from a trip away: as long as you don't live somewhere that's being torn apart by war, famine, drought or the persecution of a minority group you happen to belong to, the pull of 'my country' is a very powerful thing. Just ask the French, the Chileans, the Norwegians, the New Zealanders, the Canadians, the Scots, the Germans, the Spanish . . . need I go on?

Being born into a country means being born into a culture – and that includes language, aesthetics, religion, literature, music, the sense of humour and all the other aspects of a society's traditions, rituals and practices that make it seem different from other places. Not just different, but uniquely, reassuringly, *wonderfully* different. It would be astonishing if it were otherwise – people's attachment to their homeland is visceral, and perfectly natural. Of course Belgians think Belgium is the best place on earth; of course the Swiss, Germans and French all disagree with them. The rest of Europe might sneer at the Greek economy, but just ask the Greeks about their history, culture and heritage: believing your country was the cradle of Western civilisation certainly compensates for the passing pain of an unruly national debt.

There is a migratory urge that grips many people – perhaps because their homeland has disappointed them, perhaps because of the lure of the exotic, perhaps because they believe they can provide their children with a better life elsewhere, perhaps because they've fallen in love with a foreigner, or perhaps because of job opportunities, and Australia has been the great beneficiary of that urge. Migration is not always spontaneous or voluntary, of course. There are about 65 million refugees and displaced persons adrift in the world: some are desperate to go home; some are desperate to go anywhere but home.

Even in Australia – relatively calm, relatively stable, relatively affluent – plenty of people are on the move. About 600,000 Australians currently live overseas, and many young people are more open than their parents and grandparents ever were to the idea of living, loving and working anywhere in the world. Concepts like 'globalisation' and 'the global village' – to say nothing of the internet – encourage us to reimagine ourselves as citizens of the world, and the increasing busyness of airports might give you the impression that half the world wants to be somewhere else.

But dreams of relocation are less common than you might think. Our desire for a sense of place, closely linked to our desire for a sense of belonging, means that once we've lived somewhere for a while, we generally become attached to both place and people, and so we drop anchor. It's the familiarity; it's the habits of daily living, the reassuring little rituals that become increasingly comfortable over time; it's the quite primitive sense of security – part tribal, part territorial – that goes with being known in the place where you live.

Like people of most nationalities, we can tell you *why* this is the best country on earth, though if our journey together into the heart of the nation has taught us anything, it has surely taught us to ease back on the bragging.

Yes, we have one of the world's most robust parliamentary democracies, but our faith in it is being sorely tested.

Yes, we're a reasonably well-educated bunch and unprecedented numbers of students are enrolled at our universities, several of which are world–class, but our cockeyed approach to schools funding cries out for far more radical reform of the education system than has so far been contemplated.

Yes, we have relatively low unemployment and a high – though steadily falling – rate of home ownership. We have a sound financial system, and we've experienced a world-record period of continuous economic growth, though it has been accompanied by record levels of personal and government debt and growing income inequality, and it has engendered a disturbing level of complacency.

Yes, we have some of the best healthcare professionals in the world, and some of the best medical researchers, too. We have universal health insurance, a national disability insurance scheme and some of the world's best hospitals, but the existence of federal *and* state health departments creates unproductive tension and confusion in the system.

Yes, there's our deservedly famous physical environment: our spectacular beaches; the stark, startling beauty of the outback; the mysterious 'bush'; the rugged mountains; the mighty rivers and sparkling harbours, plus some of the world's cutest wildlife and most liveable cities. Even this list contains some inherent warnings: there's an alarming rate of species extinction or threat, the Murray–Darling river system has been abused for too long by water theft from irrigators (cotton farmers, especially), the Great Barrier Reef is under stress, and the congestion of our biggest three cities is making them less appealing places to live.

And yes – the big one – this is a place where we pride ourselves on *the fair go*. A place where we enjoy freedom of speech, freedom of assembly, freedom of the press and freedom of religion – though religious persecution rears its ugly head from time to time, and believers of all kinds are increasingly being mocked by the fashionable breed of New Atheists who are often driven more powerfully by anti-religious sentiment than by metaphysical considerations about the possible meanings of 'God'.

No wonder we occasionally allow ourselves to feel a trifle smug about our desirability as a destination for tourists, immigrants and, yes, refugees and asylum seekers as well. Why wouldn't people want to come here? After all, this is a place where it must seem, from the outside, as if the opportunities are limitless; as if the dream of equality could come true here. We're not war-torn. We're not ravaged by famine. We're not in the grip of any life-threatening epidemics. Our housing crisis is not about millions of Australians struggling to find a safe place to lay their head at night. We're not a country where getting sick can send you broke unless you can afford health insurance.

One of our greatest attractions to people eyeing us off as a possible place to resettle is the fact that we have managed to create a harmonious society out of extraordinary cultural and ethnic diversity, bringing together people from about 180 different birthplaces around the world and making it work.

All good.

And yet . . .

It would be a mistake to feel too pleased with ourselves. History tells us that smugness ill becomes a nation, as it does an individual. As Rebecca Newberger Goldstein has reminded us in her *Atlantic* essay about the hazards of rampant nationalism, 'Making Athens Great Again', Plato and his fellow Athenians were hardly the last to discover that a nation that sees itself as exceptional 'may prove unprepared to respond wisely when arrogance takes over and expectations go awry'.

No matter how much we love the place, we might as well admit that all is not well with our nation. It's a bit like any loving relationship that survives over the long haul: once the magic of romance fades and you develop a more mature, more sustainable attitude to each other, you find yourself noticing that not everything is perfect, after all. The love is still there, but it is tempered by a realistic sense that our relationship could benefit from a little work in some areas – a little give and take – though it's often hard to bring this up.

To criticise aspects of Australia is not to stop loving it. But it would be a blind and meaningless patriotism that couldn't withstand occasional confrontations with some unpalatable facts about us.

The melancholy truth, as we have seen, is that we are a society increasingly at risk of fragmentation and division. In politics, gender relations, religion, education, housing, income distribution and in the functioning of our local neighbourhoods and communities, we are less cohesive, less trustful, less cooperative – and less optimistic – than we once were.

The sense that all is not well with us is perhaps most graphically illustrated by the startling facts we confronted in chapter 2 about our epidemics of anxiety and depression. The prediction that one-third of us will experience some form of mental illness at some time in our life is sobering, surely.

But there are other, equally disturbing facts . . .

A whopping two-thirds of us are overweight (including about 30 percent who are actually obese). You don't need a degree in psychology to work out that overeating, like over-drinking, is usually a symptom of something not being okay, so there'd be a significant overlap between the epidemics of obesity and anxiety. Obesity is also associated with increased risk of cardiovascular disease and type 2 diabetes. So it's no surprise to learn that one million Australians currently suffer from type 2 diabetes, with a rapid increase in the numbers of young adult sufferers.

And while we're on the subject of diet and health, the CSIRO tells us we are not eating nearly enough fresh fruit and vegetables, and the Adelaide Institute for Sleep Health warns us that we are dangerously short of sleep, partly because we stay awake too long staring at the screen on one or more of our IT devices.

Here's another hard-to-believe symptom of 'something not being okay': our suicide rate. The good news is that the rate of suicide has recently been falling slightly; the bad news is that, as mentioned in chapter 3, somewhere between 65,000 and 70,000 Australians *attempt* suicide every year. That's the equivalent of the entire population of a regional city like Albury. Every year. As if reaching the point of wanting to end your life isn't bleak enough, people who survive suicide attempts have to live with the stigma attached to suicide in our society. According to Jackie Crowe, Australia's National Mental Health Commissioner until her untimely death in 2017, we are still a long way from developing effective psychotherapeutic techniques for dealing with the specific nature of suicidality.

None of this is easy material to confront, and here's another pair of unpalatable statistics: almost one million Australian children are living in poverty, and a 2017 UNICEF report found that 16 percent of Australian children below the age of fifteen lack secure access to sufficient, safe and nutritious food. Just put the book down for a moment and think about those two closely related facts.

Although we pride ourselves on our low rate of unemployment, we too easily overlook the problem of underemployment: about two million Australians are currently either unemployed or underemployed, and a gnawing sense of job insecurity is becoming endemic as the casualisation of the workforce and the increasing automation of the workplace proceed apace. Meanwhile, among full-time workers, overtime – both paid and unpaid – is a scandal still waiting to be addressed: every hour of overtime worked is an hour of work not being made available to the unemployed or underemployed. Job-hogging is bad for the health of those working over-long hours, and it contributes to an inherent unfairness in the labour market.

While the escalating value of our properties might bring smiles to many faces, we are pricing young first-home buyers out of the housing market in our two biggest cities, where housing loans to investors outnumber those to occupiers. Negative gearing and massive concessions on capital gains tax have continued to attract investors who drive prices steadily higher, putting home ownership even further beyond the reach of young people. This is one reason why only 8 percent of young Australians believe they will be financially better off than their parents, according to the 2017 Deloitte Millennial Survey. Economist Saul Eslake notes that our rate of home ownership has been steadily falling since its peak in 1966 and is now the lowest it has been since the mid-1950s.

Many families are now bracing themselves not only for the probability of adult children staying in the family home for longer than ever, but also for the experience of becoming three-generation households, with either new grandchildren or ageing parents being added to the core household. Perhaps they can draw comfort from the knowledge that that's how it used to be: the nuclear family household only became fashionable within the last 100 years.

Here's a bizarre thing about the housing market: as our households shrink, our houses expand. We have become a nation replete with spare rooms and also, according to the 2016 census, with unoccupied dwellings: more than one million of them stood empty on census night – that's 11 percent of our total housing stock.

Meanwhile, about 100,000 Australians are homeless, though it's an ever-shifting, hard-to-count population, so that's probably a conservative estimate. Homelessness is associated with an increased risk of mental illness in the young and Alzheimer's disease among older people. It is often also associated with a history of incarceration. Speaking of which, our prison population has risen to record levels, with a distressing over-representation of Aboriginal Australians – one of the clearest signs that we are nowhere near bridging the social, cultural and economic chasms between Indigenous and non-Indigenous Australians.

Despite falling crime rates across most categories, we still live with unacceptable rates of violence. Over two million of our women and half a million of our men have been victims of domestic violence – to say nothing of the (mostly male) child victims. A 2012 survey of rates of sexual assault in 36 OECD countries, published by Civitas, had Australia at the top of the list. Sweden was second, with alcohol abuse likely to have been a key contributing factor in both countries. Seeking an explanation for the rise in street violence, a report written by independent think tank Australia 21's Richard Eckersley and Lynne Reeder for the Victoria Police identified the night-time economy, changing patterns of alcohol and drug use, increasing levels of poverty and disadvantage, changes in the structure of families and modes of parenting as some of the most likely contributors to this unhappy state of affairs.

And the dream of egalitarianism? Given the present level of income inequality, the widening chasm between public and private education, and the growing sense of entitlement (supported by clever tax avoidance) among the burgeoning wealth class, we seem to be further from that ideal, if it is still an ideal, than we were 30 years ago. Peter Whiteford of the Crawford School of Public Policy at ANU says that, although the prospects for future inequality are unclear, 'wage disparities have continued to widen for most of the last 30 years and there is little reason to think that this trend will halt or reverse itself'. Professor Whiteford also points out that *household* income has become much more unequal over the past 30 years.

Egalitarianism is all about equality of opportunity, of course, not equality of outcomes, but when the outcome gap yawns ever wider, serious questions need to be asked about whether we have retreated from our commitment to equality of opportunity. Australia's once-famous middle-class society has given way to one where there has been steady growth at the top and bottom of the economic heap and shrinkage in the middle. As sociologist Eva Cox has pointed out in 'Redefining Inequality', an article for *Australian Quarterly*, the widening of economic inequality has negative consequences for social cohesion and the level of trust in society.

We are world champions when it comes to losing money on gambling: we squander about $25 billion each year in gambling losses – the highest per capita rate of gambling losses in the world – and 40 percent of us choose to gamble at least once a week. On top of those personal losses, the University of Sydney's School of Psychology estimates the 'social cost' of gambling at $4.7 billion per annum. Social costs include suicide, depression, relationship breakdown, lower work productivity, loss of employment, bankruptcy and crime.

While we're squirming, we'd better acknowledge that our national energy policy has been a decade-long shambles, with privatisation and competition having driven prices ever higher – the very opposite of what was promised. We've been selling so much gas to overseas markets we've created a domestic supply crisis, and there appears to be no coherent national plan for the urgently needed switch to clean and renewable energy.

Our declining trust in institutions

The power crisis is but one sign of a general loss of respect for institutions – in that case, both energy companies and governments. In fact, one of the grimmest reminders that all is not well with us is the steady erosion of respect and trust we feel towards many of our major institutions. We're by no means alone in this – the worldwide Edelman Trust Barometer reported the biggest-ever global drop in trust in governments, business, media and NGOs in 2017. But Australia experienced the second-largest drop of the 28 countries surveyed, and the study found that 59 percent of Australians feel that 'the system is failing'.

What do we mean by 'the system'? Clearly, this is a reference to the institutions we set up to regulate, serve, maintain and protect our society, whether through government, educational, commercial, industrial, religious or social enterprises. Such institutions evolve both to perform specific functions as well to preserve the ideals and traditions that express a society's values. As Nugget Coombs put it: 'Institutions provide the context within which the drama of our personal lives is played out.'

We therefore demand a high standard of integrity in our institutions: our trust in them depends on our continuing per-ception that they are working in our interests. By contrast, our respect for them declines when they are seen as corrupted by their own power and placing their institutional interests ahead of the interests of the society they are meant to serve.

For example . . .

When parliaments are seen as having become dominated by political parties and individuals more interested in power for its own sake than in serving the best interests of society at large, our trust is eroded.

When the church is perceived as having condoned corrupt behaviour (such as the sexual abuse of children) or become preoccupied with its own power and wealth, or more preoccupied with doctrine than charity, it loses the respect of the community whose spiritual and charitable needs it is supposed to be meeting.

When individual banks are accused of malpractice – manipulating the bank bill swap rate to their own advantage, turning a blind eye to money laundering by criminals or exploiting the vulnerability of their own customers through excessive fees – a cloud of mistrust inevitably descends over their entire industry. In November 2017, Federal Court Justice Jayne Jagot declared that the public should be 'shocked, and indeed disgusted' by the behaviour of ANZ Bank and National Australia Bank in relation to the bank bill swap rate scandal, but the institutional reputation of all four big banks has been tarnished by the more general perception of a reckless disregard for the greater good of the society they are supposed to serve.

When professional sport is seen to have become over-commercialised – placing corporate interests ahead of those of players or fans – or corrupted by the influence of gambling on the results of particular sporting events, or when players are perceived as being 'in it for the money', the public becomes understandably sceptical.

When trade unions are perceived as having become too powerful, too intent on feathering their own nests, or inclined to overreach in their claims for better wages and conditions, they lose public support. (For example, the ACTU's successful 1970s campaign for a 17.5 percent annual leave loading to wages was widely perceived as 'a step too far' that eroded support for trade unionism itself.)

When news-gathering organisations are perceived as having gone too far in the direction of sensationalism or having blurred the distinction between reportage and opinion, they lose the respect they might otherwise enjoy.

When universities are seen as being driven too strongly by commercial motives, questions about their academic integrity inevitably arise. Persistent stories about academics not being permitted to fail students and aggressive marketing to attract high fee-paying overseas students have tarnished the reputation of several universities. Media reports that universities have spent $1.7 billion dollars on advertising over the past seven years add to the worrying perception that many universities are being run like businesses rather than academic institutions, and some people now question whether there may simply be too many universities competing for the pool of available students.

Doctors comprise our most trusted profession, yet they are not immune from the charge of self-interest. When medical specialists' incomes reach stratospheric levels – especially when compared with the modest earnings available to general practitioners or those who work in the public hospital system – they can easily be interpreted as a sign of exploitation of the sick and vulnerable.

Commercial institutions are understood by everyone to be in business to make a profit but they, too, suffer an erosion of respect and trust when there is any sign of their unresponsiveness to the needs or concerns of employees, clients or customers, or when they become too commercially dominant, like the major supermarket chains and the four big banks. The payment of executive salaries widely perceived as excessive raises questions about an organisation's sensitivity to community standards, as does any sign of a lack of social responsibility.

While a healthy scepticism is always in order, the widespread loss of trust in institutions is an unhealthy state for us to be in. Yet research consistently shows that people make a distinction between 'the institution' and their personal experience of individuals within that institution. People can condemn the Roman Catholic Church, for instance, over child sexual abuse or any other aspect of institutional corruption, yet continue to support their local parish because of their trust in a local priest. People can condemn the banks or other financial institutions as being rapacious, yet speak warmly of their local branch or a particular financial adviser they have learnt to trust. People can mock medical specialists for their Porsches and Ferraris while their faith in 'my specialist' is undiminished.

The lesson for institutions is clear: the more remote and self-interested they appear, the more vulnerable they will be to a loss of public confidence, trust and respect. When that happens, people will inevitably begin to look for alternatives: the house church movement, non-bank financial services (including crypto-currencies), private tertiary educational colleges, amateur journalism via the internet and employment contracts that bypass trade unions. When people become cynical about the medical establishment and 'Big Pharma', they will eagerly consult 'Dr Google' and become more open to alternative (often unproven) therapies. And, as we have seen, when the loss of trust goes all the way to parliament itself, people will begin to talk seriously about different ways of doing democracy.

A troubled nation

We are in a strange state, no question; both troubled and chirpy. It's as if we're living within a paradox that gives us enough wiggle room to postpone engagement with unresolved social, economic, political and environmental issues in favour of the distractions and short-term satisfactions of materialism and hedonism. The Me culture, the coffee culture, the smartphone culture, the sporting culture . . . the culture that allows many of us to say, right now, and in spite of everything we know needs fixing: 'It doesn't get much better than this.'

On the one hand, we're self-satisfied to the point of smugness, lulled into complacency by the promise of continuing economic prosperity, most of us enjoying sufficient material comfort to insulate us from too much concern about the less well-off and to remain reasonably optimistic about 'my future'. On the other hand, we're anxious, disenchanted with politics, and losing faith in institutions that once defined and even inspired us. Many of us are verging on anger about the state of the nation and are pessimistic about its future. The most disturbing entry in that ledger is, to my mind, 'anger'. In her perceptive Quarterly Essay *Great Expectations*, Laura Tingle described us as an 'angry nation' – and doesn't history teach us that when anger takes over from cynicism or despair, revolution is in the air? Is that us? How does our anger manage to blend so bizarrely with our complacency? Are we too unsure of what we want to attempt anything revolutionary?

While politicians continue to talk admiringly of 'Aussie values', we are actually showing signs of a disturbing retreat from the values of an open, tolerant society for which we were once famous. In a comment piece published early in 2017, Michael Gordon – the then political editor of Melbourne's *Age* – described us as a 'timid society'. That's a far cry from the bold, innovative nation we were in the days when we became famous for such exemplary initiatives as giving women the vote, inventing the secret ballot and compulsory preferential voting, legislating for free and universal public education, throwing our overwhelming support behind the 1967 referendum that gave Indigenous Australians full rights as citizens, or, later, welcoming the Vietnamese boatpeople fleeing persecution and economic despair after their homeland was devastated by a war in which we were active combatants.

Gordon presented a list of things other comparable countries have that we don't, including a bill of rights, their own head of state, and a treaty or compact with their First Peoples. He also cited, as evidence of Australia's retreat from its past aspirations, the growing gap between rich and poor, the unconscionable treatment of asylum seekers, and the reluctance of Australian governments to take the lead on measures to combat climate change or to mitigate its effects. As Gordon put it, 'the plucky country lost its mojo.'

Tim Costello of World Vision Australia agreed, telling Gordon that Australia had retreated into a 'delusionary mental bubble where self-interest is a prime motivator', citing the slashing of Australia's foreign aid budget as one manifestation of this. (Indeed, our dwindling foreign aid program should be the cause of some profound national embarrassment, to put it mildly.)

Where did this edgy, anxious, angry, too-violent yet, para-doxically, timid and complacent society come from? In his book *Panic*, journalist David Marr identified 'turning fear into panic' as 'a great political art', arguing that Australians' view of them-selves as a relaxed and tolerant bunch is at odds with an underlying insecurity that makes us vulnerable to our fears – real and imagined. How does that stack up against our more robust view of ourselves? After all, 'Aussie values' are not supposed to include giving way to panic at the first sign of threat.

What are those vaunted 'Aussie values'?

We love talking up Australia's national values as if they are uniquely ours. But when you start reciting them – the fair go, justice, equality of opportunity, freedom, respect for the rule of law, 'mateship', tolerance, care for the disadvantaged and marginalised – you soon realise that these are the values of any Western liberal democracy; indeed, of any civil society. Do we really imagine that Canadians would be less concerned about the marginalised than we are? Or that Italians wouldn't help each other out in the wake of a natural disaster? Or that the French might be less committed to liberty than we are? How easily we forget that *liberté, égalité, fraternité* was forged in the French Revolution of 1789, just a year after the First Fleet arrived in Farm Cove, and that the same trinity of ideals has been enshrined in the constitution of many other countries and political parties ranging from the Republic of Haiti to Denmark's Social Democratic Party. We need to remember, when we spruik freedom, mateship and the fair go, that we are placing ourselves in a long and broad tradition.

We are at our most hubristic when a natural disaster strikes – a flood, a cyclone, a bushfire. In such situations, our leaders talk about spectacular acts of altruism and heroism as if they are somehow typical of *Australians*, rather than being what they are – typical of *humans*.

If those are not distinctively, uniquely, *our* values, then what values might qualify as ours? What sort of behaviour, reflective of our values, might set us apart from other comparable societies? If we were to be brutally honest, we'd have to say that some of the values reflected in our recent national behaviour are not terribly attractive. Here are just four that might make you wonder what we really stand for.

Imprisonment and mental torture of asylum seekers

We believe in imprisoning certain asylum seekers indefinitely in offshore detention centres, in defiance of the United Nations 1951 Refugee Convention to which we are a signatory – so you'd have to put blithe hypocrisy on the list of our political values, too. Actually, I shouldn't say 'we' believe in indefinite imprisonment of asylum seekers in offshore detention centres, since, according to a 2016 poll commissioned by the Australia Institute, a mere 22 percent of us support that appalling practice. But the senior figures in both major political parties have been intransigent on the subject, so that's our official position, and there are no sustained mass demonstrations against it, perhaps because no Australian lives are at risk or perhaps because the reality of what has been done in our name would cause us too much shame if we were to confront it.

A succession of prime ministers and immigration ministers tried to mesmerise us with a Big Lie about asylum seekers who arrive by boat by calling them 'illegal immigrants', though they have done nothing illegal at all, and by creating an association in our minds between asylum seekers and terrorists. And those same ministers, acting on our behalf, have chosen to treat asylum seekers more harshly than we treat criminals – a level of harshness amounting to cruelty at best and torture at worst.

Offshore detention of boat arrivals is the ugliest aspect of our asylum-seeker policy, but there are other shameful aspects, such as our restriction of asylum seekers' access to government employment and language services. In May 2017, the Coalition government demanded that the roughly 30,000 asylum seekers who had arrived between 2012 and 2014, and whose applications for protection had been frozen by the former Labor government, were to submit their application by 1 October, or risk deportation. In announcing this new measure, the immigration minister Peter Dutton repeated the Big Lie by declaring that these people 'have no right to be in Australia', also suggesting that lawyers offering assistance to asylum seekers were 'unAustralian'.

The government's subsequent decision to cut off welfare payments and the provision of accommodation for asylum seekers who had been evacuated from Manus and Nauru on medical grounds provoked a flood of offers for support – including accommodation and employment – to organisations like Sydney's Asylum Seekers Centre, from members of the community anxious to ensure that these people did not fall into destitution. The heart of our nation beats strongly, but it doesn't often get its adrenaline from government.

Perhaps the grimmest of all the grim aspects of our asylum seeker policy was the Turnbull government's decision in November 2017 simply to abandon approximately 600 men who had sought asylum in Australia but had been detained on Manus Island. The men were still languishing there when the detention centre was closed, after due warning, by the government of Papua New Guinea.

Our iniquitous asylum-seeker policy is often claimed by political leaders to be a success on the grounds that it has 'stopped the boats' and discouraged the exploitation of vulnerable refugees by ruthless 'people smugglers'. And so it has, though there are still an estimated 7–9000 asylum seekers arriving each year by plane who are not being kept in detention centres. But if 'stopping the boats' is the only justification for the policy, then, sadly, we would have to chalk up 'the end justifies the means' as another of our Aussie values. We wouldn't be alone in that, of course, but are we really prepared to enshrine and defend that principle as a basis for national policy? If so, we put ourselves in some pretty murky company. 'The end justifies the means' is the classic defence of torturers, assassins and corrupt dealers of every kind. That's the kind of company you find yourself in if you declare that you will imprison and torture innocent refugees in order to stop further boatloads coming here.

There are all kinds of ways we could discourage so-called people smugglers: better coordination of regional intelligence, more energetic diplomacy and policing, more regional cooperation in dealing quickly and humanely with the flow of refugees, more humanitarian aid for the countries from which refugees are fleeing. To admit that we're incapable of devising any more imaginative or humane solutions than imprisonment, abuse and mental torture of the innocent is to say something rather unattractive about our values.

Unprovoked military invasions

Here's another of our 'Aussie values': judging purely by our behaviour, we believe in launching unprovoked military attacks on other countries, when asked to do so by the US. The unwarranted and ultimately disastrous invasion of Iraq is the prime recent example, but our participation in the murky complexities of Afghanistan and Syria raise equally deep questions about what the hell we are doing there, and whose side we're on. So add 'prepared to invade other countries' or, if you prefer, 'prepared to take sides in other countries' civil wars' to the list of Aussie values.

Sledging

While we pride ourselves on being 'good sports' *(do we? still?)*, our international sporting reputation has been tarnished – most obviously in cricket, and increasingly in tennis – by teams and players who have become infamous for boorish behaviour, especially sledging. (Yes, other countries do it too, but we're famous for its elevation to 'normal'.) Football is not exempt, either: AFL player Heath Shaw, commenting on his own and others' offensive sledging in the 2017 season, claimed that sledging will always be part of AFL. That was a polite way of saying cheating will always be part of AFL, since, however you gloss it, sledging is a form of cheating, being just another one of the ways people try to prevail through tactics that have nothing to do with the skills required to play the game. The use of performance-enhancing drugs, ball-tampering in cricket, claiming to have taken a catch you knew you didn't take, rugby's 'professional fouls' or the laughably fake 'diving' in soccer, designed to deceive the referee: those are all examples of cheating in sport, and sledging belongs on that list.

Inevitably, younger players follow suit. Even in local club games, sledging is now an integral part of cricket, except where umpires have the courage to curb it. And sledging from the sidelines by parents attending their children's games – including the abuse of referees – is a disgraceful development that would be less likely to happen in a sporting culture where star players behaved well. (Why are golfers so polite, by the way?)

Abuse and neglect of First Peoples

Though plenty of other countries have a shameful record in the treatment of their First Peoples, we're historically down there among the worst. And we continue to get it wrong: as recently as 2017, we were debating whether or not to include a reference to Aborigines in the preamble to our constitution. *Wha-a-t?* If I were an Indigenous Australian . . . well, I can't pretend to be able to enter the mind of a person from such a different cultural background from my own . . . but I suspect that if I *were* Aboriginal, I'd totally reject that idea as yet another example of the invaders offering us their idea of consolation on their own terms; doing something *they* think is significant within the framework of *their* constitution – a document that was framed with no consultation with the Aboriginal population at all. If I were that Indigenous Australian, I'd be saying: 'It's never too late for a treaty. Are you ready to sit down and talk to us as equals? We don't want to be fobbed off with any more symbols; we want a *voice*.' Unsurprisingly, that's roughly what the Uluru Statement issued by the Aboriginal and Torres Strait Islanders' Constitutional Convention of May 2017 called for, and yet its proposal for a mechanism to achieve that fell, once again, on deaf ears.

As reported by Calla Wahlquist in *The Guardian*, the Uluru Statement had rejected symbolic constitutional reform in favour of a constitutionally enshrined voice to parliament – an Indigenous body that would sit outside the parliamentary structure but provide advice and consultation on issues and legislation affecting Aboriginal and Torres Strait Islander people. That proposal was dismissed out of hand by Malcolm Turnbull and his cabinet. Senior Indigenous and legal voices were understandably outraged by the government's unwillingness even to discuss the proposal: Dylan Lino from the University of Western Australia – one of the legal experts who worked on the Uluru proposals – described this summary rejection as 'a despicable act of mean–spirited bastardry'.

And now for some good news . . .

On the positive side, we *can* reasonably take pride in our creation of remarkable harmony out of extraordinary diversity. We have every right to be proud of the richness and complexity of a culture that has depended heavily on immigration. That is possibly our most distinctive achievement, and a reflection of the admirable values of tolerance, acceptance, and a willingness to restrain our instinctive xenophobia ('instinctive' in the sense that humans are naturally wary of otherness).

Yes, there are outbreaks of racism; there are pockets of intolerance; there are xenophobic prejudices directed mainly at whoever the latest arrivals happen to be or whoever seems to be most different from 'us' – usually based on an outmoded idea of what 'us' means. But such outbreaks make the news precisely because they are so rare; precisely because they are contrary to the spirit of multiculturalism that has shaped our growth and development since the 1940s; precisely because they contradict one of the deepest and loveliest truths about us – our acceptance of cultural difference.

Multiculturalism is a thing to celebrate, and we do. The Scanlon Foundation has been monitoring our attitude to multiculturalism for more than a decade through its Mapping Social Cohesion project; its latest findings show that 85 percent of Australians think multiculturalism is a good thing. Of course they do. Not everyone agrees: the 15 percent who don't support multiculturalism are divided between those who oppose it and those who have no opinion, though it's hard to imagine how you could have no opinion about the central cultural reality of modern Australia.

★

We can also feel justifiably proud of the achievements on the world stage of our medical researchers, our astronomers, our academics across many disciplines, our primary producers, our winemakers, our business entrepreneurs, our fashion designers, our writers, artists, musicians, filmmakers, actors and sports people. We win Nobel Prizes, Oscars and Olympic medals.

All wonderful. And there's more.

Though our cultural balance sheet can't ignore the ways we have been falling short of the ideal of a cohesive, united, equitable and, above all, compassionate society, we rise effortlessly to the occasion when given an opportunity to show our commitment to fairness and compassion – witness the 90 percent who voted in favour of recognition of Indigenous Australians in the 1967 referendum, and the strong support for marriage equality revealed by the 2017 postal survey. When it comes to righting wrongs, especially wrongs involving the persecution of minorities, we don't hesitate. (Perhaps we will yet be given an opportunity to right the wrongs done to asylum seekers over many years.)

Our history also suggests we are resourceful, resilient and capable of brilliant innovations and ingenious solutions when we really need to find them – the stump-jump plough, the Sunshine stripper harvester, the Snowy Mountains Hydro-electric Scheme, ultrasound technology, zinc cream, Victa rotary lawnmowers, the ute, all the way up to the creation of the Reserve Bank, the ABC and SBS, our national network of public libraries, a welfare system that, for all its deficiencies and inequities, is still a lot better than most countries offer, a world-leading census (recent wobbles notwithstanding), the brilliant environmental repair and restoration work being done by Greening Australia, and the near miracle of the merger of six sovereign states into one Federation based on the still-glorious concept of a Commonwealth of Australia.

Looking at the future we face, we are going to need some more brilliant innovations and ingenious solutions.

★

Every moment in history is unique. Every moment is fascinating for some, and frightening for others. Every moment has seemed 'modern'. Every moment has offered the potential for human advancement, or stagnation and decay.

This is our moment.

It looks as if there has never been a more exciting or challenging time to be alive, yet many of history's moments have been just as exciting and just as challenging as this one, and have carried far more danger and the prospect of far greater disruption than anything being faced by contemporary Australians.

In any case, we have the resources not merely to cope with the changes that lie in wait for us, but to thrive on them. Among those resources are our rough-hewn decency, our pioneering spirit, our sense of humour, and our generosity in response to others' needs (though, shamefully, nouveau riche Australians still lag way behind international standards when it comes to philanthropy: almost 40 percent of Australians earning more than $1 million per annum do not claim a single dollar of tax-deductible donations to charity).

But our chief resource is not uniquely Australian at all: it's our common humanity. That's what will finally assert itself in response to further threats to our social cohesion; that's what will pull us back from the brink of a mad world where we would put more faith in devices and algorithms than each other; that's what will ensure that the communities we rely on to sustain and nurture us – and keep us sane – will never fragment into meaninglessness.

11

Big hearts, open minds

Would we ever allow ourselves to become so dependent on a robot, so 'friendly' with it, that we would eventually prefer hanging out with it to spending time with other people? Would we ever decide to set a 'use-by' date for human life? Would we ever decide to call a halt to research on the frontiers of biotechnology? Would we ever decide to resist some forms of technology that would involve throwing thousands of people out of work they enjoy?

Many of the looming challenges to our way of life lie beyond our personal control. But we're not as powerless as you might think: the way we choose to respond to these challenges – in particular, the extent to which we are prepared to accept or resist technology that threatens to dehumanise us – will determine the kind of society we will become.

When we contemplate changes in our social structures and institutions and in our ways of living and working, we are really contemplating how we ourselves might be changed. Look at how mass literacy changed us; how radio and TV changed us; how social media are still changing us; how cheap air travel changes us;

how sudden prosperity – or sudden poverty – changes us. So it's a good idea to be sure that the changes we choose to embrace will produce the kind of society, the kind of people, we want to be.

We might disagree, from time to time, about the level or composition of immigration, the fairest way to deal with people seeking asylum, which side of politics has got it right (or, perhaps, less wrong) on some particular issue, the cultural and economic significance of home-ownership rates, whether China poses a threat to the security of our region . . . or about other weighty matters, like which of our four codes of football is superior, or which school of Pilates practice is the most authentic. But there are some things we could mostly agree on, aren't there? Things we'd like to be able to say about an ideal Australia? Things we'd like others to say about us?

Here's my list. Tick the ones you agree with; cross off the ones you don't; scribble your own in the margin.

- I want to live in a society where people respect each other, *especially* when they disagree, and *most especially* when they disagree on matters of politics and religion.

- I want to live in a society where kindness and compassion are regarded as normal, commonplace responses to the needs of others (especially the needs of strangers), not 'soft' or 'fringe' motivations mainly associated with do-gooders.

- I want to live in a society where the strong willingly accept responsibility for the weak; the rich for the poor; the privileged for the underprivileged; the 'main-gamers' for the marginalised; the cognitively and emotionally competent for the cognitively and emotionally challenged.

- I want to live in a society whose core values are expressed in the small courtesies of everyday life.

- I want to live in a society where equality means what it says; where people have equal rights, equal opportunities and equal access to the best we can offer – notably in education and health – regardless of their postcode, gender or ethnic heritage, or any advantage or disadvantage of birth.

- I want to live in a society in which people at any point on the gender spectrum are regarded simply as *persons* in circumstances where gender shouldn't be an issue (at work, at school, in the community at large, in religious institutions, in politics) but where gender differences are acknowledged and celebrated when it's appropriate (in reproduction, obviously, but also in social life more generally, in sport, and in some branches of the arts where the distinct representation of gender is relevant, significant and clarifying).

- I want to live in a society where we err on the side of generosity when it comes to our treatment of refugees; where we can rise to the moral challenge of dealing humanely with some of the world's most desperate, vulnerable people who manage to make it to our shores, by whatever means.

- I want to live in a society that places such a high value on education as the chief instrument of equality that we esteem schoolteachers more highly than any other professionals – training, supporting and rewarding them in ways that reflect the importance of their role.

- I want to live in a listening culture, where people make time to attend to each other, as a gift, not always wanting to cut to the chase or resort to a text or a tweet. This would be a culture in which excessive busyness would be seen as a sign of foolishness or inefficiency or perhaps as a means of escape from the responsibility of nurturing personal relationships – rather than (as now) a badge to be worn with pride.

- I want to live in a society where we are realistic about the availability of work, equitable in its distribution and prepared to compensate those for whom no work can be found – not via 'welfare' but via a basic living wage.

- I want to live in a society where eccentricity is not just tolerated, but embraced; where creative artists are valued for the messages they are sending us from our future; where breakaways, dropouts, larrikins and sceptics are acknowledged as having something potentially valuable to say about the way we are living.

- I want to live in a society, not an economy; a place where the health of the economy is judged according to how well it underpins and promotes a healthy society; where critical decisions are justified primarily in terms of the social costs and benefits, supported by an analysis of the economic costs and benefits.

- I want to live in a society where everyone has access to secure accommodation and healthy food.

- I want to live in a society (indeed, a world) where violence – physical and emotional – is regarded as a sign of weakness.

- I want to live in a society where we can trust our institutions – political, religious, commercial, educational, cultural – to understand that they exist only to serve *us*, not themselves; a place where corruption, profiteering, exploitation of workers and/or consumers and the cutting of moral corners are resisted by the leaders of all our business enterprises – large, medium and small.

- I want to live in a society in which clean air and clean water *for the planet* are regarded as pressing public health issues; a society whose power comes exclusively from clean and renewable energy sources.

- I want to live in a society where parliamentarians never resort to fear as a political weapon.

- I want to live in a nation that has its own head of state, a flag that doesn't devote 25 percent of its surface to the Union Jack, and a stirring anthem with words so inspiring that we'll wonder how we ever managed to keep a straight face while we sang 'Our home is girt by sea' (a claim that is inarguably, unassailably, true but which is also the very least you could say of an island).

- I want to live in a society where we acknowledge that perfection is beyond us — in politics, in relationships, in the social order, and especially in our private emotional states; a society where, knowing this, we turn down the heat of our unrealistic expectations. This is not to discourage idealism (can't you tell I'm a hopeless idealist myself?), but only to encourage more realistic responses to each other and to whatever life throws at us. We will all disappoint or exasperate each other in one way or another, but we can sometimes inspire each other as well. We can always do better, especially when it comes to righting wrongs, but none of us is a saint.

- Above all, I want to live in a society where we treat other people as we ourselves would want to be treated. Yes, it's the old Golden Rule — as relevant today as it ever was, and perhaps even more relevant tomorrow, when we will be so dazzled and disorientated by change that we'll be in danger of assuming the old rules don't apply.

If enough of us wanted that kind of society, that's the kind of society we would become. The process of getting there is already well underway; the big thing is not to lose heart.

References

Altman, Dennis, 'Discontents: Identity, politics, institutions',
   Perils of Populism, Griffith Review 57, Griffith University, in
   conjunction with Text Publishing, Melbourne, 2017

Andersen, Kurt, *Fantasyland: How America went haywire: A 500-year
   history*, Random House, New York, 2017

Athanasiadis, Chris, 'A man got to do what a man got to do',
   The Psychologist, British Psychological Society, June 2017

Barnes, Julian, 'Diary', *London Review of Books*, 20 April 2017

Baumeister, Roy F., Kathleen D. Vohs, Jennifer L. Laker and Emily
   N. Garbinsky, 'Some key differences between a happy life and a
   meaningful life', *Journal of Positive Psychology*, 8(6), August 2013

Billig, Michael, 'Henry Tajfel's "Cognitive aspects of prejudice"
   and the psychology of bigotry', *British Journal of Social
   Psychology*, 41(2), June 2002

Biddulph, Steve, 'How male shame drives a terrorist', *Canberra
   Times*, 14 June 2017

Bonnor, Chris and Bernie Shepherd, 'The vanishing private
   school', Centre for Policy Development, 1 February 2017

Boston, Ken, 'Our school funding system is unfair and holding Australia back. Here's how to fix it.', *The Money*, ABC website, 13 April 2017

Botsman, Rachel, *Who Can You Trust? How technology brought us together – and why it could drive us apart*, Portfolio/Penguin, London, 2017

Bracy, Jedidiah, 'This pacemaker just incriminated its owner', *International Association of Privacy Professionals* (https://iapp.org/news/), 7 February 2017

Brett, Judith, *Fair Share*, Quarterly Essay 42, Black Inc., Collingwood, Vic., 2011

Butler, Hubert, 'Beside the Nore', *Escape from the Anthill*, Dublin: Lilliput Press, 1985

Caldwell, John C., *Theory of Fertility Decline*, Academic Press, London, 1982

Cammataci, Joseph A., *Report to the 39th International Conference of Data Protection and Privacy Commissioners*, Hong Kong, September 2017

Cobbold, Trevor, 'Gonski 2.0 is the best special deal private schools have ever had', *Pearls and Irritations* (https://johnmenadue.com), 12 December 2017

Colville, Deb, 'Medicine's gender revolution: How women stopped being treated as "small men"', *The Conversation* (https://theconversation.com/au), 7 August 2017

Connors, Lyndsay, 'Are we sifting and sorting our children . . . and then scattering them among too many schools?' *EdMediaWatch* (http://www.edmediawatch.com.au), 2017

Coombs, Elizabeth and McLaughlan, Sean, 'Australia's mandatory breach notification regime imminent', *Privacy Laws & Business*, Issue 150, December 2017

Cowdell, Scott, *Abiding Faith: Christianity beyond certainty, anxiety and violence*, James Clarke & Co, Cambridge, UK, 2010

Cox, Eva, 'Feminism has failed and needs a radical rethink', *The Conversation* (https://theconversation.com/au), 8 March 2016

Cox, Eva, 'Redefining Inequality: It's the inequity of social trust, not "The economy, stupid"', *Australian Quarterly*, July 2017

Cribb, Julian, 'When optimism spells disaster . . .', *Pearls and Irritations* (https://johnmenadue.com), 4 August 2017

Daley, John, Correspondence in response to David Marr's Quarterly Essay 65, *The White Queen*, Quarterly Essay 66, 2017

De Beauvoir, Simone, *The Second Sex (Le Deuxieme Sexe)*, Gallimard, Paris, 1949

Dobbs, David, 'The Smartphone Psychiatrist', *The Atlantic*, July/August 2017

Eckersley, Richard and Lynne Reeder, *Violence in Public Places: Explanations and solutions*, Report on an expert roundtable for Victoria Police, Australia21 (http://www.australia21.org.au), 2008

Eckersley, Richard, 'Subjective well-being and the mismeasure of progress' in A. Podger and D. Trewin (eds), *Measuring and Promoting Well-being: How important is economic growth?*, ANU e-press and the Academy of Social Sciences in Australia, 2014

Eckersley, Richard, 'Is the West really the best? Modernisation and the psychosocial dynamics of human progress and development', *Oxford Developmental Studies*, Routledge, 2016

Einstein, Albert, *Autobiographical Notes* (edited by Paul Arthur Schilpp), Open Court, Chicago, 1949

Eslake, Saul, 'The causes and effects of the housing affordability crisis, and what can and should be done about it', *Pearls and Irritations* (https://johnmenadue.com), 2 May 2017

Fine, Cordelia, *Testosterone Rex: Unmaking the myths of our gendered minds*, Icon Books, London, 2017

Fitzgerald, Tony, 'If we care about our children, and theirs, we need to raise standards, beginning with federal politicians', *Canberra Times*, 13 April 2017

Friedman, Thomas L., *Thank You for Being Late: An optimist's guide to thriving in the age of accelerations*, Allen Lane, London, 2016

Gallop, Geoffrey, 'Rethinking Australian politics: Engaging the disenchanted: 13th Annual Hawke Lecture', The Bob Hawke Prime Ministerial Centre, Adelaide, 2010

Gibbs, Samuel, 'Privacy fears over "smart" Barbie that can listen to your kids', *The Guardian*, 13 March 2015

Gillespie, David, *Free Schools: How to get a great education for your kids without paying a fortune*, Pan Macmillan, Sydney, 2014

Gillespie, David, *Taming Toxic People*, Pan Macmillan, Sydney, 2017

Gittins, Ross, 'How we can do better on education', *Jean Blackburn Oration,* Australian College of Educators, Melbourne, 22 February 2017

Goldstein, Rebecca Newberger, 'Making Athens great again', *The Atlantic*, April 2017

Gordon, Michael, 'Australia has retreated into a delusional bubble of self-interest', *The Age*, 20 January 2017

Grayling, A.C., *The Age of Genius: The seventeenth century and the birth of the modern mind*, Bloomsbury, London, 2016

Greer, Germaine, *The Female Eunuch*, Farrar, Straus & Giroux, London, 1970

Gripper, Ali, 'Words on the street', *Sydney Morning Herald*, 24–25 June 2017

Hartcher, Peter, 'How a long run of economic prosperity led to complacency over economic reform', *Sydney Morning Herald*, 2 June 2017

Holt-Lunstad, Julianne, 'Loneliness: A growing public health threat', Paper delivered at the 125th Annual Convention of the American Psychological Association, Washington Convention Center, Washington DC, 5 August 2017

Horne, Donald, *The Lucky Country* (6th edition), 1964, republished by Penguin, Camberwell, Vic., 2008

Hull, J.G. and Draghici, A.M., 'A longitudinal study of risk-glorifying video games and reckless driving behaviour', *Journal of Popular Media Culture*, October 2012

Irvine, Jessica, 'Why even the free-market faithful should support gender quotas', *Sydney Morning Herald*, 26 June 2017

Johnson, Mark, 'Developing human brain functions', *The Psychologist*, British Psychological Society, November 2009

Jung, Carl, *Memories, Dreams, Reflections*, 1963, republished by Flamingo, London, 1983

Kagan, Jerome, *Surprise, Uncertainty and Mental Structures*, Harvard University Press, Cambridge, Mass., 2007

Kawachi, Ichiro and Lisa Berkman, 'Social cohesion, social capital and health' in Berkman and Ichiro (eds.), *Social Epidemiology*, Oxford University Press, Oxford, 2000

Keating, Paul, quote re neoliberalism at a dead end: see Deborah Snow reference below

Kellaway, Lucy, 'Dedicated office chat is an extinct species', *Australian Financial Review*, 3 April 2017

Keynes, John Maynard, 'Economic possibilities for our grandchildren', 1928, in *Essays in Persuasion*, W.W. Norton & Co, New York, 1991

Khazan, Olga, 'The queen bee in the corner office', *The Atlantic*, September 2017

Klein, Naomi, *The Shock Doctrine: The rise of disaster capitalism*, Allen Lane, London, 2007

Koenig, Harold G., Dana E. King, Verna B. Carson, *Handbook of Religion and Health* (2nd edition), Oxford University Press, New York, 2012

Kolbert, Elizabeth, 'No time', *New Yorker*, 26 May 2014

Lanchester, John, 'You are the product', *London Review of Books*, 17 August 2017

Leigh, Andrew, *Disconnected*, New South, Sydney, 2010

Leigh, Andrew, 'Why Scott Morrison isn't entitled to his own facts on inequality in Australia', *Pearls and Irritations* (https://johnmenadue.com), 2 August 2017

Leys, Simon, *The Hall of Uselessness: Collected Essays*, New York Review Books, New York, 2011

Llosa, Mario Vargas, *Notes on the Death of Culture: Essays on spectacle and society*, Faber & Faber, London, 2012

Louv, Richard, *Last Child in the Woods: Saving our children from nature-deficit disorder*, Workman Publishing, New York, 2005

Mackay, Hugh, *Parties & Politicians*, The Mackay Report, December 1982

Mackay, Hugh, *Reinventing Australia*, Angus & Robertson, Pymble, NSW, 1993

Mackay, Hugh, *Living with Technology*, The Mackay Report, November 1993

Mackay, Hugh, *Advance Australia . . . Where?* Hachette, Sydney, 2007

Mackay, Hugh, *What Makes Us Tick? The ten desires that drive us*, Hachette, Sydney, 2010

Mackay, Hugh, *The Good Life*, Pan Macmillan, Sydney, 2012

Mackay, Hugh, 'The "unfocussed" group discussion technique', *Australasian Journal of Market and Social Research*, 20(2), December 2012

Mackay, Hugh, *The Art of Belonging*, Pan Macmillan, Sydney, 2014

Mackay, Hugh, *Beyond Belief: How we find meaning, with or without religion*, Pan Macmillan, Sydney, 2016

Mackay, Hugh, 'Australia's Political Undertow', *East Asia Forum Quarterly*, ANU Press, Canberra, 8 (4), October–December 2016

Marr, David, *Panic*, Black Inc., Collingwood, Vic., 2011

Maslow, Abraham, *Religions, Values and Peak Experiences*, Ohio State University Press, Columbus, OH, 1964

Megalogenis, George, *Australia's Second Chance: What our history tells us about our future*, Penguin, Melbourne, 2015

Mishra, Pankaj, *Age of Anger: A history of the present*, Allen Lane, London, 2017

Niebuhr, Reinhold, *Children of Light and Children of Darkness*, 1944, republished by University of Chicago Press, 2011

Niebuhr, Reinhold, *Pious and Secular America*, WIPF and Stock, Eugene, Oregon, 1957

Osborne, Charlie, 'We-Vibe vibrator creator to pay damages after spying on user sex lives', *ZDNet* (www.zdnet.com), 14 March 2017

Page, Scott E., *The Diversity Bonus: How great teams pay off in the knowledge economy*, Princeton University Press, Princeton, NJ, 2017

Pianigiani, Gaia, 'Italy's first "social street" a runaway success that has spread', *New York Times*, reprinted in *Sydney Morning Herald*, 27 August 2015

Pors, Justine Grønbæk, 'What kind of children will we get out of this?' *Perspectives* 17, Whitlam Institute, Western Sydney University, August 2017

Prosser, Scott, 'COAG – the last throw of the dice for the Gillard government', *The Conversation*, 19 April 2013

Rogers, Carl, *On Becoming a Person: A therapist's view of psychotherapy*, Constable & Co, London, 1967

Rogers, Carl, *Freedom to Learn: A view of what education might become*, Charles E. Merrill, Columbus, OH, 1969

Ryan, Meredith, 'The Theory of Equanimity' in *Time Now to Walk Barefoot by the Blue-sailed Sea*, Musgrave & Elgara, Mosman, NSW, 2004

Salt, Bernard, 'Great melting pot: World's most successful immigrant nation', *The Australian*, 20 March 2017

Scriven, Michael, 'The compleat robot: A prolegomena to androidology' in Sydney Hook (ed.), *Dimensions of Mind*, New York University Press, New York, 1960

Seligman, Martin, 'Why is there so much depression today? The waxing of the individual and the waning of the commons', in Ingram, R.E. (ed.), *Contemporary Psychological Approaches to Depression: Theory, research and treatment*, Plenum Press, New York, 1990

Sexton, Anne, 'Consorting with Angels' in *Complete Poems*, Houghton Mifflin, Boston, Mass, 1981

Sigman, Aric, 'Time for a view of screen time', *Archives of Disease in Childhood*, 11 September 2016

Slattery, Luke, 'Silvertail subversives', *Good Weekend*, Fairfax Media, 24 June 2017

Snow, Deborah, 'Paul Keating says neoliberalism is at "a dead end" after Sally McManus speech', *Sydney Morning Herald*, 30 March 2017

Storr, Anthony, *Solitude: A return to the self*, Free Press, New York, 1988

Thompson, W.F., *Music, Thought and Feeling: Understanding the psychology of music*, Oxford University Press, New York, 2007

Thompson, W.F. & Schlaug, G, 'The healing power of music', *Scientific American: Mind*, 26(2), 2015

Tingle, Laura, *Great Expectations: Government, entitlement and an angry nation*, Quarterly Essay 46, Black Inc., Collingwood, Vic., 2012

Tingle, Laura, 'Ideology, facts and a backseat', *Australian Financial Review*, 22–27 December 2016

Toussaint, Loren L. and Everett L. Worthington Jr, 'Forgiveness', *The Psychologist*, British Psychological Society, August 2017

Twenge, Jean M., 'Have smartphones destroyed a generation?', *The Atlantic*, September 2017

Twenge, Jean M., *iGen: Why today's super-connected kinds are growing up less rebellious, more tolerant, less happy – and completely unprepared for adulthood – and what that means for the rest of us*, Simon and Schuster, New York, 2017

Van Reybrouck, David, *Against Elections: The case for democracy*, Bodley Head, London, 2016

Verhaeghe, Paul, *What About Me? The struggle for identity in a market-based society*, trans. Jane Hedley-Prôle, Scribe, Brunswick, Vic., 2014

Wahlquist, Calla, 'Turnbull's Uluru statement rejection is "mean-spirited bastardry" – legal expert', *The Guardian*, 26 October 2017

References

Wallenius, M, A. Hirvonen, H. Lindholm et al., 'Salivary cortisol in relation to the use of Information and Communication Technology (ICT) in school-aged children', *Psychology*, 1, 2010

Walsh, Richard, *Reboot: A democracy makeover to empower Australia's voters*, Melbourne University Press, Melbourne, 2017

Whiteford, Peter, 'Inequality and its socioeconomic impacts', *Australian Economic Review*, 48 (1), 2015

Williams, Joan C., 'What so many people don't get about the US working class', *Harvard Business Review*, 10 November 2016

Wilson, Sarah, *First, We Make the Beast Beautiful: A new story about anxiety*, Pan Macmillan, Sydney, 2017

Wood, Julian, 'Terence Davies: Religion, feminism and Emily Dickinson', *FilmInk*, 23 June 2017

Text Acknowledgements

Epigraph on page v taken from *Thank You for Being Late*. Copyright © 2016 by Thomas L. Friedman. Reprinted by permission of Penguin Books Ltd.

Extract on page 25 taken from 'What so many people don't get about the US working class' by Joan Williams. Reprinted by permission of Harvard Business Publishing. The full article can be read at https://hbr.org/2016/11/what-so-many-people-dont-get-about-the-u-s-working-class.

Extract on page 149 taken from 'Beside the Nore' from *Escape from the Anthill*. Copyright © 1985 by Hubert Butler. Reprinted by permission of The Liliput Press of Dublin.

Extract on page 241 taken from *Griffith Review 57: Perils of Populism*. Copyright © 2017 by Dennis Altman edited by Julianne Schultz. Reprinted by permission of Text Publishing. www.griffithreview.com.

Extract on page 243 taken from *Reboot: A democracy makeover to empower Australia's voters*. Copyright © 2017 by Richard Walsh. Reprinted by permission of Melbourne University Press.

Acknowledgements

Australia Reimagined draws on experience acquired during a 60-year career in social research, so there is no doubt about my greatest debt: it is to the many thousands of Australians who have shared with me their personal stories and their private thoughts, feelings, attitudes, values, hopes, doubts, fears, joys, triumphs, tragedies and disappointments. I have always been grateful for the time people have been prepared to spend talking about their lives to a total stranger, often allowing my colleagues and me into their homes. Their willing participation in extended personal interviews and small group discussions made my intensive style of research possible; their frankness gave it its integrity. Those encounters with my respondents also led me to develop the deepest respect for the lives of quiet heroism led by so many of my fellow citizens.

Many people have contributed, directly and indirectly, to the writing of this book – some by critical responses to early drafts of some chapters, and some by offering information or insights that have enriched my understanding of the issues. I am particularly grateful to Caroline Baum, Geoffrey Board, Christie Breakspear,

Lyndsay Connors, Elizabeth Coombs, Scott Cowdell, Geoffrey Duncan, Richard Eckersley, Mhairi Fraser, Richard Gill, Bruce Kaye, Lawson Lobb, Don Mackay, Hannah Mackay, James Mackay, Tim Mackay, Robert McLaughlin, Hilary McPhee, Keith Mason, Clare Payne, Ailsa Piper, Frances Rush, Ida Walker, Stephanie Wells and Julian Wood.

I am indebted, as ever, to Ingrid Ohlsson, head of non-fiction, and the team at Pan Macmillan – most notably the wonderfully encouraging senior editor Ariane Durkin and the publicists Léa Antigny and Clare Keighery who have been tireless supporters, and Georgia Webb who has assiduously pursued copyright permissions. I appreciate the personal interest in this project shown by the publishing director Cate Paterson and, in particular, her suggestion of the title.

Ali Lavau has been characteristically astute, meticulous and generous in helping to convert my final draft into a clearer argument and a more fluent book. The editing process was further enhanced by Libby Turner's formidable proofreading skills.

My wife, Sheila, has contributed more than can possibly be acknowledged here, through her unfailing encouragement and support, and her close reading of the manuscript at every stage of its development.

Chapters 5 and 10 include extracts from my 2017 Gandhi Oration, delivered at the University of NSW. Chapter 4 is partly based on a public lecture given in 2016 under the auspices of the NSW Privacy Commissioner and sponsored by First State Super. The section of chapter 4 on reality TV first appeared in *InPsych*, August 2017, published by the Australian Psychological Society. The section of chapter 7 on what the 2016 census revealed about religion first appeared in *Pearls and Irritations* in August 2017.

Index

Index

Index